DATE DUE

		PRINTED IN U.S.A.

AGING WISELY

AGING WISELY

Strategies for Baby Boomers and Seniors

Robert A. Levine, MD

ROWMAN & LITTLEFIELD
Lanham • Boulder • New York • London

Published by Rowman & Littlefield
A wholly owned subsidiary of The Rowman & Littlefield Publishing Group,
Inc.
4501 Forbes Boulevard, Suite 200, Lanham, Maryland 20706
www.rowman.com

16 Carlisle Street, London W1D 3BT, United Kingdom

Portions of this book were previously published in *Aging with Attitude: Growing Older with Dignity and Vitality* by Robert A. Levine (Westport, Conn.:
Praeger, 2004). © 2004 by Robert A. Levine.

British Library Cataloguing in Publication Information Available

Library of Congress Cataloging-in-Publication Data

Levine, Robert A.
Aging wisely : strategies for baby boomers and seniors / Robert A. Levine.
pages cm
Includes index.
ISBN 978-1-4422-3295-2 (cloth : alk. paper)—ISBN 978-1-4422-3296-9 (electronic) 1. Older people—Health and hygiene. 2. Older people—Psychology. 3. Aging—Psychological aspects. 4. Quality of life. I. Title.
RA777.6.L49 2014
613'.0438—dc23
2014003644

♾™ The paper used in this publication meets the minimum requirements of
American National Standard for Information Sciences Permanence of Paper
for Printed Library Materials, ANSI/NISO Z39.48-1992.

Printed in the United States of America

I would like to dedicate *Aging Wisely* to my patients.

Over the years, thousands of patients have entrusted me with their care, teaching me about perseverance, humility, and tolerance as I have diagnosed their problems and treated them. I have learned the importance of listening carefully, for patients' words usually provide the clues to their physical and emotional states— patients with terrible afflictions borne with dignity and hope, and others demanding and manipulative with minor problems. Some of the information in *Aging Wisely* has come from direct observation of my patients, while other data came from research related to patients I was seeing, or questions that they raised.

I would also like dedicate *Aging Wisely* to my wife, Anne, the source of many of my ideas and a gentle critic, who is always there, supportive and caring.

CONTENTS

1 Introduction   1

2 The Baby Boomers: Aging Reluctantly   19

3 The Greatest Generation and the Silent Generation: Life
Before the Boomers   43

4 The Impact of Time and the Aging Process   67

5 Knowing Your Enemies: Diseases and Disorders Common
with Aging   85

6 Loss: Aging's Companion   125

7 Ageism—Marginalizing Older People   151

8 The Quest: Strategies for Control   171

9 It's in Your Hands: Additional Strategies   203

10 What the Future Holds—Aging in the New Millennium   237

11 Doing It Your Way—Preparing for Life's End   259

12 Observations and Conclusions   291

Notes   299

For Further Reference   321

Index   325

About the Author   335

I

INTRODUCTION

Be like the cliff against which the waves continually break; but it stands firm and tames the fury of the water around it.

—Marcus Aurelius, *Meditations* [1]

In 1994, at age fifty-five, I was diagnosed with non-Hodgkin's lymphoma and told I had a 40 to 50 percent chance of surviving two years. Fortunately, the initial prognosis was wrong and after multiple courses of chemotherapy and a new experimental drug that is keeping my disease at bay, I'm still here. Understandably, this experience has colored my perception of life, and living with the possibility of death has perhaps given me some insights in terms of what we regard as important and what should be important. My years of medical practice have also been helpful in shaping a philosophy of life and teaching me how we might approach the aging process. I have seen many individuals who have been healthy, chronically ill, or facing death, become either paralyzed with anxiety or cope effectively with their circumstances.

At seventy-four, society considers me old. My wife, at sixty-six, was one of the first Baby Boomers to reach the age of Social Security and Medicare. Yet, neither she nor I think of ourselves as old. We both exercise regularly and are in excellent physical condition. However, the way we must look to others was brought home to us recently on the subway in Manhattan. One morning, we pushed aboard a crowded subway car on the way to an appointment and were standing amid a throng of diverse people of all ages. Suddenly, to our surprise, a young woman arose from her seat and offered it to my wife. Initially reluctant, my wife sat down and nodded to the woman to thank her. Obviously, we see ourselves differently than how this woman and most other people see us. And that's true in general for midlifers and older individuals who may regard themselves differently than the way society perceives them. This is important to recognize as it impacts the manner in which we live and how people react to us, particularly when we are doing things that do not seem congruent with our ages.

"Age is a question of mind over matter. If you don't mind, it doesn't matter."[2]

The baseball player and armchair philosopher Satchel Paige uttered the above words many years ago, when he was pitching in the major leagues in his fifth and possibly sixth decades. He was dismissing those critics who insisted that he was too old to pitch at such a high level and showing confidence in his own abilities. Indeed, the way we age and much of what happens to our minds and bodies as we grow older depends on our attitudes and feelings about ourselves and our lives. Though some elements are beyond our control, such as illnesses or the death of loved ones, to find joy and contentment we must take advantage of what we can control while dealing with the adversities that might arise. We should also not focus on our mortality and how to live longer, since survival itself is meaningless. What is really important is the quality of our lives and whether we can find satisfaction in the things we do in the time available to us.

A large segment of America's citizens, labeled the Baby Boomers, are now middle-aged or older, a major challenge for society and for these individuals. While the nation must come to grips with how to pay for the Medicare and Social Security programs for this group, the Boomers must learn how to skillfully handle aging to make their remaining years productive and pleasurable. And given the recent financial turmoil, many middle-aged Americans have lost their jobs or have seen their nest eggs depleted. This certainly complicates their planning for the years ahead, with some having to work longer and some unable to work at all despite their needs and desires. The Boomers are obviously not a homogeneous group, economically, healthwise, educationally, and in other ways that determine the manner in which they live. However, their attitudes and expectations will play a major role in whether they can age successfully. The ability to be happy and maximize their potential is theirs for the taking. But in order to grab the ring, people first have to get aboard life's carousel, instead of standing on the sidelines because of inertia or fear. The goal of this book is to show people how to get aboard, enjoy the trip, and collect as many rings as possible. And for most of us, even the trip itself can be worthwhile.

As we face the problems that accompany aging and search for solutions, we are not alone. With life expectancy increasing and birth rates declining, the population of the United States and the rest of the industrialized world has aged significantly in the last half century and will continue to do so in the decades ahead. The roles and lifestyles of midlifers and seniors have also changed dramatically—the result of both social necessity and individual desire. People who once would have been thought of as old and those of middle age today lead active, exciting lives—as rich and rewarding as the younger members of society. Some keep working past the normal age of retirement, while others follow creative pursuits, engage in competitive or recreational sports, take courses, collect various objects, or travel extensively. Though these scenarios may be more prevalent among the affluent, they are seen at every economic level. The image of an older man and woman sitting on a porch in rocking chairs whiling away their remaining days—she knitting and he perhaps reading the newspaper—in a placid but boring existence, is no longer the general rule. The Rolling Stones (Mick Jagger was recently seventy and is about to become a great-grandfather) have sung to us for years about "what a drag it is getting old."[3] But it doesn't have to be that way. From the fifties up, people are demanding more from life and from themselves, and are discovering ways to satisfy these demands.

On the other hand, many midlifers and seniors, for reasons other than illness or disability, find themselves unable to enjoy the latter decades of life in a vital fashion. Because of their own behavior and the inability to manage their lives, they often lose their pride and self-confidence. This results in diminished respect and admiration from their families and friends, reinforcing their negative perceptions about themselves. Even those midlifers and older people who are fully self-sufficient, healthy, and financially sound, may find it difficult maintaining their resolve and drive as they try to function in a world that is geared to the young. In a society that measures worth by attributes like "coolness" and youthfulness, midlifers and seniors may be less valued even though they may be quite productive. Nevertheless, self-assurance, self-respect, and dignity as we age should be universal objectives and should be attainable for almost all of us.

But you may ask, what do I mean by dignity? Dignity is an intangible characteristic, unique to each individual and manifested differently in different people. It includes feelings of self-worth and self-esteem, much of it internalized and some of it visible to others in a person's bearing and actions. An individual's dignity is his or her shield against the slings and arrows of the outside world. It allows him or her to exist within a predatory universe, inured to the insults and trauma of daily living, safeguarding his or her spirit. With dignity gone, we face the universe as naked, primitive beings, powerless and fearful before the shifting currents of our environment.

In my practice over the years, I have seen hundreds, if not thousands, of middle-aged and older individuals with various illnesses, or none at all, who have lived with positive feelings about themselves, with self-confidence and belief in their own self-worth. The same is true of friends and acquaintances in my personal life. These people did not fret over growing older and did not succumb to illness, but instead preserved their dignity while making the most of their lives. On the other hand, some individuals did not or could not make the good fight, feeling sorry for themselves or surrendering to their infirmities. And some allowed depression or anxiety to sap them of their strength and dignity, or used alcohol or drugs to deaden their discontent, becoming roadkill on the highway of life.

Below are some brief examples of how patients and acquaintances dealt with problems in mid or later life, some successfully and others ineffectually.

> L. E. was a woman in her late forties when I first saw her in my office with balance problems and numbness and weakness in her left leg. Workup confirmed a diagnosis of multiple sclerosis and her symptoms improved aside from some residual weakness and numbness in her leg. Over the next twenty-five years, she had periodic relapses even with treatment and eventually required a cane when walking. A divorced woman with two children, she continued working until age seventy as a financial planner and was quite successful in her field.
>
> T. B., a fifty-one-year-old man when he consulted me complaining of severe daily headaches, was an affluent bond trader who did

well financially even during the recession, but was under constant stress on the job. His examination, blood work, and imaging studies were all normal. Tall and heavy, a former athlete in his youth, he subsequently led a completely sedentary life. With mild tranquilizers, his headaches improved. I recommended that he start an exercise regimen and meditate or seek counseling to relieve his stress, as I wanted to get him off the medication. Over the next six months, he failed to follow my suggestions, saying that time constraints would not allow it. When I insisted that he play a more active role in controlling his headaches, he did not return for further visits.

K. B. was fifty-six years old when he and a partner decided to go out on their own and start a new business. In a happy marriage with two grown children, K. B. had prospered in his job as a salesman for a woman's sportswear firm in Manhattan, but found it tedious. With their contacts and knowledge of the product, he and his partner saw an opportunity to have their own line of clothing manufactured in China and sell to department and chain stores in the United States. Willing to take the risk of walking away from their longtime employer and using capital they had been saving for retirement, K. B. and his partner had their product line flowing and a number of large customers within a year of starting their venture. In addition to exceptional financial returns, K. B. has a newfound freedom as his own boss, with the ability to travel, spend more time with his wife and family, and play golf.

D. C. was sixty-two when he came to see me because of a slight tremor of his right arm. A wealthy, retired businessman, he was depressed because of the recent death of his wife. It was obvious to me that he had Parkinson's disease. Though initially surprised by the diagnosis and further depressed for a while, he became determined to battle the illness and enjoy life to the fullest. He began a vigorous exercise program and started dating, meeting a series of women through the Internet, one resulting in a long-term, satisfying relationship. Over a three year period, there was mild progression of his disease on medication, but no functional limitations. He also became active in the Parkinson's Disease Foundation and local support groups, contributing time and money. In spite of his illness and the loss of his wife, he says that he is happy now and looking forward to the years ahead.

S. W., a widow who lived alone in a condominium, was eighty when she came to see me because of problems with balance. She had a neuropathy (damage to the nerves in her legs) with impaired sensation and in addition, had previously had several small strokes. Notwithstanding her problems, she exercised for forty minutes every day on a treadmill or stationary bike and had a busy social life with friends and family. Over the five years that I saw her, she remained stable. An avid painter, she worked in a studio in her home, also visiting museums in the city with family members who were quite attentive. With one of her granddaughters, she was able to fly to London for an extended vacation and helped this woman plan her wedding. She refuses to allow age or her conditions restrict the way she wants to live.

R. L. was a businessman who retired at age fifty-eight because he could, intending to play golf and tennis, and spend half the year in Arizona. He figured that some of his time would also be utilized investing in real estate. However, with the financial meltdown in 2008 and the recession that followed, he was unable to pursue any real estate deals. And as time went on, he found he was getting bored with golf and occasional tennis. Unfortunately, he has no other activities or interests that appeal to him. His wife continues to work, so he cannot even travel or do things with her. At this point, he is financially secure, and neither depressed nor anxious, but lacks excitement and stimulation in his life. Without having planned ahead for his retirement, he is at loose ends and without a vision of what he wants to do.

These vignettes of midlifers and seniors describe different trajectories they followed after encountering various problems in their lives, medical and otherwise. Most of these people maintained a positive outlook and did well, and there is no reason why others, who are free of major problems or illnesses, or even with limitations, cannot also do as well, or better. The key perhaps is the belief in one's self and having the will to move forward. We must remember that as we grow older, aside from genetic predispositions we may have inherited and random illnesses or accidents we may encounter, we determine our own destiny. We are in control of the way we age and the quality of our own lives.

From the "biblical era" through medieval times, people lived an average of thirty or fewer years, reproducing as teenagers, then dying off when their children were in their midteens. (Generations were delineated as fifteen years apart, as this was the length of time for the cycle of reproduction to start again.) By 1900, life expectancy had climbed to about fifty years of age and continued to increase through the twentieth century. Now, at the beginning of the third millennium, the average life expectancy in most Western countries is in the upper seventies to low eighties. (In America in 2010, life expectancy for women was 80.5 years, and for men, 75.9 years.[4]) As the Baby Boomers reach their seventies and eighties, the population sixty-five or over will comprise 20.1 percent of the total, with those seventy-five and over accounting for 9.0 percent.[5] Put another way, in 1900, one in every twenty-five Americans was sixty-five or older.[6] In 1965 (the year Medicare was enacted), it was one in twelve. By the year 2030, one in five will be sixty-five or older. Other Western countries will have even a higher proportion of older people.

"Global aging will transform the world into societies that are much older than any we have ever known or imagined," Peter Peterson noted in his book *Gray Dawn*.[7] He warned that the aging of America and other industrialized nations will present serious economic problems. We see that now with America's budget deficits and national debt, mainly the result of the unfunded liabilities of Medicare and Social Security (though there are solutions to these problems that politicians will not consider). Pension obligations of municipalities and states are also financial burdens that may not be sustainable. In July of 2013, the city of Detroit declared bankruptcy with retirement costs a major driver of their economic woes. Similarly, in Europe the social compact has frayed because smaller numbers of young workers cannot adequately support the increased population of older people at the levels they anticipated.

Economics aside, we recognize today that growing old is normal and expected, in sharp contrast to the past, when it was uncommon for people to survive into old age. Now, those fifty and above are a substantial minority whose existence and needs must be acknowledged by the rest of society. For the most part, older people are also much healthier than they used to be. They have their own living complexes, their own organizations, their own magazines and newspapers that cater to them. Yet too often they may be disregarded by a society obsessed with youth.

WHY HAS LONGEVITY INCREASED?

Historically, infectious diseases were responsible for most human deaths, though periodically, famines and wars exacted a heavy toll. Advances in medicine, hygiene, and sanitation in the late nineteenth and early twentieth centuries controlled many of these infectious diseases in Western countries, accounting for much of the rise in life expectancy. (Improved sanitation was particularly important, with the development of sewage systems, clean drinking water, and garbage collection.) Infantile diarrhea, childbed fever, and diseases like typhoid, cholera, smallpox, and plague, which previously ravaged the citizenry in intermittent epidemics, were virtually eliminated. Leprosy, syphilis, and polio, which caused a great amount of disability as well as death, were vanquished almost completely. Tuberculosis and pneumonia, which took innumerable lives in urban centers over the centuries, were curbed greatly, though pneumonia still represents the final blow for many of the very feeble and immune compromised. Over the last fifty years, life expectancy has further increased because of progress in the prevention, diagnosis, and treatment of coronary artery disease and cancer, currently the two major killers in the developed world.

WHAT IS OLD?

Old age is a function of a person's location on a bell-shaped curve of the population in the era in which they live. When life expectancy was thirty, those considered old may have been forty or fifty—much younger than when overall life expectancy reached fifty, or seventy. In addition, with people now living longer and being productive longer than in the past, and engaged in tasks not necessarily related to physical prowess, categorizing them according to age is more complicated. When everyone in society was occupied hunting or gathering, age was regarded differently than with individuals employed as scientists, lawyers, machine operators, or computer technicians, some working productively into their seventies or eighties. "Also, individuals age at different rates; differential aging can be observed not only in changes in facial appearance, loss of hair, skin changes, but also in motor, sensory, and cognitive processes."[8]

These differences in biological aging may be due to inherited factors or related to people's working conditions, nutrition, stress, substance abuse, and so forth—a combination of genetic and environmental elements. Even in normal healthy people with similar diets and behavior, the aging process affects individuals differently. At eighty, some may be feeble and some may be vigorous, with the saying "You're as old as you feel" true to some degree. Thus, a person's physiologic age may be quite different from his or her chronological age, as evidenced by his or her lifestyle and activities. For example, a seventy-year-old marathon runner may be younger, according to many parameters, than a forty-year-old couch potato.

Of course, any designation or grouping to which men and women are assigned is usually inconsistent and based on the biases of the person doing the classifying. Nevertheless, placing people in categories can be helpful in describing certain observations and perceptions common to individuals within these groups. Traditionally in industrialized societies, life's stages have been defined by a person's assigned role. Youth was supposed to be devoted to education. In young adulthood, one started to work, with middle age the time of major accomplishments. Then old age was a period of retirement. Today, however, in this era of the Internet and social networks, the boundaries are fuzzier. There are individuals whose crowning successes in the tech world may come when they are in their early twenties. In fact, some of these people have been able to retire at age twenty-five or thirty, fabulously wealthy. On the other hand, those studying complex subjects such as medicine, science, or the humanities, may not be able to even begin their life's work until they are in their late thirties or forties.

I will arbitrarily define adulthood as starting at age twenty-one, with those below this level considered youths or children. Young adults are those from twenty-one to forty-five, those middle-aged are from forty-six to seventy, and those above seventy are old. However, given the growing number of older people, old age can be further divided into the young-old, those from seventy-one to eighty-five, and the old-old, those above eighty-five. (There have been previous definitions of the young-old as from sixty-five to seventy-four and the old-old as above seventy-five[9] and other classifications as well.)

As one would expect, people's outlooks and concerns change at different stages of their lives, shaping their actions and behavior, including

Table 1.1. Classification of Ages

Childhood		Through age 20
Adulthood	Young	Age 21 to 45
	Middle-Aged	Age 46 to 70
	Young-Old	Age 71 to 84
	Old-Old	Age 85 and Over

patterns of spending and saving. In general, young adults tend to be preoccupied with career development, having and raising children, and buying and maintaining a home. For most men and women, middle age is more a period of consolidation. Children have left the nest and interest centers on achieving economic security. Occupational issues and the desire to be "successful" still persist, but wind down toward the latter part of this stage. In old age, one's career is over and there are fewer responsibilities. The opportunity to acquire significant financial assets is usually gone. The focus now is on how to live with what one has and how to enjoy retirement, perhaps moving to a smaller home or condominium, a special community, or even to a new region of the country. Without the stresses of children and careers, there is potentially more freedom during this time, though not everyone takes advantage of this. In terms of preparation, most people feel ready for aging when they have hit sixty-five. Those above sixty-five are more afraid of becoming dependent, or living with pain or disabilities, than they are of dying.

Of course, midlifers and seniors are not a homogeneous group. They differ not only in age and activity levels, but also in terms of health and finances, whether single or married, and whether living in rural, suburban, or urban areas. People's physical, cognitive, and emotional status and the way these elements interact are important in determining how they carry on their everyday lives. Aside from those in midlife who are unemployed or underemployed, financial pressures affect older people to a greater degree than the young, since they usually live on fixed incomes and cannot return to work to earn more money if the need arises. And their family situations and the presence or absence of a spouse and/or children are critical as people grow older, and may be major factors in how their energy is directed.

Because men die earlier, there is a higher percentage of women beyond middle age that increases every decade. After age eighty-five, there are five women for every two men.[10] Among the older population are individuals who were never married, divorcees, and widows. And those who are still married may have relationships that run the gamut from unpalatable to wonderful. A spouse may also be ill and have to be cared for. This task may be borne cheerfully with love, or there may be resentment because of the previous history and ambivalent feelings toward the spouse. Relationships with children vary as well and influence peoples' emotional states. But notwithstanding the differences that exist among older people and those in midlife, certain common patterns and needs run through their lives. These can be explored to aid us in understanding the process of aging, to give us some degree of control.

In the past, both the Judeo-Christian tradition and Eastern religions instructed their adherents to hold those who were older in esteem, as did most primitive cultures. Age was equated with wisdom and, in myths, literature, and art, sages were depicted as old men. There was a gender bias to this, however, with old women less appreciated than men and often called by derogatory names—for example, crone, hag, or witch. Of course, since men and women died earlier in life, there were not many older people in the community and they did not constitute a significant burden on society. Those who reached old age were believed to have special qualities that allowed them to survive and perhaps they were venerated because there were so few of them. Families and the community not only revered the elderly, but if necessary, cared for them and met their needs as much as they were able. (There were exceptions to this rule in some primitive societies, such as the Eskimos.)

Starting in the nineteenth century, attitudes toward older people changed, owing to various social currents, both secular and religious, which will be discussed later. This led to a tendency to devalue seniors in many ways. (There is a divergence here between midlifers and seniors, with the former more respected and providing leadership in the political and economic realms, as well as in other areas.) Instead of regarding older people as wise and acknowledging their experience, they are often thought of as senile, or near senile, with their infirmities exaggerated (aside from special cases like a Warren Buffet or Henry Kissinger). Indeed, there is a bias against older people called *ageism* (a term first used by the geriatrician Dr. Robert Butler in 1968), which makes it more difficult for them to work or realize their potential in other ways. Their expertise is usually not utilized by the community, or even their families, and they are frequently relegated to standing on the sidelines when leadership is needed or decisions are made.

That our culture lionizes youth is reinforced daily on television, in music, in the movies, and in the print media. Fashion and styles are also created with the young in mind, giving little consideration to the tastes of older people. Youth is good, age is bad. Young is beautiful, old is ugly. But other factors as well may make seniors feel out of the loop. The language and terminology of the young is different from that of older people, further hindering communication between the generations. And the revolution in computers, mobile phones, and social media has left many of the older population behind, unable to comprehend just what is going on. Social networks are foreign to some of them and the Internet may not be a major factor in their lives. Many of them have no idea how Facebook or Twitter work and may not care to learn. On the other hand, most midlifers have had plenty of experience with the new technologies through business or their private lives, and are adept in utilizing them.

Unlike midlifers, as seniors search tentatively for a place in today's complex world, they are often reluctant to speak up and let their views be known. But whether or not their opinions are sought by others in society, or they are disdained as being "over the hill," they should put in their two cents on the issues of the day, making their feelings evident and their voices heard. They should be secure in their wealth of experience and recognize that they are wiser in many ways than those who are disinclined to listen to them. They understand more about the intricacies of life—its pleasures and its pains, and what makes the world go round. And midlifers should pay attention to the struggles of older people and be supportive, since soon they themselves will go through the same hoops to be seen and heard.

With the degree of mobility in America, the extended family has also been vanishing over recent decades to the detriment of older people. Older parents often don't live near their children and may not have frequent contact with their grandchildren. The familiarity and emotional ties among family members and the structure of the family unit, which were related to proximity, encouraging love and solicitude among the generations, is no longer there. Many children feel less responsibility toward their parents and no longer want to take care of them when there are problems. Indeed, physical or emotional abuse of elderly parents by children or grandchildren is not uncommon.[11] So-called granny-bashing cases are seen in hospital emergency rooms and, at times, relatives have been known to abandon demented older people without identification. Children also take funds or material possessions from older parents and use them for their own ends, sometimes impoverishing their fathers or mothers. This shameful behavior by children was publicized by the case of the socialite Brooke Astor. In her last years, she was defrauded out of millions of dollars by her son, Anthony Marshall, who was subsequently convicted in 2009 and sent to prison for his actions.[12]

The United States encompasses many individual ethnic cultures, as well as the prevailing culture. Attitudes toward older people and how they are treated by their children and younger individuals differ greatly from subculture to subculture. However, as the second and third generations are assimilated, their opinions and beliefs tend to track the dominant culture. Midlifers who are generally independent and still working, whatever their ethnic backgrounds, for the most part do not yet have to worry about assistance from their children.

Though people are surviving longer, the quality of their lives may diminish as they age, particularly when they attain the status of being old-old (over eighty-five). Some have chronic illnesses, such as arthritis, diabetes, Alzheimer's, Parkinson's disease, or residua from strokes, which leave them infirm to varying degrees. And if their impairments are severe enough, their lives may be bereft of pleasure. Before the era of modern medicine, most of these individuals would have fallen victim to infections (usually pneumonia) and died prior to reaching this stage. But with ventilators and IVs to sustain them and antibiotics to combat the bacteria, many now manage to escape death, while passing from crisis to crisis. As the famed physician William Osler noted in 1898, "Pneumonia may well be called the friend of the aged. Taken off by it in an acute, short, not often painful illness, the old escape those 'cold gradations of decay' that make the last stage of all so distressing."[13] (By "taken off by it," he meant dying.)

However, those with *severe* disabilities constitute a minority of the older population and most individuals in this age group have at least the potential of leading rich, rewarding lives. And midlifers have even fewer physical and cognitive problems to hold them back. Interestingly, people's attitudes about aging appear to improve as they grow older, as a recent study involving over one thousand older adults showed.[14] Though many had some type of impairment, as they got older there was an improvement in how they self-rated whether they were successfully aging.

Older individuals or midlifers with mild to moderate impairments or various aches and pains can usually function fairly well and be active in numerous ways. Indeed, aches and pains are a normal part of aging and signal that a person is still alive and able to feel things. If they are not significantly ill, older people largely hold in their own hands the level of activity that they pursue. While some take advantage of the opportunities offered to them in terms of continued growth, too often older adults are lacking in goals or objectives over and above their daily existence. Without work to lend structure to their lives, they do not have a routine and do not make long-range plans. They refuse to consider options that are not easily attained or that may require physical or mental effort. They are unwilling to be challenged or to explore new worlds, instead allowing their lives to become mechanical and automatic, with an absence of passion and little that is exciting or stimulating. In short, they permit themselves to fall into a rut and then find that climbing out may be a formidable task. On the other hand, many midlifers may be too busy in their jobs to develop other interests, which are so necessary after retirement.

Numerous seniors also become dependent emotionally or physically on a spouse, children, or friends, when they are actually able to fend for themselves. Taking the easy way out, they have others do things for them that they are quite capable of doing themselves. Sometimes, this may happen when a person is depressed or anxious, but it can be simple laziness as well, or even manipulative in nature. For those older individuals who feel lonely and irrelevant, this may be a way for them to gain recognition and to control other people.

In addition, some older persons, and occasionally midlifers, may be excessively fearful—afraid of death or illness or of being alone. They see peers dying or disabled and wonder when their turn will come. The associated anxiety may dominate their daily lives and interfere with their ability to function normally and communicate with others, changing the nature of their relationships. Fear may chain them to their homes and they may be unwilling to take any chances or expose themselves to any threats, further isolating themselves. Life entails taking chances and putting oneself at risk in one way or another, and those unable to do so also deprive themselves of pleasure, settling instead to exist with a relative absence of pain.

Some seniors and midlifers resent how their lives have played out and the situations in which they find themselves. It may or may not be their own fault, but that does not lessen their feelings of bitterness. (Of course, it is always easier to blame someone else than accept responsibility for one's own fate, particularly when the results have not been what one had hoped for and one cannot change what has happened.) This was supposed to have been their "golden years," but they wonder who named it so when life is difficult and they are unhappy. They claim it is golden only for those who are healthy and economically sound, or not burdened with caring for another person. Anger and depression float to the top of their cups, the scent paralyzing their wills. And they are unable to move forward and find joy in the years remaining, instead feeling sorry for themselves and bringing sadness to those dear to them.

In his 1992 book *The Journey of Life*, Thomas R. Cole queries whether old age has lost its meaning in this era when science tries to answer all questions and sees aging as merely a problem to be solved. The spiritual aspects of aging—its mystery, and its special significance as a part of life—seem to have been forgotten. He notes that "no amount of biomedical research and technical intervention can bring aging fully under the control of human will or desire. Growing old and dying, like being born and growing up, will remain part of the cycle of organic life, part of the coming into being and passing away that makes up the history of the universe. Human freedom and vitality lie in choosing to live well within these limits, even as we struggle against them."[15]

Though much attention in recent years has been paid to the manner in which we die, there has been less concern voiced about how we can "live with dignity," vitality, and self-respect as we grow older, a process that lasts longer and presents more dilemmas than dying. Indeed, a large and increasing portion of our existence is spent in midlife and old age. Using that time wisely by getting the most out of those years, in terms of personal growth and satisfaction, productivity and enjoyment, may determine whether or not we view our lives as having been "successful."

A book with the title *Successful Aging* was published in 1998 by Dr. John Rowe and Dr. Robert Kahn addressing these concerns. According to the authors, successful aging connotes an overall happiness with one's life, and the ability to operate at a high level and with a strong self-image as one grows older. Rowe and Kahn believe this necessitates an engagement with life, an avoidance of disease, and maintaining high cognitive and physical function.[16]

What do I mean by *living with dignity*? Is there a special lifestyle or way of living required as one grows older? Not at all. Though remaining independent and autonomous is important, many different lifestyles and individual approaches to life can be rewarding. Each of us has to find the path that is right for him or her and follow that path. If it leads to a dead end, one must search for another road and take it as far as one can. And we must resist attempts by others we encounter during our journey to rob us of vitality and self-respect. This includes family members with good intentions who do things for us and take away our independence as they try to be helpful. It is obviously easier to be independent or to change course in midlife, but still possible even when one is older, if one has the will to do it.

All human life has an inherent dignity and worth and there are those who feel that no matter how our lives evolve as we grow older, we should accept our situations and try to be comfortable with who we are. They say by not making an effort to modify our circumstances, or the manner in which we live, we will not have to deal with the possibility of failure. I disagree. I believe we should all try to play a role in shaping our lives at every stage and should endeavor to change the way we live if we are not generally content. This entails finding activities and pursuits that are satisfying for us and participating in those we enjoy.

But life is not all pleasure and we should also try to do things we believe are meaningful and rewarding—for ourselves, for others, and for society at large—giving of ourselves to make the world a better place. We should attempt to fulfill our remaining potential to the best of our abilities, whatever our age or status. This includes making our presence known and having our voices heard debating the issues of the day, shouting loudly rather than allowing ourselves to drift quietly into irrelevance. If we are unsuccessful in some or all of these efforts, at least we tried. As Dylan Thomas wrote,

> Do not go gentle into that good night,
> Old age should burn and rave at close of day;
> Rage, rage against the dying of the light.[17]

As a practicing neurologist for forty-three years, I cared for middle-aged and older patients over long periods of time. Listening to their fears, their hopes, their despair, and their joys, I learned a great deal about what growing old means to people and understood more about how aging affects them. I have also watched three grandparents advance in years and eventually die (one had died before I was born), my parents age and then die. Now I am witness to my own aging along with that of my wife and our peers, both friends and relatives. Our aging is on our minds every day, with offhand remarks, frequent discussions, and attempts at humor about our limitations. With each birthday and New Year that marks the passage of time, we tell ourselves that things are not really so bad. And perhaps that is true. But at seventy-five, I can visualize my parents in their seventies and remember thinking how old they were. Yet though I know I am old chronologically and I have some limitations, life is very stimulating and for the most part quite pleasant, and I look forward to every day.

SYNOPSIS OF THIS BOOK

The next two chapters will survey the factors that shaped the Baby Boomers, the Greatest Generation, and the Silent Generation, and how they lived, to try to better understand how they have aged and will age. They currently comprise the midlifers and seniors. In the chapters that follow, I will examine the barriers, both internal and external, which are placed in the paths of all of us as we grow older, making it more difficult for us to enjoy life and live well. I will explore strategies that can be used to overcome these obstacles and empower people to reach the individual objectives they set for themselves. I will describe various actions that can help us age gracefully, even zestfully, as we live life to the fullest while retaining our pride, self-esteem, and dignity.

This is not meant to be a "how-to" book that instructs people on the best ways to grow old. It is more a philosophy of aging and observations about people derived from my own experience and personal beliefs. However, it also provides information about necessary exercise, nutrition, and medical treatments for conditions that may be encountered. While the book is meant to be helpful for midlifers and older people, it is also written for younger men and women who have the ability to prepare themselves for what lies ahead and then confront aging with the advantage of being ready.

2

THE BABY BOOMERS:
AGING RELUCTANTLY

Virtue may choose the high or low degree.

—Alexander Pope, "The Triumph of Vice"[1]

Time Line: Born 1946–1964
Influences: Cold War, Sexual Revolution, Rock and Roll, Alternative
Lifestyles, Vietnam War, Political Cynicism, Civil Rights Movement,
Feminism
Age Range in 2014: 49–67 (Midlifers)
Age Range in 2014: 85–100

The Baby Boomers may be aging reluctantly, but they are aging nonetheless. And the demographic bump they represent, with a huge portion of the population leaving the workforce and entering retirement, presents a challenge for society as well as for the men and women in this group. How the individuals included in this stratum handle the aging process will determine their self-esteem and contentment as they grow older and will also set a standard for those who will follow.

Who exactly are the Boomers and how are they different from and similar to the generations before and after? Some of their virtues, or vices—depending on the observer's perspective—were their independence, unusual lifestyles, and willingness to experiment in seeking self-fulfillment when they were younger. This was certainly at variance with their parents' and grandparents' general conformity and desire to "fit in." Will the attributes that characterized them in youth affect the way the Boomers age? Baby Boomers have been called Generation Change, Generation Spend, the Entitled Generation, the Reinvention Generation, and the Greediest Generation by various commentators. However, Boomers generally do not attach labels to themselves and most rarely remember that they belong to a particular group.

DEFINITION AND DEMOGRAPHICS

Baby Boomers are middle-aged Americans in a challenging period of their lives, with retirement on the horizon or already having been reached. Most analysts use this classification for those born after World War II, usually from 1946 to 1964. Because the group encompasses a large span of time, some observers also divide it into an early and later phase, each comprising nine years, as the cultural influences and economic situations were dissimilar for the two segments. As of 2014, some Boomers had already reached their midsixties, while others were only in their late forties. Obviously, the experiences that shaped these midlifers varied greatly depending on their ages. And where they are now in their lives, where they are going and what is important to them, is quite different. However, we should remember that the term *Baby Boomer* is an artificial construct; an attempt to categorize a segment of the population to make it easier to analyze and write about them, and target advertising to sell things to them.

There are currently seventy-nine million Baby Boomers in the United States, or 26 percent of the total population,[2] a disproportionately larger percentage compared to other named segments. Throughout history there has been a large increase in births after a war when men return home. And there were sixteen million Americans in the military during World War II who came back to their wives and girlfriends and began procreating. This was also a time of unheralded affluence in the United States that favored couples having children and larger families. In addition, during the Depression before the war, many men and women had delayed starting families. Thus, what happened in the period afterward can be considered as an attempt to catch up. And because of numbers alone, Boomers' aging will cause a reexamination of the process and what it means to be old. According to a Pew Research survey, the average Boomer considers old age to start at seventy-two.[3]

And 61 percent of them say that they feel younger than their chronological age by an average of about nine years.

CULTURAL INFLUENCES

For any generation, or any group of people, culture is an interactive process. Individuals absorb information, social mores, customs, acceptable behavior, likes and dislikes, what is fashionable and what is not, from the general pot of stew from which everyone gains intellectual and emotional nourishment. However, individuals also contribute their own ideas, creations, and practices to that stew, influencing others even as they themselves are affected. And this interactivity is certainly true of the Baby Boomers who added to the constantly changing mix even as they were shaped by the prevailing culture. Boomers grew up in a time of great social ferment in America, which they aided as well as absorbed, some of them in fact becoming cultural icons.

One of the important factors in the evolution of the Boomer generation that made them different from preceding generations was the explosion of knowledge and the ability to access information. They were the first segment to grow up with television, and personal computers became ubiquitous at a later point in their lives. The burgeoning of news outlets and the willingness of journalists, photographers, and cameramen to go anywhere in search of news, allowed Boomers to see the Kennedy assassination shortly after it happened, watch the Vietnam War unfolding in almost real time, follow the development of Watergate, and President Nixon's resignation. In the later decades of the twentieth century, the twenty-four-hour news cycle presented a continuous flow of information about the world, the nation, and local events.

Their exposure to the seamier side of politics, the harshness of the political dialogue and the rhetoric of extremist politicians, made Baby Boomers cynical about government and politics. In fact, many of them were unwilling to participate in the political process when they were younger. However, as they approach retirement age or are already retired, more have become engaged in politics and apparently more conservative in their outlook.[4] This is particularly true of older Boomers, 69 percent of whom voted in the 2000 and 2004 presidential elections, with the majority choosing Bush.[5] Only 56 percent of younger Boomers voted in these elections. Subsequently, Boomers narrowly favored Obama in 2008, then returned to the Republicans by an eight point margin in the interim elections of 2010.[6] Increase in conservatism appears to be almost universal as people age, and Baby Boomers are no different in that aspect than their predecessors. Though this is the generation that participated in the sexual revolution and grew up with drugs and rock and roll, in this period of their lives they crave stability and are fearful of the way the world is changing around them.

Among the events that impacted them when they were younger were the assassinations of the Kennedys and Martin Luther King Jr., along with the shootings of Ronald Reagan and George Wallace. For many early Boomers, the Cuban Missile Crisis was a formative experience, with the threat of nuclear annihilation a real possibility. And the continued overhang of the Cold War caused people to build bomb shelters in their backyards, with children going through drills in school in preparation for an atomic war. There was also the long arc of the Vietnam conflict and its divisive effect, with nation-wide demonstrations and the Chicago antiwar riots at the 1968 Democratic convention. Draft-dodging and the refusal to serve in the military caused some young men to move to Canada. The oil embargo, Watergate, and President Nixon's eventual resignation in the 1970s, then Iran-Contra in the 1980s, fed citizens' distrust of the government. Along with these were the sexual improprieties of Bill Clinton and the impeachment debacle in the 1990s, Enron, 9/11, and the War on Terror in the new millennium along with the Afghan and Iraq Wars, and the Great Recession. The debate over global warming has also been unsettling. These developments played out in front of the Baby Boomers as they happened— unexpurgated and continuous, day in and day out.

Of course, Boomers were and are actors on the political stage, with many still prominent in this arena. They enacted the laws of the land and decided on the nation's policies, showing the interactivity of the Boomers politically as well as culturally. Among the more influential players in the older tier were Bill Clinton, George W. Bush, and Mitt Romney, with Barack Obama just making it in on the younger end. Chief Justice Roberts with a majority of his associates on the Supreme Court are also Boomers who will be sitting in judgment of us for decades to come.

At the same time the political world was in upheaval, the technological revolution was in full swing. Not only was knowledge expanding geometrically and becoming more available, but the machines being utilized were also improving by leaps and bounds. The advent of personal computers and the Internet changed everything for everyone, from the way we communicated with each other, the way we shopped, the way we searched and stored information, and the way we created documents of all sorts. We had desktops, then laptops and tablets, which allowed us to carry our offices and work with us wherever we went. Microsoft and then Apple and Google became leading players in the information game, with Boomers Bill Gates and Steve Jobs in the vanguard of the revolution. And as the Internet evolved further, social networks, such as Facebook, LinkedIn, and Twitter, were part of people's everyday lives.

Flat screen TVs with higher definition also became the norm, with a plethora of cable channels. Boomers listened to music on records, then tapes, then CDs, then iPods and smart phones, with phonographs and stereos becoming obsolete. And communication was enhanced by cell phones and smart phones, e-mails and texting, to the point that no one was ever out of touch, unless he or she chose to be. There were also the advances in transportation with jumbo jets and high speed trains (though not in the United States), the interstate highway system, along with safer cars that burned less fuel. The journeys into space and landing on the moon also changed the Boomer's view of the universe and man's place within it.

The civil rights movement with church bombings in Birmingham, the murders of civil rights workers in Mississippi, Emmitt Till and other racially motivated killings of blacks in the South, children blocked from attending school by government officials, the integration of schools both in the North and the South, all influenced the Baby Boomers. Feminism was another current that rippled across America, empowering women to demand equality and control of their lives. Women were able to enter professions that were once the province of men, as well as to advance in the corporate world. Another social insurrection that gained traction during the Boomer years was the Gay Pride movement, with gays coming out of the closet and gaining mainstream acceptance.

Of course, the battle for equality on all of these fronts continues, with segments of the population unwilling to endorse or acknowledge the changes that have occurred. But no matter how individual Boomers perceived of these movements and whether or not they were sympathetic to the objectives, the struggles still impacted this entire generation's thinking and behavior.

In investigating the cultural factors that helped shape the Baby Boomers, events in the 1960s and 1970s had the greatest effect on the older cohort of that generation. The concepts and conduct that emerged in those decades were more earth-shattering, transforming accepted social mores to a greater degree than anything before or after. These also influenced Boomer men and women when they were younger, at a time when their thinking was more malleable. Still, since culture is a constantly evolving manuscript with a plethora of authors, the 1980s, 1990s, and the years thereafter certainly played a role in molding the Boomers, determining their beliefs and outlooks on life, and how they might age.

When most people think about culture, what comes to mind are music, art, theater, movies, and literature. Of all these creative endeavors, music probably had the greatest influence on the Boomer generation. Rock and roll was the defining sound of their youth. Even today, concerts by some of the early groups bring Boomers, filled with nostalgia, back to the auditoriums and stadiums. While country music, hiphop, rap, and other genres certainly have their adherents, rock is almost universally appreciated. The musicians and bands of that era are too numerous to list all of them, but some of the notables include Elvis Presley, Bob Dylan, Jimi Hendrix, Janis Joplin, Bruce Springsteen, the Beatles, the Rolling Stones, the Grateful Dead, the Eagles, and the Beach Boys, along with the singers and groups of Motown.

Of course, along with the music was the use of drugs by many of the youthful Boomers; hard drugs, only by a small percentage. Psychedelic drug guru Timothy Leary urged young people to "turn on, tune in, and drop out" during the 1960s, encouraging them to try drugs for their life-altering experiences. And "sex, drugs, and rock and roll" was a mantra for some in this generation, perhaps given greater credence in retrospect by those looking back on their lives. However, early Boomers were thought of as the Woodstock Generation with all that represented, and as the unwashed generation, hippies who were always high and with long hair and ragged clothes. To reinforce their behavior, there was also a maxim for some of the young people immersed in the 1960s lifestyle that stated, "Never trust anyone over thirty." (Wonder what they think of that maxim now?)

Movies during the 1960s and 1970s were another part of the cultural milieu that engaged and influenced young Boomers. Though generating revenue was the main objective of the film industry, some of their creations helped to form viewers' perceptions of themselves and the world around them. *The Godfather, Jaws, The Exorcist,* and *Bonnie and Clyde* were among the most popular films, but probably had no lasting impact upon moviegoers. On the other hand, films like *Star Wars* and *2001: A Space Odyssey* brought home the reality of space travel, expanding the possibilities of what science could achieve. The downside of modern science, however, was evoked by *Dr. Strangelove*, which soon after the Cuban Missile Crisis reminded Boomers that nuclear Armageddon could be just around the corner. *The Graduate* in 1967 was a film reflecting the times, presenting the concerns of young people about careers and the future in a world of sexual and economic philistinism. Other films of cultural interest include *Easy Rider* and *Midnight Cowboy* that were released in 1969. From the 1970s there were *A Clockwork Orange, American Graffiti, Chinatown,* and *Apocalypse Now.*

There were a number of authors of cultural and literary importance during this era, their effect upon readers difficult to assess. Some include: Saul Bellow, Norman Mailer, John Updike, Phillip Roth, and Joyce Carol Oates. But certain individual books, mainly nonfiction by various writers, had more of an impact upon society because of their subject matter. Among these were *Beyond Freedom and Dignity* (B. F. Skinner), *The Feminine Mystique* (Betty Friedan), *Capitalism and Freedom* (Milton Friedman), *Silent Spring* (Rachael Carson), *Unsafe at Any Speed* (Ralph Nader), *The Autobiography of Malcolm X* (Malcolm X and Alex Haley), *In the Shadow of Man* (Jane Goodall), *The Complete Book of Running* (Jim Fixx), and *Bury My Heart at Wounded Knee* (Dee Brown). Alex Haley's *Roots*, though fictional, provided an awareness of the African American experience.

Another book that had a profound influence upon the Boomer Generation was Dr. Benjamin Spock's *The Common Sense Book of Baby and Child Care*, originally published in 1946 and rereleased numerous times. It was a bible many parents used in raising their children. Two other significant titles for Boomers were *Everything You Always*

Wanted to Know about Sex (David Reuben) that came out in 1969 and *The Joy of Sex* (Alex Comfort), first released in 1972. Though Reuben's book was filled with misinformation and value judgments, both his and Comfort's books contributed to the sexual revolution by making sex an acceptable topic of conversation.

Even more important for the sexual revolution of the 1960s and 1970s was the availability of oral contraceptives that freed women from worries about pregnancy. And television coverage of Woodstock with pictures of half-naked women and stories of free-sex communes titillated the general public. Though many Boomers disapproved of this behavior, others saw it as the dawn of sexual freedom, sparking changes in their own conduct. Certainly, society's sexual mores morphed during this period. Women became less fearful and awakened to the pleasures of sex. And as they have aged, Boomers have been more open about sex than preceding generations and more interested in continuing sexual activity.

At the same time that sexual freedom for women became more mainstream with the belief they should control their own bodies, *Roe v. Wade* became the law of the land in 1973, opening up a large wound in society that is still festering. In fact, the ability of women to obtain abortions has been slowly shrinking over the last forty years, with social conservatives in a number of states enacting various laws restricting abortion rights. And pressure or violence by religious militants has forced many women's clinics to close.

America is basically a religious nation and generally as people grow older, they tend to become more observant. Is it the same for the Baby Boomers? Their coming of age in the 1960s and 1970s was associated with spirituality, cults, and "New Age" beliefs, a virtual cornucopia of religious choices. Some of the exploration by Boomers was perhaps due to their living under "the shadow of the atom bomb,"[7] with the possibility of mass annihilation hanging over them like the Sword of Damocles. And some of it was perhaps a reaction to their parents' quest for material things and adherence to traditional religions. (Yet later on, the Boomers were also materialistic.) Though it was a time of Hare Krishna, Scientology, Kabbalists, Transcendental Meditation, the Unification Church, and so forth, it was also a period when megachurches appeared and grew, and evangelicalism flourished. Werner Erhard and EST

(Erhard Seminar Training) promoted a "conversion" process to help people transform themselves.

In 1993, a report noted that about 42 percent of Boomers had rejected formal religion, a third had never left their churches, and a quarter had returned to religion, but were less reliable than traditional church members.[8] And as they've grown older, Baby Boomers remain less likely to affiliate with organized religious groups than the generations before or after.[9] Another study in 2011 showed that 41 percent of Boomers were "unchurched,"[10] and that although a majority was involved in some way with organized religion, just 38 percent attended church regularly. While as a group, Baby Boomers may be less religious than past segments of the population, there is a wide spectrum of behavior and practices regarding faith that will continue as Boomers age further.

LIFESTYLES

The independence of the Boomers and their reluctance to accept the societal constraints of their parents have been mentioned. However, not all of them chose to turn on and drop out in alternative lifestyles. Even many of those that did, at some point resumed a more customary existence to raise their children and earn a living. Of course, the decisions Boomers made and continue to make will impact the way they age, as changes in lifestyle and behavior even later in life are often possible if the will is there.

Education

Boomers are considerably more educated than any of the population segments that preceded them. Given the explosion of knowledge, jobs of consequence in business and manufacturing required skilled people who could utilize relevant information to deliver the best outcomes for their employers. In the professions as well, more years of schooling and training became essential. For example, physicians who previously would have taken a year's internship after medical school and started a general practice, chose residencies of three to six years to specialize after their internships. And sometimes these were followed by fellowships of an additional year or two. For the later cohort of Boomers, the lure of the financial world and the chance of obtaining outsized salaries led some of them to pursue MBAs or other degrees after finishing college.

The fact that society and parents were more affluent permitted students to spend the extra years in school, instead of going to work early. Children could thus devote more time to improving their own prospects. However, not every child followed through on the opportunities provided, while some were never given a chance. As it turned out, 27 percent of Baby Boomers have four or more years of college, with 88 percent graduating from high school, far surpassing any previous generation.[11] The choices Boomers made early in life regarding education, as a rule determined their success in the workforce and their financial status, and will be a major factor in how they age and manage their retirements.

Employment

As the 1960s and 1970s faded in the rearview mirror, material success became important to most of the Boomers, considered hard working, competitive, and goal oriented by their employers. Besides generating income, work helped to define their identities and feelings of self-worth. This is why, in addition to the financial hits and problems finding new employment, losing jobs in the last recession devastated them. However, this generation has also been considered independent and self-reliant, which allowed many of them to reinvent themselves or make a comeback in various ways.

I have seen this resiliency in some of my patients and personal acquaintances, though of course not everyone has had the strength or ability to rebound. For example,

> R. R. was a fifty-one-year-old man whose position as a corporate salesman with a major tech company was eliminated in 2008. Within two months, while searching for new openings, he established himself as a consultant for businesses interested in buying software and high-tech equipment. As of October, 2013, he had not found a job with any company. However, his income working as a consultant had grown to 80 percent of his former salary. He now has the freedom to

set his own hours, is often able to work at home, and does not have an hour's daily commute each way.

While the trajectory of the economy was and is the most important factor in terms of the job market for Boomers and the overall population, other factors also play a role. These include the kind of employment held or sought, and the person's age, education, and training. Offshoring of manufacturing by United States corporations and the use of technology in factories have meant that fewer workers are needed in this sector of the economy. As a sobering reminder, the nation's GDP derived from manufacturing dropped from 28.3 percent in 1953 to 11.7 percent in 2007.[12] Whenever the economy takes a dive, factory workers and construction crews appear to be the hardest hit and the ones with the most trouble finding jobs, made worse if they are midlife or older.

Somewhat paradoxically, with so many Boomers approaching retirement or already having done so, there is concern in various industries as well as the public sector that there will not be enough skilled employees to handle the workload and provide services. There will be heavy losses of managers, technicians, engineers, machine operators, and personnel throughout the health care industry and educational system. The median age of American workers increased from thirty-five in 1985 to forty-one in 2008, evidence of aging in the workforce.[13] There is also fear that the depleted labor supply as Boomers age will jeopardize United States competitiveness and growth.[14] Prior to the recent recession, this may have been more of a problem, but because of dwindling assets many Boomers will work longer. Social Security reforms that raised the retirement age to sixty-seven and increased benefits for those who waited longer, along with changes in employer-provided benefits have also encouraged later retirement.[15] Yet in spite of the need in some areas, the job market remains closed for most older workers once they have been laid off.

Partly as a result of more education and partly because society as a whole has been more affluent, Baby Boomers' household incomes are 35–53 percent higher than their parents'.[16] However, those who did not graduate from high school had incomes decline 12 percent compared to those with a similar background in their parents' generation. Because the economy was stronger at the time the older Boomers started work-

ing and for a while afterward, they generally have done better financially than the younger Boomers.

Housing

During the last half of the twentieth century, following their parents'
leads, Boomers bought into the American dream of a house in the
suburbs to raise their children, in safe towns that provided superior
education. Mainly a Caucasian phenomenon initially, minorities joined
the parade to the suburbs in the last few decades. However, some
pioneering Boomers, both white and black, did elect to stay in the cities
in prosperous areas, or reclaim older, rundown sections, which have
subsequently increased in value.

Now, because of the Boomers, the suburbs are growing grayer, with
40 percent of suburbanites forty-five or older according to the 2010
census, compared with 34 percent ten years earlier.[17] This transformation has implications both for older residents and for the towns they live
in. Unlike the cities, public transportation systems in the suburbs are
inadequate, if present at all, which makes it difficult for seniors to get
around when they can no longer drive. In addition, health care and
various social services are required as more Boomers age. This means
competition for resources with the younger population in suburban
towns, in which education is the most expensive budget item.

Though younger men and women often intend to move to other
areas when they retire, when the time actually comes, most remain in
place. This may be because of local support mechanisms, children and
grandchildren nearby, financial reasons, or simply because they are
happy where they are. AARP in 2011 reported that 90 percent of older
Americans want to stay in their homes as they continue to grow older.[18]
However, this may not turn out to be practical and people often change
their minds. Even so, Boomers may be forced to remain in their residences because of difficulty selling them at the desired prices. Of
course, for the more affluent Boomers, moving to assisted living complexes or gentrifying city areas can be attractive options.

Another alternative that some couples are pursuing is building a
home with an apartment for parents, which they themselves might use
when they are older.[19] In this way, three generations of families are
together, as was often the norm in the past. Sometimes, the couple and

their parents split the costs of construction and sometimes it is done by one or the other. In this setting, grandparents often provide child care and do some meal preparation. Later on, their children can assist them if they become disabled.

Health and Fitness

While the connection between health and fitness has been repeatedly reinforced by medical studies over the last several decades, many Boomers have not heeded this information and do not exercise regularly. Thirty-six percent of them are obese, compared to 25 percent of the generations before and after, and a large percentage of those who are not obese are overweight.[20] Both the lack of exercise and obesity are associated with the development of many chronic diseases. In addition to higher mortality from these conditions, increased morbidity affects quality of life. People who are sedentary and obese also have predilections for cognitive impairment and dementia.

A poll of over fourteen thousand Baby Boomers in June of 2011 reported on some of their concerns related to aging.[21] Twenty-eight percent said the worst thing about getting older were changes in their physical abilities, while 26 percent said the worst thing were health issues. They were most worried about maintaining physical independence and about being able to afford medical costs. Forty-two percent were comfortable with growing older and 38 percent were unhappy.

The prescriptions for maximizing health for midlifers are the same as for older people and will be discussed further in subsequent chapters along with the evidence favoring these actions. But a brief overview given below describes what Boomers have to do to stay healthy and enhance their quality of life. Regular physical exercise is probably the most important factor in improving and maintaining health. The earlier in life it's started and the longer the daily regimen is (within limits), the more effective it will be. (Some recent studies suggest that moderate exercise three or four days a week may be sufficient from a cardiovascular standpoint, but these studies do not address cognitive function.) Aside from an occasional day off, one should aim for at least an hour of aerobic exercise daily. Running, walking, biking, swimming, or any other brisk repetitive activity is worthwhile. Switching off now and then, both for novelty and to prevent injuries, is reasonable. And to preserve upper body strength and to counter osteoporosis, everyone should include lifting weights several times each week as part of their routine.

A proper diet is essential to good health as well. This includes portions of fruits and vegetables every day and fish several times each week. The amount of red meat should be kept to a minimum, with protein coming from fish, chicken, turkey, and occasional eggs. Salt intake also needs to be watched. In addition to these suggestions, total calories should be monitored, for even a few extra calories daily will lead to accumulated poundage over time. However, sporadic deviation from these dietary recommendations will not cause problems and there is nothing wrong with enjoying a special meal here and there without feelings of guilt. But aside from a rare indulgence, fast food, with its dependence on harmful, high-caloric ingredients should be avoided.

Prevention and/or early treatment of chronic conditions such as hypertension, diabetes, and elevated cholesterol are critical, as is weight reduction in those who are obese. If not controlled, these will lead to heart attacks, strokes, peripheral vascular disease, and a higher incidence of dementia. Midlifers who are symptom free should visit a physician or health clinic once yearly to be checked for these chronic problems, and more frequently if something is found that requires medical intervention. Guidelines for screening tests such as mammograms, pap smears, and colonoscopies are constantly changing, and the need for these should be discussed with your physician. The value of routine annual physicals has also been questioned.

As is well known, smoking cigarettes is self-destructive behavior inimical to good health, causing lung cancer, heart disease, and other conditions. Never starting is preferable, but if one is a smoker, it should be stopped as soon as possible, with or without medical assistance. Reversal of the damaging effects will begin the day cigarettes are abandoned. Addiction to street drugs or prescription drugs is also associated with early deaths and disabilities, and medical help should be sought. On the other hand, though excessive drinking of alcohol is comparable to drug addiction in its deleterious effects, in moderation alcohol is beneficial, reducing the incidence of heart attacks and strokes, as well as cognitive decline and dementia.

Relationships

While the 1960s and 1970s may have been a time of sexual freedom, promiscuity was potentially life threatening after the specter of AIDS raised its head in the 1980s. Initially believed limited to the gay community, it soon became evident that IV drug users and heterosexuals who were sexually active were also at risk. Though AIDS may have been a consideration in how single Boomers assessed sexual liaisons and relationships, sex became less of a force in their lives anyway as they grew older and hormones ebbed.

The divorce rate for all Americans peaked at 50 percent in 1979, with many of the new divorcees being Boomers.[22] However, for the last twenty years, the divorce rate among Baby Boomers has continued to swell, while stabilizing or decreasing in other segments of the population.[23] About one third of adults ages forty-six through sixty-four were single in 2010—divorced, separated, or never having been married. This compared to 13 percent forty years earlier. One in four people getting divorced now are over the age of fifty, while in 1990, it was only one in ten.[24] And divorce rates are twice as high among Boomers who were previously married.[25] In the future, more divorces among midlifers and older couples can be anticipated, though in the past this was an unusual occurrence. Unmarried Boomers are five times as likely to live in poverty as married couples, and three times more likely to depend on food stamps, public assistance, or disability payments.[26]

There are a number of explanations why divorce may be more prevalent among Boomers than in previous generations. They, like younger Americans, are more likely to believe that "the main purpose of marriage is mutual happiness and fulfillment rather than child rearing,"[27] and they are willing to walk away if their objectives are not being met. Problems communicating are the cause of many of the breakups, and since men and women are living longer, they don't want to face the possibility of being locked into sterile, unhappy relationships for decades. Women are also more independent than in past generations and experience less social pressure to stay married. Some of them actually feel liberated when they walk away from a bad marriage. In addition, unlike their parents, there is no stigma for women to be divorced later in life. Retirement may be another impetus to ending a marriage since, when couples spend more time together, routines are disrupted and conflicts may become more manifest. Incompatibility regarding financial matters can lead to breakups as well. And of course, infidelity is a frequent cause for couples splitting. The following is an illustration of a midlife divorce:

> A married woman in her midfifties came to see me because of headaches that responded to mild muscle relaxants and exercise. She had a disabled teenage child and was embroiled in an unhappy relationship with a verbally abusive husband. Though she generated a reasonable income from her jewelry business, for years she had been afraid to end her marriage. When she finally filed for divorce, it felt like a great burden had been lifted from her and her headaches vanished. Her son did fine afterward, her business flourished, and she began dating, albeit quite cautiously.

In addition to financial difficulties experienced by many single Boomers, having no spouse to rely on means they may have to fend for themselves for everything, including shopping, cooking meals, cleaning their residences, and so forth. Men seem to have more problems accommodating to these routines than women. Making living alone even more of a challenge after a divorce, the friends the husband, wife, or both, had as a couple may no longer be there for them when they are single, as the dynamic of the friendships have changed. Searching for a new mate or companions of the opposite sex is easier for men than for women, as more women are available.

Following the lead of younger singles, over the last decade Boomers have embraced online dating sites as a method of meeting people. Many marriages and long-term relationships have started this way. There are general sites and ones for specific religious, racial, or ethnic groups, or gays. Many Boomers find online dating a better way to become acquainted with people than going to bars. However, there are problems with this process, including false personal data given to obtain dates, and predators of various sorts who frequent these sites, searching for those who are vulnerable.

For the majority of Boomers who remain married, the quality of their relationships run the spectrum from wonderful to intolerable, though hopefully most of the latter will be sundered by divorce. In marriages where both partners are content, the signature aspect is good communication, where spouses are able to verbalize their needs, as well as their dissatisfactions, to each other. There must also be respect for the other person, along with love and trust. When relationships work, spouses are kind and understanding, accepting their mate's imperfections that are invariably there. There is also a willingness to "go the extra mile" to make one's partner happy, knowing that person will reciprocate when the opportunity arises. That this is done out of self-interest as much as out of love makes it no less worthwhile if happiness is the end result.

Gay Boomers

While gay relationships became more acceptable to the general public as Boomers aged, it was not until recently that civil unions and gay marriages became part of the national discourse. However, even today, because of religious opposition, the majority of states still prohibit gay marriage. Along with this, gay couples have difficulty adopting children and obtaining their partner's benefits. In addition to the legal problems gays encounter in various states, gays also experience all the trials and tribulations long-term heterosexual relationships have. Being older, single, and gay presents special concerns, as individuals may be isolated within the larger community. However, some organizations now work with older gays, and housing complexes and assisted living arrangements that cater to gays are starting to be available.

FINANCIAL STATUS

Unemployment

Boomers were hit particularly hard by the recession in 2008, then hurt by the slow economic recovery as they approached retirement. Many suffered a double whammy, in losing their jobs and seeing savings and other assets dwindle, including the value of their homes. Of midlifers, 57 percent reported a worsening of their financial situation and a higher proportion of them cut their spending compared to other population segments.[28] Among Boomers ages 50–61, 60 percent said they might have to postpone planned retirement.

While older workers are less likely to be laid off than those who are younger, their chances of being rehired are much worse.[29] Since the start of the recession, the number of unemployed workers ages fifty to sixty-five has more than doubled. The longer they are unemployed, the worse their chances of ever working again, down into the single digits and with a significant pay cut if they do find a job. Since 2010, over 50 percent of older workers who are unemployed have been so for more than six months; the overwhelming majority, for over a year.[30] Employers say that expensive health benefits and the lack of computer skills are the foremost reasons older workers are not hired. The time and cost of training new personnel who may only be working for a few more years is also a concern. Laws are now on the books to protect against age discrimination, but they are difficult to enforce. However, workers have legal recourse if they believe they were let go because of age.

The stress of unemployment takes a toll in many ways, including divorce and higher death rates. In the years after an older male worker loses his job, there is a 50–100 percent increase in expected mortality, with displaced workers in midcareer living about a year and a half less on average than those who remain employed.[31] Suicide is one of the major reasons. And the probability of divorce is increased by 18 percent if a husband loses his job and 13 percent if a wife is laid off. Older workers who have difficulty finding jobs often retire early, resulting in lower Social Security and pension benefits and a greater possibility of impoverishment. Many apply for disability payments, which precludes their working. By taking early payments and not contributing to the Medicare and Social Security funds, the midlife long-term jobless exacerbate the government's budget deficits and the national debt, as well as their own financial problems.

Assets

Boomers have also been labeled the "sandwich generation," since some of them have provided financial assistance for both children and parents, reducing their own assets. As of December 2011, only 24 percent were saving for retirement, while 58 percent were helping elderly parents with their bills.[32] In addition, adult children were receiving money for car payments, insurance bills, utility bills, college loans, tuition, and so forth. And many children live with their Boomer parents rent-free and receive meals at no cost, since recent college graduates and other young people have had difficulty finding jobs and supporting themselves. Though parental aid is understandable, it means that compassionate midlifers may have to keep working longer if they are employed and may be strapped financially when they are older.

Some Boomers have also fallen prey to Ponzi schemes, like those of Bernie Madoff and Alan Stanford. Two conclusions can be drawn from these acts of betrayal by apparently solid money managers. The first is that one should be critical of investment advice, no matter who it comes from. Analyze information or investment prospectuses carefully before committing capital to a financial advisor. Even people who are financially sophisticated can be duped and it is important to have a knowledgeable family member or friend review any significant investment before committing funds. The second conclusion is that money is not everything and acquiring more wealth should not be a primary objective in life. As author Geneen Roth, who was defrauded by Madoff wrote, "It turns out the focus on me-me-me getting more-more-more leaves us empty-handed and poverty stricken. Equating 'net worth' with 'self-worth' can lead to negative outcomes and strong regrets."[33] More money does not lead to more happiness, and we can find fulfillment and satisfaction in life without being wealthy.

A few years ago, a Boston University economist, Lawrence Kotlikoff, set off a firestorm with an article in *Forbes* that labeled Boomers the "Greediest Generation" because the entitlement programs, Medicare and Social Security, which will have to increase their payouts as Boomers age, could bankrupt the country if spending for them is not brought under control.[34] In 1962, excluding interest payments, 32 cents of every federal dollar spent went for investments such as infrastructure and 14 cents went for entitlements.[35] In 2012, less than 15 cents went for investment and 46 cents was utilized on entitlements. It will only get worse in the future if these imbalances are not addressed. Though there are straightforward ways to do this, such as raising the retirement age for Social Security, or changing the cost of living adjustments, they would be painful for retirees. Thus far, pressure on politicians from Boomers and older Americans has kept any measures from being enacted. But solutions must be found out of necessity, which may mean additional financial stress for Boomers depending on the changes made.

Boomers have also been called "Generation Spend" because of their proclivity to buy and accumulate "stuff," often using credit cards to run up debt. However, most people by midlife are no longer as interested in accumulating things as when they were younger, and focus more on "consuming experiences" such as travel and dining out.[36] This has implications for the United States economy that is driven by consumer spending. However, the financial services sector should benefit by Boomers' need to save and increase their assets.

Households headed by people ages fifty-five to sixty-four saw the biggest decline in income, 9.7 percent, since the start of the last recession.[37] In addition to the contraction of income, savings, pension funds, and 401Ks, many Boomers lost another chunk of their assets with the drop in housing prices. Homes have always been a major portion of middle-class Americans' worth, with prices and people's equity increasing annually. Unfortunately for midlifers, the recession interrupted this seemingly inexorable upward path when the market was flooded by foreclosed homes. It may take a number of years before the prices of homes return to their prerecession levels, providing Boomers with some needed financial security.

Reemployment

Several things should be considered when a midlifer looks for a job after having been laid off, or when deciding to go back to work after retirement. Is money the primary object, or does he or she want to find an interesting position to provide stimulation? If money is needed, then the job seeker may accept offers of employment perhaps below his or her level of competence and qualifications, and at a lower salary than for previous work. With the job market so constrained, sometimes Boomers have to swallow their pride and take work they would have considered beneath them. But there are also opportunities out there, either to work for oneself as a consultant, as an entrepreneur, or in other areas. For example:

A former sales executive we know is now a photographer for an online news service. Though he makes considerably less money, he loves the work.

A successful surgeon who was an acquaintance took a job as a hospital administrator when he felt that his surgical skills were eroding. His income is reduced, but he's glad he can work in a hospital doing something he enjoys.

A friend's son lost his job in public relations for one of the major financial firms when it went bankrupt in 2008. A year later, when his severance package ran out, he established his own public relations business that was rapidly successful.

As a consultant, you can generally tailor your schedule and work in a way that gives you free time to pursue other interests. And if no jobs are available in your field and you are not comfortable working as a consultant, you can go back to school to gain competency in a completely different area. A lawyer can become a teacher; or an engineer, a journalist; or a banker, a carpenter. Health care, education, and computers are fields where jobs often outnumber applicants. A number of government programs help unemployed workers with retraining, so financial assistance may be available if you decide to return to school. Some companies also recognize the value of mature workers and are willing to hire them if the fit is right.

On the other hand, if income is unimportant and one is bored, or wants to get creative juices flowing, or has a need to be with people, volunteering may be the way to go. Many positions at nonprofits are intellectually demanding, emotionally satisfying, or both. And it's nice to know you have the ability to set your own hours and spend as little or as much time as you want.

A friend of ours who was a public relations guru now teaches English as a second language and loves it.

Several retired physician acquaintances volunteer at AmeriCares's free clinics and find it very gratifying.

A woman who was a high-powered office manager says that she finds volunteering at a nearby hospital exciting.

A former lawyer mentors underprivileged girls.

Opportunities for volunteering abound. If you can't find anything that interests you, you are not looking very hard.

Retirement

Retirement was once labeled the "golden years," when people could enjoy life and reap the benefits of the time spent working. However, it must be remembered that when Social Security's retirement age was set at sixty-five in the 1930s, people had only a few more years on average to live. Now, if a person retires at sixty-five, it is likely he or she will survive for another two decades or more. Obviously, this extended life expectancy is cause for celebration, but it is attended with some concerns for retirees. These include financial security, occupying time with pleasurable or productive activities, maximizing health and quality of life, and enhancing relationships. Though these areas have already been explored to some degree, they will be covered in more depth in subsequent chapters. Suffice it to say that for most of us, one quarter of our lives on average will be spent in retirement, making it essential that we prepare for this time. Some aspects, such as illness or the loss of a spouse are beyond our control. But if retirement is approached in a haphazard fashion or not given sufficient consideration, painful consequences that are avoidable may result in discontent and unhappiness in the latter stages of our lives.

> P. J. was a hard-driving surgeon forced to retire by his group at the mandatory age of sixty-five. His entire life had been devoted to medicine and in retirement he found little to do. He joined a local men's club, played golf in the warm weather, but felt isolated and unhappy, with no particular interests to motivate him. His wife was involved in a book club, was active in an arts group, and spent a lot of free time painting. Unwilling to interfere in his wife's pastimes, he kept searching for something to do that would excite him. He regretted his past singular focus on medicine and that he had never developed any hobbies or activities.

Debt and lack of income-producing assets are forcing more Baby Boomers to put off retirement and continue working if they are employed. A survey by CareerBuilder in 2010 found that 72 percent of workers over the age of sixty were delaying retirement because of financial problems.[38] However, over two-thirds of those not retiring said part of the reason was because they were happy with their jobs and enjoyed working.

Attitudes

An AARP analysis in December 2010 revealed that Boomers are generally satisfied and optimistic about what lies ahead for them.[39] Of those turning sixty-five in 2011, 78 percent said they were content with the way their lives were going, 70 percent reported accomplishing most or all of what they wanted out of life, with 26 percent achieving some of what they had hoped for. Only 3 percent reported attaining little or none of what they had wanted in life. On average, Boomers expected to live about another twenty years. Unlike their parents, a significant number of midlifers want work to be part of their retirement and many say they do not ever want to retire. Sixty-two percent of Boomers were very happy regarding relationships with family and friends, while 38 percent reported it as the single most important aspect of their lives.[40] Only 32 percent were content with their physical health, and just 22 percent, with their personal finances.[41] Only 40 percent were very satisfied with their work or career, and 30 percent, with their leisure activities. Though 91 percent of higher income households (over $75,000) were satisfied with their lives in general, somewhat surprisingly, so were 68 percent of those with household incomes under $25,000.[42] Education seemed to make little difference in attitudes, with 86 percent of college educated midlifers content with their lives compared to 80 percent of those less educated.

How well Boomers age and whether they are happy will be determined by their health, financial status, and relationships, as is true for the older segments of the population. And it should again be emphasized that longevity should not be the goal when aging, but maintaining a good quality of life for as long as possible. How to achieve a good quality of life and maximize one's potential will be explored further in subsequent chapters, after examining the barriers that are present.

We must accept that we can only control what we can control.

3

THE GREATEST GENERATION AND THE SILENT GENERATION: LIFE BEFORE THE BOOMERS

Everything that exists is in a way the seed of what will be.

—Marcus Aurelius [1]

The Greatest (G. I.) Generation
Time Line: Born 1910–1929
Influences: Great Depression, World War II, Atom Bomb, Korean War, Cuban Missile Crisis, Economic Expansion Post WWII, Radio, Early TV
Age Range in 2014: 85–100

DEMOGRAPHICS

The *Greatest Generation* was a term conceived by the journalist Tom Brokaw in a book published in 2004. It described the population cohort that weathered the Great Depression of the 1930s and fought the enemy on two fronts in the 1940s, bringing victory to the Allies in World War II. Previously, it had been called the *G.I. Generation*. Some historians include people born as early as 1901 as part of this group, but the core of this demographic is formed by those born from 1914 to 1927. The earlier portion that lived through World War I and experienced the Roaring Twenties has also been called the *Lost Generation*, a term that originated with Ernest Hemingway. The surviving members of the Greatest Generation are now mostly in their eighties and nineties, their numbers dwindling. Of 16 million American veterans of World War II, only about 1.5 million were still alive in 2013.

INFLUENCES: CULTURAL AND POLITICAL

Many members of the earlier segment of this generation have clear memories of Prohibition and the Roaring Twenties. This was a boom time for the country, with high levels of employment and some individuals able to accumulate great wealth. It was also a period of financial inequality, another "Gilded Age," as depicted in novels like *The Great Gatsby*. With the stock market soaring, people bought stocks on margin or poured their savings into the market on tips, hoping to make financial killings.

The crash of 1929 was a life-altering experience, when the world changed dramatically for both affluent and ordinary citizens. Numerous highflyers became penniless overnight and the rate of suicide among them soared. An unemployment rate of 3.2 percent in 1929, along with the low rates during much of the 1920s, climbed to 25 percent at the height of the Depression, remaining at 15 percent in 1940.[2] Underemployment and low wages were also the norm, with deprivation for the majority of Americans. Men struggled to feed themselves and their families, willing to take any kind of work. This time of economic depression also describes people's emotional state, with men and women wondering if the American Dream was just a myth. Also during the 1930s, the Dust Bowl of the Great Plains devastated millions of acres of farmland due to drought and overfarming, increasing rural poverty and migration to the cities. African Americans also migrated north, hoping to find ways to earn a living.

With much of the public blaming the Depression on predatory banks, Wall Street, and corporate America, people looked to the government to provide answers for them. President Roosevelt, while demonized by some, was seen by many as almost a God-like figure who was interested in the little guy. While government programs such as the Works Progress Administration and Civilian Conservation Corps did provide work for millions and mitigated hunger to some degree, there was still great suffering throughout the land. During this period, however, Social Security was enacted to provide a safety net for older people, and rural electrification was increased with projects such as the Tennessee Valley Authority. Greater scrutiny and supervision of the banks and financial institutions by the government gave citizens a greater sense of security, reassuring them that the stock market crash and the run on the banks would be unlikely to happen again. The Federal Deposit Insurance Corporation was formed to protect bank deposits, and the Securities and Exchange Corporation, to make public corporations truthful in their filings and to provide more transparency regarding stocks for the small investor.

The Japanese attack on Pearl Harbor on December 7, 1941 signaled the beginning of American involvement in World War II, a conflict that would totally engage the nation over the next four years. American military forces, which grew quickly with the draft, fought the Japanese in the Pacific and the Germans in Europe. In both arenas, bloody battles with high casualties profoundly shaped the outlook of the survivors.

On the home front, the nation's manufacturing machine was ramped up to work at full capacity to produce armaments and military hardware. Women were recruited to work in the factories, including many who had never been employed before. Rosie the Riveter was their icon, the symbol of a woman competently doing what had been a man's job. For some women, their success in the workplace and their ability to produce the necessary war materials for the nation's fighting forces became a vision of what could be. But they rarely followed up after the war when the men came home and reclaimed their jobs, though perhaps women passed on some of their experiences to their daughters.

The detonation of the first atomic bombs over Japan and reports and pictures of the Holocaust also affected the Greatest Generation's perception of life. Then the onset of the Cold War, with the Soviet Union acquiring nuclear weapons, made the threat of nuclear war a reality. Only five years after the end of World War II, the Korean War required American men to put their lives on the line again, this time to fight communist North Korea and China. This brutal war lasted over three years, with heavy casualties on both sides. In the next decade, the Greatest Generation lived through the Cuban Missile Crisis and then

Vietnam, for the most part as observers too old to participate in the fighting.

The events of the 1960s and 1970s certainly influenced the Greatest Generation, but in general, the strengths and weaknesses of their personas had already been hardwired by the Depression and two wars. In spite of everything they had endured, a sense of optimism and a "can do" feeling inspired these Americans, as the economy expanded and prosperity returned. They were also patriotic, with a sense of the shared sacrifice they had all lived through. Of course, this was before questions over Vietnam and the Nixon presidency shattered belief in the government and turned many citizens into cynics.

For the most part, this generation was religious and affiliated with traditional houses of worship throughout their lives, such as the mainline Protestant denominations and the Catholic Church. In fact, in 2010 about 95 percent reported a connection to some religious institution.[3] Seventy-one percent were certain that God exists and three quarters believed in an afterlife. This generation has also been described as "father worshipping and heavily male fixated."[4]

The music favored by the Greatest Generation was both mellow and soothing. It did not address the problems of the era as did the musicians and singers later on, and was not anti-establishment. With Americans undergoing great hardships during the Depression, followed by the war, the music focused on love and longing, with dances like the fox trot, jitterbug, and rhumba. Big bands playing swing music were popular, led by The Dorsey Brothers, Benny Goodman, Count Basie, Glenn Miller, among others. Crooners such as Frank Sinatra, Bing Crosby, Perry Como, and Nat King Cole also had large followings. Mass communication was limited to radio until television made an appearance in the late 1940s and became more ubiquitous in the 1950s. Wrestling and variety shows, along with the news, were the staples of the new medium until sitcoms began to make an appearance.

Cinema was generally positive in its outlook during the 1930s and 1940s—comedies and musicals with happy endings, along with Westerns and crime stories. Some films of social significance were also produced, such as *Citizen Kane* and *Of Mice and Men*, but these did not induce changes in the political milieu. And during the war, movies about combat and espionage were used to energize citizens and spur the war effort. In literature, top authors included John Steinbeck, Ernest Hemingway, Edna Ferber, Pearl Buck, and Sinclair Lewis, with Margaret Mitchell's *Gone With the Wind* heading the charts as a book and movie. Though these writers all had followings, their published works did not appear to have much impact in terms of societal change or people's behavior. Having come through the Great Depression, most individuals were mainly concerned with making sure they could provide for themselves and their families.

The symbiosis of the Greatest Generation with government never really came to an end. In spite of Watergate and other corrupt activities, acceptance of the role of government remained mostly intact. Government had helped men get jobs during the Depression, had organized the military forces that won World War II, and had defeated Communism. They had assisted people with housing and education under the G.I. Bill and had passed Social Security and Medicare. Of course, the national debt also soared because of government programs, but paying that off was not the Greatest Generation's responsibility.

This generation also grew up with scouting, 4-H, fraternities, sororities, and other social and neighborhood groups, and saw the strengthening of the union movement. This gave people a belief in organizations and community building, in counterpoint to the individuality of the Boomers. They were joiners who also wanted to be "regular guys," blending in with everyone else.

LIFESTYLES

Education

The G.I. Bill after World War II helped many returning veterans go to college, but compared to succeeding population segments, a smaller percentage actually received degrees. With well-paying jobs available in manufacturing and construction, there was less reason to pursue higher education. And during this period, many managerial and administrative jobs did not require college degrees. Though postgraduate education was necessary in the professions such as medicine and law, few men saw the value of MBAs or other advanced degrees to help them climb the corporate ladder. In science and academia, however, it was a different story, with master's degrees and PhDs required.

Unlike their daughters and granddaughters, most women were uninterested in careers, and education was not a priority. The ideal for most of them was to be stay-at-home moms taking care of their families. In fact, a standard joke was that when women went to college, the degree most of them sought was an MRS rather than a BA or BS. Of course, many women did want to work for at least awhile when they were young. Teaching and nursing attracted them mostly—professions that required additional education after high school, but not necessarily college. However, some women did go on to college and occasionally obtained further degrees to work in academia or the professions.

Employment

Though unemployment was rife during the Depression in the 1930s, jobs were plentiful after the war. American manufacturing surged as companies switched their factories from armaments to consumer goods and exported products all over the world. Domestic consumption of virtually all goods increased almost exponentially to make up for previous lean times. As the economy grew, credit expanded both to businesses and individuals. Appliances and televisions flew off the shelves and automobile ownership soared, providing work in these industries. Middle America and the "rust belt" states were riding high, their factories in overdrive. Construction also boomed, with new homes in the suburbs and development of the nation's infrastructure. Out of financial necessity, women who had joined the workforce prior to their expected marriages continued to work if they remained single. Aside from teachers and nurses, they were usually secretaries or held low-level administrative positions.

The men and women of the Greatest Generation were generally hard workers, happy to have jobs after having lived through the struggles of the Depression. Financial security for themselves and their families was the overriding consideration for most of them. Given the time that many of the men had spent in the military, they knew how to take orders and were respectful of authority. There were no feelings of entitlement, that certain things were owed to them, or that they were special in any way. They were generally loyal to the firms for which they worked, often remaining with a single employer throughout their working lives. This loyalty was usually returned by their companies who kept workers on until retirement. Before the advent of the multinational corporations searching for low-cost labor, businesses once were glad to have productive, competent American employees manufacturing their goods.

At this time many families also engaged in farming and a significant part of the workforce lived in rural areas. Over the last half of the century, however, as farming became more mechanized, with large corporate farms that required less labor replacing family holdings, men left the farms to find work in the cities. Aside from small businesses, such as gas stations, grocery stores, and local firms, there was little entrepreneurship, though some large corporations, such as Walmart and McDonald's, did get their start during this period.

Housing

With GIs returning from the war and starting families, the American Dream for many couples was a house in the suburbs, providing a safe place to bring up children, with decent K–12 educations as part of the package. The prewar national fertility rate during the Depression was low, jumping after the war and driving the need for housing for these larger families. However, moves to the suburbs reinforced patterns of segregation. As young white couples departed, predominantly impoverished minority populations remained behind, the tax bases dropping. It was not until the 1980s that urban living again became popular. Waves of gentrification resulted from older people returning to the cities, as well as young couples with and without children.

In the late 1940s and 1950s, Levittowns and other tract housing developments, along with custom-designed homes, sprang up throughout metropolitan regions, made more accessible by the growth of the Interstate Highway System. Men commuted by car or train into the cities or nearby suburbs to their jobs and reappeared for dinner with their families.

As the men and women of the Greatest Generation aged, many of them continued to live in their homes, though some clustered in retirement communities. The support mechanisms of the extended family were not often present in either case. Though those in the Greatest Generation had taken care of their own aging parents, many of their Baby Boomer children had moved away, making it difficult or impossible to offer assistance. In addition, in many Boomer families both spouses worked. Of course, some seniors were able to live with their children or move nearby, where family members could help them navigate the difficult tasks of daily living. And if their children were not available, assisted living facilities or nursing homes provided other options.

Health and Fitness

Coming out of the Depression, when many people had barely enough to eat or went hungry at times, and World War II, when there was food rationing, most members of the Greatest Generation were not concerned with consuming healthy foods. Hearty meals of meat and potatoes were considered ideal dinners, with ham and eggs or sausages and eggs with a side of toast for breakfast. Smoking cigarettes was acceptable behavior, as its devastating effects were not yet known. Drinking to excess was also more common in this generation that had lived through two major social upheavals. Control of cholesterol and triglycerides were not even on the horizon during the early years of members' lives. Similarly, regular exercise was not part of most people's routines. All of this changed during the final three decades of the twentieth century when eating right and exercising were heralded as important to maintain health. For the majority of aging individuals in this population segment, it was too late to alter fixed habits, though some did begin to walk and watch their diets. Below are two examples of how my patients dealt with medical problems.

> At eighty-six years of age, L. R. had several seizures due to a minor stroke that caused no discernible deficits. The seizures were controlled with medication. Ninety-three on his last visit to my office, he lived with his wife, a year younger than he, in a small home they had occupied for over fifty years. Her vision was not good and he did all the driving when they went shopping or saw friends. Whenever the weather permitted, he and his wife walked outside for exercise. They were not affluent and did not travel much, but were bright and articulate and still enjoyed life. He had an excellent sense of humor, delighting in verbal repartee. His standard comment when I asked how he was doing was, "I can't complain. I'm in fine shape for the shape I'm in."

I lost track of J. G. several years ago after he had been a patient of mine for five years. Tall and lanky, he was ninety-two when I last saw him, a widower living on his own in a condominium. He had come to me because of pain in his neck and shoulder, the result of cervical arthritis. I treated him with medication and physical therapy that relieved his pain, though it recurred at times and required renewal of medication. In spite of complaints of minor difficulties with memory, J. G. was quite sharp and able to care for himself. Always nattily dressed, he went into his office at a local law firm several days a week to handle some cases. He also read extensively, mainly biographies, and loved crossword puzzles. Physically very active, he walked daily and went swimming four or five times a week. Every winter, he traveled down to Florida and spent three to four months there with a group of friends. Though he joked about not having much time left, he was always positive about the future, making plans to do things months in advance.

Mental illnesses, particularly depression, were often kept hidden and seen as signs of weakness by people in this generation, with medical help generally not sought. In fact, psychiatry was thought of as akin to quackery by some individuals, with only "crazy" people seeing these specialist physicians. Useful drugs for treatment of mental illness were not available, so talk therapy was employed along with shock therapy for those severely depressed. This changed in the 1950s, when Thorazine was approved for the treatment of psychosis and Miltown for anxiety disorders, with Valium part of the armamentarium later on.

Effective drugs to treat cholesterol and blood pressure came onto the market as men and women of this segment of the population grew older, reducing deaths and morbidity from vascular disease. Surgical techniques such as CABGs (coronary artery bypass graft) and stenting of blood vessels (putting in artificial tubes to widen arteries) resulted in longer life spans as well, as did improved treatments for some types of cancer. The use of antibiotics to treat pneumonia and other infections were also important factors in extending life. However, living longer meant more Alzheimer's disease and dementia, Parkinson's, and other degenerative processes, producing a poor quality of life for many of these survivors. It also increased medical expenses for many families. This sometimes led to bankruptcies, until Medicare and Medicaid lifted these financial burdens from the shoulders of most of the elderly in the mid 1960s. But the burden was shifted onto the federal government as the cost of medical care continued to escalate.

Relationships

"'Til death do us part." The Greatest Generation believed this ideal vision for relationships, and frowned upon premarital sex. "Nice girls" didn't have sex prior to marriage as most men wouldn't want "damaged goods." Of course, premarital sex did take place and marriages were sometimes the result of unplanned pregnancies. But marriages usually occurred for the same reasons they flourished throughout history: A man, a woman, and children formed an efficient economic unit. Certainly there was love and fulfillment of sexual needs, but the family unit worked fairly well with a division of labor.

Fixed roles for the man and woman were expected after marriage. The man was the breadwinner, out of the house working, and "bringing home the bacon," while the woman was the homemaker, taking care of the house, preparing meals, and raising the children. Both the man and the woman put in long days, but were happy for the most part with what they had, remembering the hardships of past years. On the family farms, both the wife and children usually shared the workload.

Given this cohort's early years of want and scarcity, once there was adequate food on the table, material things became important to people. Besides a home of their own, automobiles, appliances, TVs, and so forth were all desired by married couples, indeed signs of success. Keeping up with the Joneses, or even ahead of the Joneses, was a game that many played, perhaps an overcompensation for the period growing up when things had been tough. Yet at the same time, there was a streak of frugality; an ambivalence about spending. (I saw that in my father's reluctance to buy a new car in 1948, when his old one was nine years old and falling apart.)

Socializing for most couples was usually insular, involving family, friends from work or the neighborhood, or old school chums. With neighborhoods homogeneous from a racial and ethnic standpoint, friendships across these lines were unusual.

Looking at Greatest Generation marriages from the outside, most couples seemed happy and projected auras of wonderful relationships. This was because the façade of perfection was important; to show that you were doing as well or better than your friends and neighbors. But behind that façade, many couples remained bound in unhappy marriages since divorce was seen as shameful and divorced women were not socially acceptable in various groups. Religious reasons also held people back from making the final break. After all they had gone through, there was an element of loyalty as well that kept many couples together in the face of discontent, even with physical or emotional abuse, or alcoholism. Another factor was that women felt tied to their husbands financially, afraid of having to support themselves if the marriage faltered. Sometimes, later in life, couples finally separated or divorced after years of unhappiness. Infidelity of course, did occur, but was often kept concealed and did not necessarily lead to divorce. It was important for individuals and families to keep problems hidden and not provide peers with ammunition for gossip, or for cutting a person or family down to size.

Because of the way roles were defined for men and women, communication between them could be difficult at times, with men focusing on work and women on bringing up the children. Control of finances was thought to belong in men's hands as they were the ones making the money. Certain topics, such as sexuality and sexual needs, were rarely discussed. For many couples, sex was not as fulfilling as it could be because of a sense of modesty, embarrassment, and a failure to speak out. This lack of communication about sex and other topics caused friction within some relationships that was often accepted as the way things were.

In my medical practice, I often saw the problems couples of this generation had talking about sex. Once, when Viagra first hit the market, an older couple was seated in my office, the man with mild Parkinson's disease. As we were finishing the visit, he asked if I would write a prescription for Viagra for him. While he was speaking, his wife stood up behind him frantically waving her hands and shaking her head to indicate I should not order the medication. Obviously, the two of them had not discussed their sexual relationship beforehand. On other occasions, men wouldn't mention sexual issues while their wives were present as they were too embarrassed to discuss them. Only when their wives were out of the room would they confide in me about their problems. And women of this generation, unlike subsequent ones, never asked sexual questions or opened up about sexual dysfunction or sexual tension with their husbands. It was too private a matter and too uncomfortable to bring up. Parents also had trouble speaking to children about their bodies and about sex, and education about these topics usually came from unenlightened peers and from the streets.

Financial Status

Many couples of the Greatest Generation, because of frugality, hard work, and steady employment, were able to secure nest eggs over the years for comfortable retirements. Unlike their forebears who had no Social Security backup, they counted on it to be there to assist them financially in later life. And Medicare's enactment in 1965 freed them from worry about bankruptcy from medical expenses when they were older. Many workers also had decent pensions from their companies to supplement their incomes after retirement. Because they grew up during the Depression, for the most part they avoided debt and were avid savers, fearful that another financial catastrophe was inevitable, but they would be prepared. They were also not wasteful, using things up before throwing them away and seeking value when making purchases. Though initially reluctant to buy goods on credit, with the economy booming and people doing well, they eventually utilized credit cards liberally.

Starting in the early 2000s, it was believed that as the members of the Greatest Generation died off, there would be a significant transfer of wealth they had accumulated to their children, mostly the Baby Boomers, through inheritance. It was assumed this "greatest wealth transfer ever" would help to rescue the Boomers who had not been saving adequately for their retirements. However, this has turned out to be a mirage for several reasons.[5] First of all, members of the Greatest Generation are surviving longer and spending their money during their lives. Secondly, many of those who are still alive took big financial hits during the last recession, with their stock portfolios drooping and their homes under water. In fact, some of the surviving members of the Greatest Generation have come to depend on their children for monetary assistance, as Social Security has not been enough to keep them afloat in an increasingly expensive world. But it appears that the majority of them have remained self-sufficient financially in their final years, though certainly not free spending.

Retirement

Though some members of the Greatest Generation saw their resources depleted and required financial help from children, the latter were often unable to provide physical and emotional support when it was needed, because they had moved away. Extended families with members living in proximity had become a thing of the past. Some affluent Greatest Generation retirees went to retirement communities or assisted living residences. But many chose to spend their last years in their own homes, whether widowed or as couples.

Relationships between spouses after men and rarely women retired, depended on many factors, similar to other population segments. If spouses were kind and loving toward each other in the past, and enjoyed each other's presence, it usually carried over into retirement. If they merely tolerated each other previously, or were abusive, having both of them home in retirement likely made things worse. As with all relationships, communication was the key to making retirement go smoothly. If either spouse was unable to discuss problems and be honest with his or her mate, aggravation was sure to follow. Complicating matters was the usual strict delineation of roles that had evolved while the man was working. And of course, the overall reticence and self-containment that were common traits of this generation often made connecting more difficult.

In retirement, with both the husband and wife at home, would he be willing to help with some of the household chores, or would he be even more demanding? Indeed, many women continued to play subservient roles, accepting the husband's dominance and a willingness to serve him on a regular basis, though perhaps not happily, to avoid conflict. Another important factor was whether either spouse had a chronic illness requiring the other to act as a caregiver. Again, the previous relationship usually determined how this burden was managed. But a sense of loyalty was hard to overcome in this generation, no matter what the previous feelings had been.

Other factors that impacted relationships after retirement were whether or not the spouses had activities that engaged them outside the home, and how large their living space was. If the two spouses were involved in volunteer work, or had part-time jobs for remuneration, hobbies, or interests that kept them occupied, it was likely that things at home would be better. Or if they had friends outside of marriage with whom they could socialize, the pressure would be off the other mate to interact with them constantly. And having more space in the house made it easier not to be in each other's hair when both were at home.

The inscription on the Iwo Jima monument lauds America's military during World War II—"uncommon valor was a common virtue."[6] Whether or not the "Greatest Generation" was greater than other generation is a matter of conjecture. They certainly endured great hardships, living through the Depression and defeating the Axis powers in World War II, then building an industrial powerhouse that dominated the twentieth century. But the lives of individual members have run the gamut in terms of happiness, financial security, and satisfaction as might be expected. Have they aged well? Given that they have lived unexpectedly longer than previous generations, and given the uncertainty, anxiety, and traumatic events they have experienced, most of them have shown resiliency and done remarkably well. Overall, they can be thought of as a generation of survivors who weathered the century's greatest storms and were able to raise families and pursue careers, with the remnants now living on with memories of a completely different world.

The Silent Generation
Time Line: Born 1930–1945
Influences: Korean War, Cuban Missile Crisis, Assassinations of the Kennedys and Martin Luther King Jr., Early Days of TV, Civil Rights, Anticommunist Investigations, the "Beats"
Age Range in 2014: 68–83

The "Silent Generation" was so named because of their supposed dearth of political activism, compared to the segments before and after them. Born in 1939, I'm considered a member of the Silents, who are also known as Traditionalists and the Post-War Generation. The starting point for our group is blurred, overlapping with the Greatest Generation. Some analysts mark its beginning as the mid-1920s, others as the early 1930s, one of its characteristics being that few in our generation saw action in World War II. Of those born in the early 1930s, many have at least some recollections of the later years of the Depression.

The end point for this demographic is 1945, with the Baby Boomers following in 1946.

The appellation *Silent Generation* was first used in November 1951 in a *Time* magazine cover story about the youth of that period.[7] Subsequently, it was employed by Strauss and Howe in their book *Generations: The History of America's Future, 1584 to 2069.*[8] Mirroring their parents, men and women of the Silent Generation were seen as conformists and risk averse, but unlike them, did not have any unifying major experiences in common. Though the members of the previous cohort were role models because of their accomplishments in saving democracy and shaping the modern world, the Silents had to find their own way and build their own legacies. However, wedged between the Greatest Generation and the free-spirited Baby Boomers who came after them, they found it difficult to establish an explicit identity.

DEMOGRAPHICS

Individuals in this segment were conceived during the economic crisis of the Depression and the stress of World War II, with estimates that its population reached about fifty million,[9] fewer than the preceding generation and the one that followed. This was because of the low birth rate that hit its nadir during the last years of the war, 1944 and 1945. The majority of the Silent Generation, now in their late sixties, seventies, and eighties, are retired and a small percentage have already died. However, a significant number continue to work, either out of necessity or because they enjoy what they are doing. My sister (who is four years younger than I am), many cousins, and most of my friends, many of them still healthy and gainfully employed are of this generation. Given the advances in medical science, the average life expectancy for members of this generation will exceed that of the previous generation, but will be shorter than that of the Boomers and more recent generations.

INFLUENCES

Many parents of the Silents were overprotective and exerted pressure on them as children to conform and fit in. Though older members of the Silent Generation endured the last vestiges of the Great Depression and the effects of World War II, they were not responsible for support- ing themselves and their families during those years, or for fighting the war. Still, these events had a lasting impact that may have shaped their future behavior. Some of the men were called upon to fight in Korea and some in Vietnam, and all lived through the anxious days of the Cuban Missile Crisis and the drawn-out years of the Cold War. But these events affected them as adults, and although atomic war with the Soviet Union was in the back of people's minds, life went on pretty much normally.

Though college campuses during the late 1940s and 1950s were not the hotbeds of political activism evident in the 1960s, it must be empha- sized that the Silent Generation was not wholly silent. Numerous stu- dents spoke out on the issues of the day and were politically involved, with some later having careers in politics. Opposition to the anti-Com- munist witch hunts led by Senator McCarthy and the House Un- American Activities Committee was widespread at colleges, as was par- ticipation in the nascent civil rights movement. But with a climate of paranoia around universities related to the Congressional inquisitions, it is possible that an element of fear was partially responsible for the relative silence and avoidance of politics by most undergraduates. Also, after the upheavals of the Depression and World War II, the majority of college students were just interested in obtaining their degrees and going out into the world to make a living. A professor described the serious young adults of this period as "a generation with strongly mid- dle-aged values."[10]

Most of the cultural and political influences that shaped the Baby Boomers during the 1960s and 1970s also affected members of the Silent Generation, though not during their formative years. Much of the music, movies, and literature was the same for both generations. However, the 1950s with its early rock and roll, highlighted by Elvis Presley, Jerry Lee Lewis, Fats Domino, Chuck Berry, The Platters, The Drifters, Bobby Darin, and so forth, produced the sounds that the Si- lent Generation grew up with and formed the basis for later rock and roll. These were also the nascent years of television with Milton Berle, Ed Sullivan, and other variety shows providing entertainment. And crooners such as Frank Sinatra, Eddie Fisher, and Johnnie Ray caused hysteria among teenage fans known as bobby-soxers. Among the popular female singers were Patti Page, Rosemary Clooney, and Doris Day.

Again it must be emphasized that culture is an interactive process. Those who influenced the outlook of the Silent Generation were also influenced by their own contemporaries and the popular culture of the times. Included among important figures of the generation were Martin Luther King Jr., and Robert Kennedy, Marlon Brando, and James Dean, Marilyn Monroe and Elizabeth Taylor, Gore Vidal and William Buckley, Andy Warhol and Muhammad Ali, Neal Armstrong, the members of The Beatles, Bob Dylan, Gloria Steinem, Jimi Hendrix, James Brown, Newt Gingrich, John McCain, Dick Cheney, Ted Kennedy, Ron Paul, and so forth.

In *Brown v. Board of Education* (of Topeka, Kansas), the Supreme Court ruled in 1954 that school segregation was unconstitutional, changing the law of the land. The civil rights movement grew stronger and more active afterward, with almost all of its leadership coming from the Silents. And the obstruction of integration of Little Rock high school in 1957 by Governor Faubus and the National Guard had a profound effect upon the Silents. This played out on television, along with President Eisenhower's use of the army to enforce integration in Little Rock. Subsequently, after much conflict and violence, acceptance of integration gradually became more widespread in both the South and the North, though some resistance still exists today.

The 1950s were also the time when the Beats came to prominence with writers such as Jack Kerouac, Allen Ginsberg, and William Burroughs. With its emphasis on spirituality and the extensive use of drugs and alcohol, this movement had its origins in New York City and San Francisco. The free flow of modern jazz was an integral part of the Beat singularity as was promiscuous sexual liaisons. Materialism was scorned and many of the Beats eschewed the normal patterns of daily existence. They dropped out and traveled "On the Road," emulating Kerouac and living from hand to mouth. Though the hippies and many of their ideas in the 1960s were generated from the Beat movement, the Beats were less politically active and did not have as much social impact as their more numerous successors.

Midlife may have been a particularly unsettling time for some of the Silents, with their parents being lauded for their accomplishments and many of their children experimenting with sex and drugs. Perhaps there was a twinge of envy over the sexual revolution taking place that had passed them by. There were also those who tried to participate and may have wound up looking silly or out of place. But the Silent Generation still did not have any defining characteristics or unifying experiences that allowed them to stand out. Perhaps their uniqueness was simply the fact that they were not unique and were labeled as ordinary by some observers. However, though as a group they may have been considered conventional, there were plenty of individuals who went against the grain to make their mark on and engage in the issues of the day. After all, it was not only the Baby Boomers who demonstrated against the Vietnam War or for civil rights, and were disgusted by the conduct of Nixon and his administration. The "not so Silents" were also on the front lines.

Now, in their later years, some of the "traditionalist" Silents are unhappy with the direction of society. They are disappointed in what they believe is irresponsible behavior, evidenced by the explosion of government and individual debt, as well as the conduct of executives in the financial industry and business in general. They often perceive the way compensation is determined as unfair, bearing no relation to performance. Many of the Silents also experience a feeling of impotence— of being unable to change what they see as a deterioration of the social order. And though the Silents have held many important posts in government and business, their generation has not produced a president and have already been bypassed by the Boomers—Clinton on the older end and Obama on the younger end.

Though religion has played an important part in the lives of most Silents, compared to the preceding generation, there has been an erosion in the percentage affiliated with religious institutions and in the belief in God. And their children are even less likely to be connected.[11] As the Greatest Generation, the Silents have tended to support social stability, which for the most part meant established religions. However, regular attendance at church services has decreased when measured against their parents.

LIFESTYLES

Education, Employment, and Housing

The Silent Generation was a transitional segment between the Greatest Generation and Baby Boomers, encompassing characteristics of both. Reaching adulthood in a time of affluence, they were more educated and worldly than the preceding generation. However, jobs that paid middle-class wages were still available in both administrative positions and factories that did not require higher education. But to advance up the corporate ladder, college degrees or even MBAs were becoming necessary, and scientists and engineers with college or postgraduate degrees were in demand. Innovations by the men of this generation kept the economy humming, with soaring growth of national wealth.

For the most part, unemployment was low and jobs paid decent wages during this period of economic expansion and industrialization. In fact, from a financial standpoint this generation was more successful than either their parents or children. As noted by Strauss and Howe, "from age 20 to 40, Silent households showed the century's steepest rise in real per capita income and per-household wealth."[12] Because the economy was good, pensions and benefits from many businesses reflected this, in addition to providing healthy salaries. The low birth rate during the Depression and the war meant that workers in many fields were in short supply and companies tried to do whatever they deemed necessary to keep employees happy. Many men remained with the same firms throughout their lives, satisfaction with the status quo being characteristic of this generation. Workers of this cohort were also generally industrious with a strong work ethic similar to their parents. Ambition, however, drove some men to become "workaholics" willing to neglect their personal lives to achieve success in the business world. More women pursued careers than previously, but when married, most of them preferred to stay at home and raise their families, their husbands concurring.

If they had the financial wherewithal, couples usually opted to live in the suburbs, as their parents had, rather than the cities. Single-family homes, with greater space and safe environments for children, remained part of the American Dream for young marrieds. First-class schools were a priority, with better school districts sending more of their students on to college. And rural areas continued to bleed slowly as farms became even more mechanized, many residents migrating to urban areas and securing factory, construction, and other blue-collar work.

Health and Fitness

As the members of this generation grew older, the value of exercise and the negative effects of sedentary lifestyles became general knowledge. More men and women began to run, walk, or bike, either alone, with partners, or in groups. Membership in Ys and gyms began to grow, and new for-profit exercise establishments sprouted all over. Still, many individuals of this generation did not include exercise as part of their daily routines. It was too much trouble, or people were lazy or refused to believe it would make a difference. This was particularly true for those in the older age range. The need for intellectual activities to aid in maintaining memory and cognitive function also became known, and while some individuals took this to heart, others did not.

As a practicing neurologist, I became aware of the way many people in the Greatest and Silent Generations were resistant to exercising. A number of patients of mine in this population group who had suffered mild strokes or had minor problems with memory refused to start exercise programs, even after the benefits had been explained at length. I would tell them that I was prescribing exercise as a treatment, just like medication, and that I wanted them to be compliant. They would agree and perhaps do it for a short period, but would not persevere. It was difficult for them to change their habits after years of sedentary living. On the other hand, some patients found that they enjoyed physical activity; it made them feel stronger and more secure and they thanked me for having urged them to start.

> R. D. was a sixty-year-old man with mild hypertension when I saw him in the hospital with a right hemispheric stroke that had caused left-sided weakness. A sedentary administrative worker, he regained 90 percent of function within three days and was started on physical therapy, aggressive blood pressure control, and a baby aspirin. He was also told to start exercising. Resistant at first, he began walking in the mornings before work, gradually increasing his time and dis-

tance. For the last nine years, he has done well, walking four miles every day as part of his routine.

Medical science continued to progress as the Silents aged and many therapeutic options that their parents lacked were available for them. Surgical techniques and diagnostic studies improved and better medications were developed to reduce blood pressure and cholesterol, and treat diabetes. Not only did these advances keep people alive longer, but they also enhanced the quality of people's lives. Of course, in order to prevent strokes and heart attacks, and to control diabetes, people had to adhere to their medical regimens, see physicians regularly, and follow their orders—not always an easy sell.

> T. R., a patient from this generation under my care, was an executive of a major corporation in his late fifties when he had a small stroke. A two-pack-a-day smoker, he refused to give up his cigarettes. Over the next five years, every twelve to eighteen months and while still smoking, he continued to have small strokes with minimal deficits. This was in spite of blood pressure control, cholesterol lowering medication, and blood thinners. Finally, after a large stroke had caused right-sided paralysis and slurred speech that prevented him from working, he said he would stop smoking—an example of closing the barn door after the horse had escaped.

Relationships and Retirement

Couples in the Silent Generation tended to marry early, the average age for men being twenty-three, and twenty for women.[13] However, as was true for the Baby Boomers and beyond, those who attended college or went for advanced degrees tended to marry later. With lengthy commutes to and from their jobs not unusual for executives and managers, work often stressful and requiring long hours, some men spent little time with their families and many marriages became troubled. Greater business travel and increased hours at work in close contact with members of the opposite sex presented more opportunities as well for affairs. Perhaps the lifestyles of the succeeding generation also influenced some Silents to embark on sexual adventures.

As the stigma associated with divorce decreased, it became more common and more accepted. State "no fault" divorce laws jumped dramatically because of this. Individuals born between the mid-1930s and early 1940s had the biggest age bracket increase in the divorce rate.[14] But divorces occurred in all segments at any age, sometimes later in life when the accumulated years of offenses finally moved one or the other spouse to take action. A problem with communication was again often the sore point for many couples. Still, lifetime companionship remained the norm, with most marriages intact until the death of a spouse, even when important aspects of the relationships were wanting.

Though most individuals and couples continued to live in their homes during retirement, the growth of retirement communities, particularly in the warmer parts of the country, became alluring for many Silents. Some moved South permanently, and others went South during the winters and back North when the weather relented, becoming known as "snowbirds." In addition, living in the cities became fashionable, as urban areas underwent a renaissance and many run-down districts became gentrified. (Parts of Brooklyn and Harlem became so expensive they were priced out of the reach of the middle class.) Cities were cleaner than they had been and had less street crime. Other urban advantages included public transportation, cultural events, and better medical facilities. It was also easier for seniors to live in "high rises," with no maintenance necessary. Whether residing in the cities or down South, air travel and the interstate highway system meant that there were fewer impediments to visiting children and grandchildren.

One of the hindrances for this generation in later life, limiting those who wish to continue working, has been the impression they have difficulty dealing with technology. Since they did not grow up with computers and the new hardware and software, it is believed they have a hard time adapting to the way business is now being conducted. Because of this, employers have been reluctant to hire them, even if they had previously performed well. In reality, most are able to learn to use all of the new systems if they are taught properly. And they are motivated and productive workers even when older.

Silents have political power disproportionate to their numbers, as seniors go to the polls and vote in higher percentages than other groups. Because of this, politicians court them and generally support programs that benefit them. Whether Silents tend to favor Republican candidates or Democrats, preservation of Medicare and Social Security are sacrosanct issues for them, as for the generations before and after them, that can influence how they vote.

Financial Status

The Silents were previously described as having a strong work ethic and focus on financial security. They were also fortunate that numerous opportunities were available for them because of low birth rates and fewer workers during the expansion of the economy. Thus, compensation and benefits for employees were better than in the past and allowed many of them to accumulate savings. Adding this to pension payouts and Social Security, most Silents have been able to maintain middle-class status in retirement. Inflation has also been relatively tame since 1992, preventing excessive erosion of assets and income. But as with the Baby Boomers, some of the men and women of this generation have had to help support their parents or contribute to the upkeep of adult children, which might have sabotaged long-standing financial planning. The recession in 2008 also negatively affected many Silents who for one reason or another did not adequately safeguard their resources. And if assets were depleted during retirement or late in a person's working life, there may not have been enough time or opportunities to recoup the losses. Though some Silents did attempt to go back to work, others were forced to change lifestyles at an age where change did not come easily.

As noted, the Silent Generation is for the most part retired, though some of this cohort continue to work. They were never as silent as they were depicted and though they did not have the defining experiences of the Greatest Generation or the Baby Boomers, they have generally been successful, particularly from an economic standpoint. Though most are now in their seventies, there are still miles for them to travel on the road of life and accomplishments yet to come. Whether each of them will be content to ruminate about his or her past pleasures and triumphs or seek new ones will depend on the individual and his or her values. A passive existence may be less demanding, but meaningful physical and intellectual activities will result in more productive and satisfying later years.

In subsequent chapters we will further discuss what midlifers and older people need to do to maximize the quality of their lives, and keep their minds and bodies working at peak efficiency.

4

THE IMPACT OF TIME AND THE AGING PROCESS

Everything about him was old except his eyes and they were
the same color as the sea and were cheerful and undefeated.

—Ernest Hemingway, *The Old Man and the Sea*[1]

Old age is an unnatural state for most species. Only human beings, or animals we have domesticated and keep in a protected environment, away from nature's primitive hands, are generally capable of growing old. And they are able to live even if they are significantly impaired or disabled. Out in the forests and the jungles however, it is the young, strong, and wily who survive. As animals age and become weaker, unable to run as fast or see as well, they are destroyed through the natural selection process by predators, disease, or by simply not being able to feed themselves adequately. For survival of the species, nature has programmed animals to live through sexual maturity and reproduce themselves. Any existence afterward is merely fortuitous.

As Ralph Waldo Emerson noted, "Nature abhors the old, and old age seems the only disease."[2]

Civilization allows homo sapiens to enjoy a major portion of their lives after propagation and child rearing, including individuals who are no longer economically productive. The more complex and compassionate the social structure of a particular nation, the longer its citizens can potentially survive with arrangements made for the care and support of its elderly. Thus ideally, in a modern, democratic state, barring illnesses, we can live as long as we are able, without worrying about predators or starving to death.

To understand how the aging process affects our vitality and ability to function, we have to know what happens to us with normal aging and common diseases of the elderly. Since the mid-twentieth century, gerontology, the study of aging, has made great progress in delineating the changes that occur as we grow older. Much of the knowledge that has been obtained through painstaking research projects has been observational in nature, with scientists reporting on the cellular and molecular transformation that organisms undergo over time. Unfortunately, the reasons why this metamorphosis takes place (perhaps the key to unlocking life's secrets) remain unclear. We know a great deal about what happens, but not why. In this chapter, I will look at the changes seen on a cellular level, then briefly discuss some of the theories on aging. I will also survey the alterations that take place in human organs and organ systems over the years. This is not meant to be all-inclusive, nor encyclopedic in its descriptions, but to provide a general idea of what happens to us as we grow older.

CELLULAR AGING

The trillions of cells in our bodies are smaller subunits (building blocks) of our tissues and organs, each one individually unique and with its own mission to perform in support of the entire organism. During our lifetime, most of our cells divide periodically to replace those that are damaged or no longer functioning properly. However, all of our cells are constantly active from a metabolic standpoint, even when we are sleeping—like miniature factories, producing various substances, destroying others, moving molecules in and out, and utilizing vast amounts of energy. "In life, entropy [the degree of disorder in a substance or system] . . . is in a constant war with biological forces that try to maintain a well-controlled 'homeostatic' environment for the cell. Homeostasis is the tendency for a biological system to keep things steady and unchanged."[3] This battle requires the cell to always be at work to preserve a steady state among different elements. Proteins in particular are being created and broken down during every moment of a cell's existence as its needs vary in response to internal and external conditions.

This unceasing activity results in differences in the cells over time, as parts of the biologic machinery are perhaps worn out.

Though we are able to recognize aging when we look at someone, the changes responsible for what we see occur at a microscopic level, involving cells and their components, and fractions even as small as molecules. "Normal cells have only a limited capacity to divide and function."[4] When that impediment is approached, cells have become old. In other words, a cell's age can be determined by its ability to divide further in the future. "It takes about forty doublings of a fertilized egg to produce a full-grown human adult, allowing all the cells that are shed from our bodies during a lifetime."[5] Fifty cellular divisions are about the maximum that embryonic human cells can manage, far more than is required during a person's life span. This barrier to infinite cell division is known as the *Hayflick Limit* after the scientist who discovered this phenomenon. The genetically predetermined biologic clock that controls the process resides in the DNA (genes) of the nucleus, in a structure called a *telomere*. Each species has its own genetic program with longevity dependent on the number of possible cell divisions.

Work on cellular aging has focused on the telomere in determining the limits of cellular division, with some discoveries that have implications for the aging process and the cancerous transformation of cells.[6] For instance, "[T]he life span of human cells is mainly set not by their chronological age, but by how often they divide. At each division the telomeres—strings of special purpose DNA at the ends of the chromosomes—get shorter, until at a particular minimum length a signal is somehow touched off that forces the cells into the phase of aging and decline known as senescence."[7] This usually occurs at about fifty cellular divisions. An enzyme called *telomerase* can prevent the telomere from getting shorter as the cell divides, thus maintaining its youthfulness, with all the characteristics of young, healthy cells. It appears that telomerase may be able to extend the life span of human cells (in culture) indefinitely, but the significance of this is uncertain. (Telomerase is also produced by cancerous cells, allowing them to multiply unrestrained.)

Telomeres and telomerase are not the complete answer to the question of why cells age. Some cells in the body supposedly did not divide after birth (muscle and nerve cells), yet still showed the changes of aging, which should not be related to a shortened telomere. So other mechanisms are probably involved. However, some studies have found that nerve cells may be able to divide and reproduce themselves under certain conditions and this may be true as well for muscle cells. Research into the different genetic components that affect aging is ongoing.

Just as cells in different individuals age at their own distinct rates, the cells of different tissues in the same organism do not deteriorate uniformly on the road to malfunction and cellular death. Cells that have divided repeatedly and are near their limit (shortened telomeres) undergo changes that influence all of their metabolic and biochemical processes, affecting proteins, carbohydrates, fats, enzyme systems, and DNA. Generally, metabolism slows in older cells and the production of proteins is reduced. Their performance then falters and makes them and the entire organism more subject to disease. The tissues or organs that age most rapidly usually determine how long the organism itself will live, particularly if they serve a vital purpose.

THEORIES OF AGING

In searching for the causes of aging in large organisms such as human beings, it is important to remember that although the rate of change that takes place may vary among individuals, it is a universal process. One must also differentiate between the normal changes seen with aging and changes caused by diseases that are common in older people, but not universal. In addition, it must be appreciated that when changes or substances are found in aging cells or aging organisms, it may be difficult to determine whether they are actually causing aging or simply byproducts of the aging process.

Though the role of the telomere in aging is intriguing, a number of different theories have been propounded as to why aging occurs. These remain speculative, with hypotheses falling in and out of favor, and with no proven cause to date. Ultimately, it may be found that several mechanisms are involved and that their interaction produces aging, rather than one specific factor. There are three main theories.[8] However, it should be emphasized again that evolution has primarily designed our bodies and its components to last until our reproductive period is over and has not been concerned with longevity.

The first theory posits that aging and cell death are programmed in genetically. This can be perceived as though a biologic clock within our bodies and cells predetermines the course of aging we will follow. However, this does not exclude environmental factors such as illnesses or exposure to toxic substances from accelerating the process, or a proper diet, better sleep habits, and exercise from slowing it down. The second theory holds that mutations and genetic errors accumulate in cells over time to produce aging. Mutations are constantly occurring in the billions of cells in our body as they divide and re-divide, observed by scientists for decades and considered as chance variants. (Some of these mutated cells will produce cancers if they do not die off spontaneously, or are not killed by other cells or our immune system.) But as these mutations increase, they cause cellular and organ dysfunction and aging. Again, random events in the environment such as exposure to toxins or radiation may enhance the rate of mutations and make us age faster.

The third theory, the antagonist "pleiotropic theory," propounds that "late-acting deleterious genes may . . . be favored by selection and be actively accumulated in populations if they have . . . beneficial effects early in life."[9] In other words, genes that are helpful for survival when individuals are young will be acquired by a species even if they are hazardous when individuals are older and past the stage of reproduction. A variety of other theories fall under the umbrella of these three major categories, though some stand alone.

Free Radical Theory

Free radical compounds may be implicated in age-related changes as well as being linked to a number of disease states. As a consequence of cell metabolism, various molecules combine with oxygen to form free radicals—unstable molecular fragments that react with other cellular substances to cause significant damage and interfere with normal cell activity. Free radicals have been demonstrated to injure genetic material (DNA), are involved in the production of the characteristic plaques of Alzheimer's disease, and in the generation of age pigment. Older animals produce more free radicals with resultant damage to DNA, and resistance to oxidative stress has been linked to longevity in some species.[10] Antioxidants, like vitamin E and vitamin C, are compounds that interfere with the formation of free radicals and have been shown in some *experimental* circumstances to retard the changes seen with aging and to increase longevity. To date, they have not been shown to enhance longevity in humans and studies involving specific diseases have been ambiguous. There is no hard evidence that antioxidants actually affect aging or reduce any of the diseases associated with aging.

Changes in the Immune System

Some biologists have theorized that alteration of the immune system induces aging, perhaps programmed in by atrophy of the thymus gland in the chest. The immune system protects us against invaders like viruses and bacteria, and also combats dangerous internal threats by destroying cancerous cells. Specialized cells of the immune system (white blood cells) and certain proteins generated by the immune cells (antibodies, compliment, and the like) are the bulwarks that safeguard our bodies. If the immune system goes awry, it can attack healthy tissues, by failing to distinguish between what is foreign and what is self. In these instances, it produces "autoimmune diseases" such as rheumatoid arthritis, multiple sclerosis, myasthenia gravis, certain types of diabetes, and other ailments. If the immune system is dysfunctional, an individual may be more susceptible to infections and less able to suppress neoplastic (cancerous) changes when they occur. Though the immune system is generally less effective as we grow older, there is no evidence this transformation is a significant factor in aging.

Errors in the Cellular Reparative Processes

This hypothesis, congruent with the second major theory, proposes that errors in the cellular reparative processes cause aging. As would be expected in a living, vital organism, there are constant breakdowns in various components of human tissues with subsequent repair. This cycle is ongoing. The mechanism for restoration of damage lies in the genetic DNA in the cell nucleus that replicates itself and is necessary for the production of proteins within our cells. Over time, after going through multiple cycles of repair, imperfections known as mutations are seen in the complex structure of the DNA. These may lead to errors in cellular proteins whose generation is controlled by DNA. The flaws produced may be even further exaggerated over additional cycles in the unending sequence that is life. The proponents of this construct believe these cumulative mistakes are related to the aging process and when severe enough result in certain diseases. Exposure to environmental factors over the years, such as sunlight, radiation, various chemical substances, and the like, may initiate the mutations in the DNA.

Other Theories

An additional theory suggests that an inability to effectively handle waste materials by the cells may be the key element in aging; like factories no longer able to dispose of their byproducts. These substances then accumulate within the cells and may be toxic, producing cellular dysfunction. While it is true that lipofuscin (age pigment) is found increasingly in neurons (nerve cells) and cardiac cells in elderly people, this may just be an epiphenomenon (something associated with a process) rather than the actual cause of cellular aging.

Cross-linking is seen in complex proteins like collagen in older cells. This may also occur in genetic material (DNA) in the cells. But is it cause or effect? These occurrences could impair cellular replication or metabolism in older people and cause the changes inherent in aging.

Other hypotheses have implied that aging may be related to hormonal signals that originate in the brain and act on tissues and cells all over the body.[11] The hormones direct the cells to burn glucose, producing free radicals that result in cellular damage and aging. Another proposal is that wear and tear to cells and tissues due to the cumulative effects of repeated small injuries, even at a molecular level, are responsible for aging. Of interest is the observation that in lower organisms like rats, restricted caloric intake and lower body weight has been shown to prolong life span by about 40 percent.[12] There have been suggestions that this is also true in higher primates. However, a study in 2012 demonstrated that caloric restriction does not increase longevity in primates.[13] Why this occurs in rats is uncertain, but may be related to a specific gene, SIR 2 (silent information regulator), and a protein it produces that silences gene activity. The bottom line is that no research has yet come up with a definitive answer as to why we age.

However, one would not know by the proliferation of special reme-
dies available to halt or reverse aging that an explanation for the aging
process has not been found. Various products with secret formulas and
exclusive methods promise to keep us from growing older, or at least
delay the consequences of time. But there is nothing on the market
today of proven value as an antidote to aging. For some people, the use
of antioxidant vitamins, such as C and E may provide psychological
benefit, though there have even been suggestions of deleterious effects
from these. On the other hand, the use of unregulated patent medicines
is definitely detrimental to one's pocketbook and some of these may be
physically or cognitively harmful.

Investigators have discovered substances that appear to have the
potential of prolonging life, though availability for humans is years
away.[14] One of these is resveratrol, found in red wines, which works by
activating a class of proteins called *sirtuins*.[15] A number of other compounds are also being studied. Some of these substances act in a manner similar to a very-low-calorie diet, but again, efficacy in humans
remains uncertain.

Also of interest are those rare genetic diseases that cause accelerated
aging. The most striking of these is progeria, caused by a mutation in
the LMNA gene that results in a defective type of protein named *lamin
A*,[16] seen in about one in eight million newborns. In this condition,
aging occurs at about seven times the normal rate, with a ten-year-old
child having the cardiovascular, pulmonary, and musculoskeletal system
of a seventy-year-old. These children appear elderly with baldness,
wrinkled skin, pinched noses, small faces and jaws, dwarfism, and ar-
thritic joints, as well as generalized atherosclerotic vascular disease.
Death usual ensues in the teenage years. Unfortunately, though this
syndrome mimics premature aging, it has not provided answers to investigators as to the riddle of aging.

NORMAL CHANGES IN ORGANS AND ORGAN SYSTEMS

There is a Yiddish word for complaining called *kvetching*. The term can
be used as either a verb or a noun. Thus, someone who kvetches constantly is also known as a "kvetch," a disparaging description. Unfortunately, some older people are perceived as kvetches because of their

frequent complaints about physical ailments, making them less sympathetic figures. In fact, the response to complainers is usually negative and others tend to avoid those who are chronically lamenting their lot in life. On the other hand, people admire those who bear their crosses with good humor and minimal grumbling. That does not mean that one should not express sadness about one's limitations, or not reveal feelings that are present. But complaining should not be a constant refrain, for it will sour relationships, driving away friends and relatives.

General Changes Seen with Aging

Loss of height occurs universally starting at about age thirty, with most of us reluctantly surrendering several inches by the time we enter our eighties. Much of this is due to shrinkage of the intervertebral cartilaginous discs up and down the length of the spine. Alterations in posture and bowing of the legs also play a role. Total body fat increases, with a difference in distribution noted as well, particularly greater abdominal girth. Lean muscle mass is reduced and the body's metabolism falls, as does oxygen consumption. A lessening of abdominal muscle tone adds to the bulging seen in older people.

The Brain and Nervous System

With aging, everyone's brain weight diminishes. Atrophy is seen at autopsy in pathological specimens, and in CAT scans (computerized axial tomography) and MRI scans (magnetic resonance imaging) of the living. The gyri (the convoluted tissue that makes up the surface of the brain) shrink, the sulci (the fissures between the gyri) widen, and the ventricles (the cavities in the brain) dilate. The number of neurons (brain cells) in the gray matter decrease, particularly in the frontal regions. Subcortical neurons (deep in the brain) are lost in greater proportions and the white matter appears to shrink. The production of certain proteins declines, among them enzymes that are important neurotransmitters (chemicals that transmit impulses between nerve cells), such as acetylcholine and dopamine, in systems that control memory and motor activity (movement, balance, coordination, and so forth). Accumulation of amyloid protein is also seen extracellularly in older brains, though much more prominently in individuals with Alzheimer's disease. The reason for this is unclear, but the accumulation may be a waste product of cellular metabolism.

In the past, it was believed that neurons were immutable and incapable of regeneration when damaged. However, studies have shown this to be untrue, raising the possibility that with the proper stimulus, injured nerve cells in the brain and spinal cord may be able to be induced to regenerate. Data suggest that the adult central nervous system may be capable of self-repair, encouraged through activity or rehabilitation.[17] In fact, new cells have been shown to develop in a part of the brain involved with memory (the hippocampus) with aerobic exercise, a truly exciting discovery.[18] (This will be discussed further in chapter 8.)

From a functional standpoint the outstanding effect of aging on the brain is that increased time is necessary to perform various tasks. As we grow older, "there is continual loss in speed of learning, speed of processing new information, and speed of reaction to simple or complex stimuli. There is loss of sensory functions, . . . in muscle strength and motor efficiency."[19] Though central processing within the brain is slowed, most tasks can be accomplished and new information learned. It just takes longer. As Hayflick notes, "[L]oss of mental capacity with age is not inevitable. The old idea that senility is a normal accompaniment of age is simply wrong."[20]

Memory is affected to some degree in virtually everyone, starting in the fifties and becoming more pronounced with each succeeding decade. Explicit memory (where there is intention to recall) is particularly involved, with long-term and working memory remaining remarkably intact in numerous older people. Many individuals are quite concerned regarding their memory problems, believing they herald the onset of Alzheimer's. But they are normal occurrences and not commonly disabling. Often, there is also rigidity in habits and daily routine and difficulty in adapting to new situations.

Balance generally deteriorates with age, though the level of dysfunction varies. Those who are physically active tend to have fewer difficulties. Hand coordination and fine movements are frequently impaired as well, usually due to a combination of both brain and musculoskeletal factors, with arthritis often playing a role. In addition to changes in the brain, there is a delay in the conduction of impulses in the sensory and motor fibers of the peripheral nerves. This may also contribute to some of the decline in motor abilities (strength and balance) and sensory perception (touch, pain, cold, heat). But usage and activity can help maintain function.

Sleep patterns controlled by the brain normally change as we grow older. Hormonal alterations may be partially responsible. The total time we sleep each night lessens with a decrease in the percentage of deep sleep. Because of a need to urinate, repeated interruptions of sleep may occur, with awakenings also originating in the brain. The elderly generally arise earlier in the morning, even if they go to sleep late at night, though most do retire earlier. Napping during the day is characteristic and quite refreshing for many individuals.

The Heart and Cardiovascular System

The incidence of cardiovascular disease in the general population is directly related to age. The older you are, the more likely you are to have problems. In the absence of heart disease however, the ability to pump blood does not change to any major degree as we grow older and our hearts are able to work surprisingly well. But heart muscle has been found to lose some of its elasticity and becomes somewhat stiffer and thicker. The maximal heart rate declines, though cardiac output can go up when necessary demands are made. This happens by raising the quantity of blood pumped out with each contraction. The heart may also not respond as quickly to various stimuli. All of these factors make vigorous exertion more difficult. Some of this is often due to deconditioning from lack of exercise and those who are physically active may be able to retard many of the alterations seen with aging.

Atherosclerosis in older people, commonly known as hardening of the arteries, is due mainly to deposition of fatty materials on and within the walls of the arteries. Calcification may also occur. Though in the past atherosclerosis was felt to be an expected part of aging, in reality it is a diseased state that is minimal in healthy individuals. The changes seen are related to cholesterol and lipid metabolism, with genetic predisposition and diet playing roles. However, there is normally some thickening of the lining of the arteries (intima) in older people and some rigidity of the blood vessel wall. Systolic blood pressure (the higher of the two blood pressure numbers) may also be somewhat elevated. The normal changes in the blood vessels of older people probably make

them more susceptible to atherosclerosis. Studies also suggest that inflammation plays an important role in the process.

The Respiratory System

As we age, lungs become less elastic because of a transformation in the
connective tissues (collagen, elastin). This leads to increased pulmonary
volume and expansion of the thoracic cavity, recognized in some older
people as a barrel-like chest. Vital capacity of the lungs also diminishes.
Calcification occurs between the ends of the ribs and the sternum
(breastbone), resulting in reduced flexibility of the chest wall. Because
of this, less air moves with each breath, necessitating more work in
breathing, particularly the deep excursions accompanying strenuous activity. Many of the small terminal sacs (alveoli) deep within the lung
tissue become damaged or collapse with age, compromising the surface
area where air and blood interface. Thus, the transfer of oxygen from
the air through the membranes of the lungs into the blood becomes less
efficient and oxygen levels in the blood decline. Again, exercise can
prevent and even reverse some of these changes.

The Gastrointestinal System

> A man hath no better thing under the sun than to eat,
> and to drink, and to be merry.
> —Ecclesiastes 8:15[21]

The gastrointestinal system makes it possible for us to eat, drink, and be
merry. Our nutritional status depends on this allied group of organs
involved in the intake and digestion of food and the elimination of
waste. It consists of the mouth and oral cavity, salivary glands, esopha-
gus, stomach, small and large intestine, liver, gall bladder, and pancreas.

In older people, the swallowing mechanism may be impaired to a
minor degree and the act may take longer. Emptying time of the stomach may be increased and less acid produced. Atrophy of the lining of
the large and small intestine can be seen along with small sacs in the
wall of the large intestine (diverticula) that can become inflamed if food
lodges in them. Because the muscles and contractile function of the
walls of the intestine weaken with age, the passage of food takes longer

and there is a higher incidence of constipation. Gas and eructation (belching) are also more common. All the glands in the gastrointestinal system (salivary, stomach, intestines) are reduced in number and secrete decreased amounts of enzymes, which may lead to problems with digestion and food absorption. The liver shrinks in size and there is less blood flow to this organ and less enzymatic activity. Since the liver is responsible for the metabolism of many chemical compounds, older people are often more sensitive to medications and may require lower doses and careful adjustments of prescribed drugs. The pancreas may also atrophy and the production of its enzymes may decline, particularly lactase, which digests the sugar in dairy products.

The Genitourinary System

In the urinary tract, the kidneys passively and actively filtrate liquid waste and excrete it as urine. It then passes through the ureters into the bladder where it is stored until it is released through the urethra. The genital system in the male consists of the testes with its various tubules, the prostate, and the penis. The female genital system is made up of the ovaries, fallopian tubes, uterus, cervix, vagina, and clitoris.

With age, our kidneys shrink, and blood flow and renal function decrease. This may cause problems in eliminating some medications. Concentration of urine is more difficult to achieve and we may have trouble regulating salt. Because the kidneys do not work as well, older people are more prone to dehydration. They may also find it more difficult to urinate and empty the bladder because of weakness in the muscles of the bladder wall. Changes in urinary sphincter tone may cause problems in controlling urination and lead to incontinence. Enlargement of the prostate gland around the urethra in older men can cause urinary frequency, nocturia (a need to urinate during the night), hesitant urinary flow, and even urinary retention.

Normally, as men grow older there is a decline in frequency of sexual intercourse and a reduction in sexual hormone levels (testosterone). However, sperm counts in ejaculates are unchanged. Some scar tissue develops in the prostate and penis, and blood flow to the latter diminishes as well. The penis may be less sensitive to tactile stimuli, and sexual daydreaming and fantasizing may decline, which appears to correlate with sexual desire. General erectile ability may be impaired and the refractory period after orgasm increases considerably (the time before an erection and subsequent orgasm can be achieved). "There is some belief that intercourse maintains the prostate in good condition. This prompted one urologist to suggest that his male patients remember the three stages of sexual activity: tri-weekly, try weekly, and try weakly—but do try."[22]

Women generally go through menopause in their late thirties to midfifties with a reduction in estrogen levels and a halt in ovulation. The ovaries tend to become atrophic and the drop in estrogen can lead to hot flashes. Lack of female hormones results in shrinkage of the uterus and vagina, with thinning of the walls of these organs and diminished vaginal secretions. This may lead to discomfort with intercourse (dyspareunia) unless corrective measures are taken. One of my professors used to joke that "dyspareunia is better than no pareunia at all." But this pain is no joke to the women who have it, leading to avoidance of sexual intercourse and possible strains on relationships. Breast tissue shrinks as well after menopause, with the breasts becoming smaller and flabbier. In some women, libido is decreased, resulting in a decline in sexual activity.

The Endocrine System

The pituitary is the body's "master gland" regulating the production of hormones. However, the pituitary itself may be controlled by a part of the brain called the hypothalamus. In addition to the pituitary and reproductive glands (testes and ovaries), the endocrine system includes the thyroid, adrenal, and insulin producing cells of the pancreas. A feedback loop exists between these glands and the pituitary-hypothalamus that determines how much of various hormones are manufactured and released. As we grow older, almost all our glands produce diminished amounts of hormones. In the past, this was felt by some to be responsible for the aging process and growth hormone, testosterone, and estrogen, were given in an attempt to reverse the changes of aging. But these have not been shown to be of significant benefit.

In spite of this, a number of clinics and physicians continue to give hormone injections in an attempt to retard aging.[23] In fact, an American Academy of Anti-Aging Medicine exists and claims to have 8,000 physicians as members. The injections given are usually a combination of growth hormone (which is produced by the pituitary gland) and the sex hormones, testosterone for men—estrogen and progesterone for women—along with melatonin, vitamins, and antioxidants. There is no question that increased muscle mass, loss of fat, and heightened vigor and sex drive can result initially from these treatments. But the long-term results are less certain and they do not appear to make people stronger, do not improve cognitive ability, and do not increase life expectancy.[24] (In animal studies, those with increased growth hormone died earlier.) And a growth hormone causes significant side effects including joint pains, swelling of the legs and feet, elevated blood sugar or diabetes, and high blood pressure. Testosterone may induce or worsen prostate cancer, and estrogen can have the same effect with breast and ovarian cancers. It is possible that further studies may come up with a hormonal formula helpful in slowing the aging process with minimal side effects, but for the time being evidence does not favor their use.[25]

The Musculoskeletal System

The musculoskeletal system is comprised of bones, cartilage, joints, muscles, ligaments, and tendons. As we age, we lose bone tissue, usually starting in the fifties, though the degree of this loss varies. Normally, there is a balance between the production of new bone and reabsorption of old bone. With aging, this equilibrium is altered; slowing bone growth and thinning bones result in osteoporosis. Women are affected much more than men, particularly after menopause.

Alterations in the joints occur frequently in older people, manifest as osteoarthritis. The cartilage undergoes chemical changes and some of this tissue is lost. Though much osteoarthritis can be attributed to excessive wear, it is not present universally. As we grow older, muscle as a percentage of body weight diminishes, along with strength and stamina, evidenced in the performance of different tasks requiring these elements. Though some of this is an integral part of the aging process, considerable enhancement of performance can be fostered with proper exercise and dietary intake.

The Skin

Our skin protects and insulates our bodies and is visible to the outside world as an indicator of age. However, the changes seen are not uniform throughout the population and certain factors cause alterations disproportionate to a person's chronologic age. The most important variable is exposure to ultraviolet rays that are part of sunlight. Thus, people who are outdoors a lot without adequate protection are more likely to have damaged skin that appears old. The loss of a protein called "collagen" and an increase in another called "elastin" cause wrinkles, for many the first sign of aging. There is also a loss of some subcutaneous fat and thinning of the skin, which becomes less flexible over time and sags. Age spots (senile keratoses) appear more frequently, particularly in the old-old. Though aging skin may not be as esthetically appealing as young skin, it functions quite effectively in the job for which it was designed.

Fingernail growth slows in most people in their later years. Color may change to a yellow or gray and the nails may look duller than previously. There are also differences in hair color and patterns of growth. (Male pattern baldness occurs in younger men who have a genetic predisposition and high levels of testosterone.) Hair becomes thinner on the scalp and generally over the body, though it may increase in the nostrils, ears, and eyebrows. Women may grow more facial hair after menopause. Of course graying of the hair is another marker of age, but is variable in terms of time of onset and degree. Graying results from the decline of cells in the hair bulb that produce melanin, the pigment responsible for coloration of the skin and hair.

NORMAL CHANGES IN THE SENSORY SYSTEMS

With aging, acuteness of sensation is blunted to differing degrees in all of us as our vision diminishes and our hearing fades, usually a slow decline that allows us to remain functional.

Vision

For most people at midlife, a change in the lens of the eye is noted and it becomes thicker and less flexible. This results in difficulty focusing on near objects (presbyopia), easily correctable with eyeglasses. Problems seeing in dim light or in the presence of glare, or adapting to the dark, also arise more often as we age.

Hearing

Structural changes also develop in our ears as we get older. The eardrum becomes thicker, the canal atrophies, and degenerative changes may take place in the small bones of the middle ear. Higher frequencies of sound are not heard as well (presbycusis) because of these differences. Pitch discrimination also becomes impaired, which may make it more difficult to locate sounds and understand speech, particularly when background noises in the environment mask them, such as in a crowded room.

Smell and Taste

The ability to perceive different odors and tastes declines markedly later in life.[26] The diminished sense of smell may be due to changes in the areas of the brain responsible for interpreting smell, or to the loss of cells that detect various odors. This impairment of smell is potentially hazardous in the elderly if they are unable to recognize toxic elements, gas, burning, and the like.

The tongue atrophies somewhat as we age, though this does not appear to affect our taste buds. But because the sensation of taste is partially dependent on smell, it also becomes muted. This can lead to less enjoyment of food and sometimes to poor eating habits and impaired nutrition.

Touch

The appreciation of light touch and pain sensation also lessens with age. Whether this is on a peripheral basis (delayed nerve conduction) or of central origin (loss of neurons in the brain or spinal cord) is uncertain.

DENTAL PROBLEMS

The loss of teeth with aging is widespread, with seniors often depicted as edentulous (toothless). However, this does not occur universally and with proper dental care, can be avoided. For many people, the loss of teeth is undesirable for cosmetic reasons and in terms of self-image. Tooth decay and cavities usually result from poor oral hygiene and when severe may require teeth to be extracted. Periodontal disease (problems with the gums and supporting structures) can also cause tooth loss. Regular dental examinations and care, proper oral hygiene, and fluoride additives for children may all be helpful in maintaining teeth in our later years.

CONCLUSION

Having reviewed the normal changes that occur with aging, one might believe that the prognosis for all of us is poor as we grow older. But that is not the case. For most of us, our fate remains in our own hands to a large degree until the last stages of our lives. However, we must remain physically active, mentally stimulated, and socially engaged to have a positive influence on the course of our aging.

5

KNOWING YOUR ENEMIES: DISEASES AND DISORDERS COMMON WITH AGING

Growing old ain't for sissies.

—attributed to the actress Bette Davis[1]

Growing old is like going for a walk on a cool, cloudy day. Suddenly, it begins misting, but that's not bothersome. As you continue walking, the mist becomes a steady drizzle. You debate whether or not to turn around and go home, but it's not heavy enough to warrant that. You persist and the rain gets stronger. You wonder about seeking shelter, but convince yourself it's not that bad. Perhaps it'll let up a bit or even stop in a while. So you keep on trudging through the rain until it's pouring and you're wet and cold, and far from home. There's no turning back as we grow older and are slowly dampened, then finally drenched by old age. At each stage, we convince ourselves it isn't that bad until we're completely soaked. And there's nowhere for us to go to dry off.

For many, growing older is not easy. Normal aging takes a toll and then we have to deal with various diseases and disorders that may attack us when we are vulnerable. It takes courage and spirit to face down the enemy, battling him to a standstill whenever possible and overcoming him when the opportunity is there. But to fight back, we have to know our adversaries, in order to devise strategies and marshal our forces, to emerge victorious whenever we can.

People do not die of old age. Death is caused by diseases that affect us when we are older (see table 5.1). These are abnormal conditions and the older we get, the more likely we are to be stricken by one or more of these disorders, since the aging process makes us more susceptible to illnesses and injuries. Many people whose cause of death is listed as a particular problem may have several diseases concurrently.

Less serious problems that interfere with quality of life are also common in many seniors. In assessing disabilities among older people who live independently, one study found that 38 percent had arthritis, 29 percent had hearing impairment, 20 percent had vision impairment, and 29 percent had heart conditions.[2] Yet in a survey published in an important medical journal in 2000, it was found that overall quality of life and health in people who were living longer was getting better.[3] We should keep that in mind as we explore the diseases and disorders of older age. People are generally living longer and their quality of life is better than at any time in the past. To make aging even less onerous, though we cannot influence some of the changes that occur with aging,

Table 5.1.   The Ten Leading Causes of Death, 2000

		Number	Death Rate (per 100,000 people)	Percentage of Total Deaths
	All causes*	2,403,351	873.1	100
1.	Heart Disease	710,760	258.2	29.6
2.	Cancer	553,091	200.9	23.0
3.	Stroke	167,661	60.9	7.0
4.	Chronic Respiratory Diseases	122,009	44.3	5.1
5.	Accidents	97,900	35.6	4.1
6.	Diabetes Mellitus	69,301	25.2	2.9
7.	Influenza and Pneumonia	65,313	23.7	2.7
8.	Alzheimer's Disease	49,558	18.0	2.1
9.	Kidney Disease	37,251	13.5	1.5
10.	Blood Poisoning	31,224	11.3	1.3

Source: National Center for Health Statistics, U.S. Department of Health and Human Services, The World Almanac and Book of Facts (New York: World Almanac Books, 2003), 76.
*Minor causes are not included in the table.

we can modify our responses to these changes and the way we conduct ourselves.

DISEASES OF THE BRAIN AND NERVOUS SYSTEM

Alzheimer's Disease and Dementia

Dementia, a general impairment of cognitive function, has a number of different causes. One report notes three quarters of those afflicted by dementia have Alzheimer's disease alone or in combination with cerebrovascular disease.[4] Generally, it is believed about two thirds of patients with dementia have the changes of Alzheimer's and about one quarter to one half have vascular disease. Other major causes include Lewy body disease and fronto-temporal dementia (Pick's disease). The ravages of dementia do not spare the wealthy, nor the famous, with Ronald Reagan, Rita Hayworth, and Charlton Heston among those who have been victims of Alzheimer's. However, those with higher levels of education or intelligence may have some degree of protection from the disease, or perhaps a greater reserve before dementia is evident.[5] Interestingly, a report in the journal *Neurology* in July 2013 shows that those with more frequent cognitive activity across their lifespans are less likely to suffer cognitive decline later in life.[6]

Dementia is not a normal accompaniment of aging; it is the result of specific illnesses whose incidence increases with age.[7] It is estimated that 4 to 5 percent of the population of the United States over age sixty-five has dementia. The highest rate of involvement is in the old-old over eighty-five, with 25 to 50 percent said to be affected. There is a hereditary predisposition to Alzheimer's, particularly when it develops at a younger age (that is, seventy or below). A clear association has also been shown to exist between the APOE E4 genotype and Alzheimer's disease, with much greater risk in those who are homozygous for APOE E4 (have two copies of the gene).[8] A study published in *The New England Journal of Medicine* in 2013 also shows that genetic variants in TREM2 (triggering receptor expressed on myeloid 2 cells protein) are associated with an increased risk of Alzheimer's.[9]

The incidence of mild cognitive impairment (MCI) in the older population may be higher than actual dementia, and many affected individuals with the amnestic form progress to Alzheimer's.[10] MCI causes problems with intellectual functioning, but generally allows those afflicted to live independently and care for themselves. Many investigators feel this condition is really pre-Alzheimer's disease and one study shows a majority of those with amnestic MCI evolve into dementia over two to three years.[11]

> R. T., a divorced woman who was a secretary at a law firm, came to see me when she was sixty-two with complaints of forgetfulness, misplacing things, and minor problems at work. Examination was normal, with a score of 28/30 on the Mini-Mental State Examination (MMSE). MRI showed minor brain atrophy and a few white-matter changes, concordant with her age, and a diagnosis of MCI was made. A year and a half later, she had to leave her job because of difficulty functioning. Over a four-year period, she had progressive impairment of memory and started getting lost driving. Greater atrophy was present on MRI and her MMSE worsened, consistent with a diagnosis of Alzheimer's. Her children eventually paid for a full-time caregiver and she was able to remain at home.

More than any other aspect of aging or any other disease process, dementia robs the involved person of all vestiges of dignity and functional ability. Alzheimer's disease causes a decline in all parameters of intellectual performance, with memory and ability to reason most severely compromised. Most investigators think that deposits in the brain of a substance called *amyloid* extracellularly destroys cells and interferes with the transmission of signals between neurons. (A study published in 2013 in the journal *Brain*, however, shows that some people with large amyloid burdens in their brains at autopsy did not have Alzheimer's.[12]) A substance called *tau*, which may play a role, is also present within the cells. However, some neuroscientists believe Alzheimer's is related to diabetes and disordered glucose metabolism. Microscopically, one sees amyloid plaques outside the cells and the neurofibrillary tangles of tau intracellularly scattered throughout the brain. These are concentrated in areas that control memory and thinking, increasing as the disease progresses. Cell death multiplies over time and the brain atrophies. The initial symptoms may be partially due to diminished acetylcholine, a chemical that transmits signals between brain cells.

At the onset, those who are ill may seem mildly forgetful, though able to operate at a fairly high level. They may understand that things are not completely right, but full insight is usually lacking. It is often the family, rather than the patient, who brings the condition to the attention of a physician. At this point, affected individuals are generally able to manage their own lives, perhaps with minimal assistance. However, as the disease progresses and they become more compromised, they gradually lose the capacity to function independently, requiring assistance and supervision for their most basic needs.

Driving may be one of the first skills to go, with difficulty reacting to conditions in traffic or on the highway. Soon, even local driving with familiar landmarks cannot be negotiated without getting lost. Usually, a family member will then attempt to take away the car keys and there may be verbal battles between the family and the individual with dementia before he or she is willing to surrender driving privileges. Periodically, one sees articles in the papers about a person with Alzheimer's disease who went out for a drive and wound up in another state. (I had a patient with Alzheimer's who took the car one day to pick up medication for his sick wife at a nearby pharmacy. The couple lived in a town on the Connecticut shore. After an hour, when the patient did not return, the police were called. But the patient was not found until a day and a half later when he was discovered driving around the streets of Brooklyn with no idea how he had gotten there.)

Over time, memory and executive functioning (the ability to plan and act) worsens. Language ability is impaired and affected individuals are unable to communicate their needs or understand things. When objects are lost or a spouse is away there may be paranoid ideation, with accusations at times of infidelity. Disinhibition is common, with behavior that may be inappropriate. Latent personality traits may come to the fore, with obsessive conduct or impulse disorders. Some patients wander outside the house without a notion of where they are, getting lost in the neighborhood, and deadbolts or special locks on the doors may be necessary. Incontinence is common as the disease progresses and attention to hygiene is lacking. Balance and motor ability are usually involved rather late, following which patients may become bedridden. Death usually intervenes mercifully through pneumonia or other intercurrent infections.

In addition to the clinical picture, diagnosis may be aided by imaging. Besides changes in brain volume and anatomy seen on MRI, there are substances that bind with amyloid in the brain and when tagged with a radio-isotope will show up on PET scan.[13] These studies can also reveal patients with MCI who are most likely to progress to Alzheimer's. In addition, normal patients at younger ages can have these changes that predict future Alzheimer's. This can be helpful in developing preventive therapies. Levels and ratios of amyloid and tau in the spinal fluid and other proteins also have predictive value for Alzheimer's disease. Biomarkers are being sought in blood as well.

At this point, Alzheimer's disease or dementia has no cure and it usually runs its course over a number of years. In the early phases, drugs may improve memory somewhat and may slow the disease's progression, but effects generally last for only a year or two.[14] As Alzheimer's advances, other medications may be useful in controlling agitation, paranoia, or behavioral changes, aiding caregivers with management. The medications temporarily helpful include cholinesterase inhibitors—Aricept (donepezil) and Exelon (rivastigmine), and an NMDA receptor antagonist, Namenda (memantine). A 2012 study suggests that a high intake of caffeine may slow the progression of MCI to dementia.[15] However, this needs to be investigated further. Exercise and cognitive therapy may also be of some value.

Two experimental approaches to treating Alzheimer's are potentially encouraging. One is with monoclonal antibodies that attack and destroy amyloid, though early studies with one agent, bapineuzumab, have been disappointing.[16] The second is to block the enzymes that produce amyloid and allow its deposition in large amounts in the brain.[17] A number of different compounds are currently being tested to this end.[18] Trials with other substances, such as growth hormone, to improve cognition are also going on, though their benefits are yet to be proved.[19] A vast number of scientists are working on ways to prevent and treat Alzheimer's and other cognitive problems. Hopefully, major breakthroughs will be seen in the near future.

Since 1996, there has been a focus on another cause of dementia that only received minor attention in the past. This is chronic traumatic encephalopathy (CTE) that results from concussions and head injuries at an earlier age.[20] The condition has been publicized because of the high incidence in National Football League players, but can be seen with any sport or occupation that results in trauma to the head and brain. It was previously known as *dementia pugilistica* because of its occurrence in boxers. Prevention is the answer to this condition since there is no known treatment of value.

Strokes

Strokes are caused by cerebrovascular disease—atherosclerotic changes within the blood vessels supplying the brain. They are also known as *CVAs* (cerebrovascular accidents). Risk factors are the same as for atherosclerosis in general (this will be discussed under "Coronary Artery Disease"). Stroke is the third leading cause of mortality in the United States and the primary cause of disability. Stroke incidence rises exponentially with age, with a the highest rates in the eighth and ninth decades. However, a 2012 study shows that 18.6 percent of strokes occur in people under age fifty-five.[21] About one in four men and one in five women can expect to have a stroke if they live to age eighty-five. A lack of blood flow to an area of the brain due to blockage of an artery, or bleeding into the brain from the rupture of a blood vessel cause strokes. Emboli, or clots that originate elsewhere (in the heart, for example) and travel to the brain arteries and obstruct them, are also responsible for strokes. The problems that result depend on the severity of the insult and the region of the brain involved.

A stroke can vary from temporary loss of function with no residual difficulty, in which case it is called a *TIA* (transient ischemic attack), to massive permanent deficits, or death. The chances of developing a stroke after a TIA can be predicted by what is known as the ABCD2 score (age, blood pressure, clinical features, duration of symptoms, and diabetes) that stratifies a patient's risk.[22] Paralysis, sensory loss, inability to speak or swallow, dizziness, problems with balance, or visual dysfunction can all be seen. Improvement may occur over time, or there may be little return toward normalcy. Partial or total disability may result with a need for full- or part-time care. In the worst instances, a nursing home or round-the-clock assistance at home may be required.

Since 1995, evidence has shown that some strokes treated within three to six hours with drugs that dissolve the clot blocking the involved arteries may result in long-term improvement in outcome. This treatment, however, has associated risks and only a small percentage of stroke patients are candidates for these compounds. The medication may be given intravenously or intra-arterially. Several types of blood thinners may also be utilized as therapy. And sometimes, a clot may be removed from a blocked brain artery with a catheter guided radiographically, or surgically.

Once a major deficit is present for more than six hours, however, chances for a return to normal function are not good. Because of this, prevention of strokes in susceptible individuals is exceedingly important. Reduction of high blood pressure, lowering of cholesterol, proper diet, adequate exercise, and cessation of smoking can all contribute to stroke prophylaxis. Aspirin on a regular basis also lowers the incidence of strokes. In some people who have significant narrowing of the carotid arteries (the major arteries in the neck that go to the brain), surgery to open up the blood vessels may be beneficial. It should be emphasized that all strokes do not result in permanent disability, even those that initially seem severe.

> An eighty-two-year-old man in my practice, L. E., had an acute stroke with significant left-sided weakness, difficulty speaking, and an inability to see things on the left, which improved dramatically over a period of days. His only residual symptoms were a mild limp while walking and minimal thickness of his speech. After a short course of rehabilitation, he was able to return to his apartment and continue living independently.
>
> Another patient of mine, P. P., a woman of eighty-five, had mild problems with balance after a stroke, requiring the use of a quad cane to make her feel more secure. She was also able to live completely independently afterward and care for herself. In addition, she travels alone to various cities around the country to visit her children and grandchildren, and even went with her family on a vacation to Ireland.

A further example of triumph over stroke is the actor Kirk Douglas. He returned to making movies, even though his speech was somewhat slurred because of the CVA that affected the motor area of his brain that controls speech.

Small vessel ischemic changes (from reduced oxygen supply) scattered throughout the white matter of the brain are ubiquitous among the elderly population on brain imaging (CAT scans and MRI scans).

These are due to diminished blood flow in the smallest arteries and may be responsible for some of the cognitive difficulties and problems with balance seen so often in this age group.

Any substance or activity that reduces the incidence of atherosclerosis will reduce the incidence of stroke, including exercise, statin drugs, antihypertensives, and so forth. A study published in the journal *Neurology* in 2012 also suggests that high levels of lycopenes, which are found in tomatoes and tomato-based products, decrease the risk of stroke, though this needs further validation.[23]

Parkinson's Disease

Parkinson's disease is also known as "shaking palsy." There are more than 300,000 patients with Parkinson's in the United States (based on a population of 300 million) with approximately 50,000 new cases each year. A number of factors probably contribute to the development of this condition. All of them cause a loss of cells in a part of the brain called the *substantia nigra*, and reduced production of a neurotransmitter called *dopamine* that transfers impulses between neurons in the extrapyramidal system (a related group of nerve cells that influence motor activity and balance). New techniques that evaluate the presence of dopamine in the *striatum*, an area of the brain affected by Parkinson's, can help make an early diagnosis (DAT scans). Because of this missing chemical, people exhibit problems walking: a stooped posture, small steps, and unsteadiness. Speech volume is low, there are difficulties with fine movements and coordination, and a resting tremor is often present. All motor functions slow and cognition may be impaired in the later stages. As the disease progresses, patients may require help with the tasks of daily living and greater degrees of care. If another unrelated illness (heart attacks, cancer, and so forth) does not intervene, death can result from pneumonia or other infections, usually after the Parkinson's has run a prolonged course.

Parkinson's disease may affect a person's spirit and self-image. Many people are embarrassed by the tremor, especially early in the course of the disease before they are disabled in any way. Drooling may also be bothersome. As Parkinson's evolves, mobility diminishes and trouble arising from a chair or turning over in bed increases, along with more difficulties with walking and balance. Eventually, patients may need assistance with some motor tasks. Hallucinations and confusion (caused by the disease and the medications) and general cognitive decline may develop, imposing further loss of autonomy. However, medications and exercise may be able to hold the disease at bay for years, and deep brain stimulation may also help some patients, particularly in controlling the tremor.[24] The severity of the symptoms and the rate of progression vary greatly, and many patients are able to function at a high level for many years after a diagnosis is first made.

Treatment is directed toward replacement of the chemical that is deficient. In the early phases, patients may appear quite normal, with or without medication. But at some point, it becomes necessary to give a drug called *L-dopa* (usually in combination with other drugs), which is converted by the brain to dopamine, the substance that is lacking. Medications that act similarly to L-dopa (dopa agonists) may also be utilized, and several other drugs may be helpful as well. As the process advances, higher dosages of L-dopa or dopa agonists become necessary. In time, patients may become refractory to treatment and greater disability occurs. Even so, with current therapy, life expectancy has improved dramatically and disability usually does not appear for many years.

There are many examples of people in public life who have had Parkinson's disease and continued functioning at a high level. Living with Parkinson's disease, Pope John Paul led the Catholic Church and followed a hectic schedule. Janet Reno, with Parkinson's disease, served as attorney general of the United States and was able to campaign vigorously in a Democratic primary for governor of Florida (which she eventually lost). The actor Michael J. Fox, who developed Parkinson's at an early age, has worked to increase funding for research in Parkinson's disease, while continuing his acting career.

Essential Tremor

Midlife and older people may have shaking of their head or hands called "essential tremor," which is unrelated to Parkinson's disease. (The actress Katharine Hepburn had this condition.) Though it can occur in any age group, it is more prevalent as people age. Stress or anxiety makes it briefly worse. Usually of familial origin, it can also result from a severe head injury, a period of cerebral anoxia (lack of oxygen supply to the brain), encephalitis, and various other types of pathology. Bringing a spoonful of soup to the mouth may be an adventure when the tremor is pronounced, and it can interfere with handwriting and fine movements. Though it does not cause any major disability, from an emotional standpoint it may be very distressing. However, certain drugs and surgical procedures can reduce the shaking significantly.[25] Mild tremulousness and involuntary movements around the mouth are also noted at times in an older population.

Peripheral Neuropathies

Damage to motor and sensory nerves is seen frequently in older people, more often in the legs, resulting in numbness, tingling and weakness, and problems with balance and walking. Diabetes and cancer chemotherapy are the main culprits, but a host of other metabolic, nutritional, and inflammatory processes can also be responsible. Control of the underlying condition and physical therapy can sometimes be helpful. Often when the elderly complain of trouble with balance or walking, multiple factors are involved, including peripheral neuropathies, cerebrovascular disease, arthritis, and other degenerative disorders. Various medications, including different anticonvulsants and anti-depressants, help in reducing the pain and discomfort associated with neuropathies.

CARDIOVASCULAR DISEASES

Cardiovascular diseases in combination are the leading cause of illness, disability, and death among people sixty-five and older.[26] About half of deaths in this population result from these conditions; 45 percent of men and 52 percent of women.[27] Cardiovascular disease encompasses coronary artery disease, high blood pressure, peripheral vascular disease (arterial disease of the lower limbs), abdominal arterial disease, and strokes. Even alone, coronary artery disease is the number one killer in the United States. In 1993, it was reported to be responsible for 743,460 deaths, one third of all the deaths in the country.[28] Though these numbers seem huge, death rates from cardiovascular disease have actually declined dramatically, a major public health triumph. "In 1950, the death rate from heart disease was 307.4 per 100,000 people. In 1996, it was 134.6. In 1950, the stroke death rate per 100,000 people was 88.8. In 1996, it was 26.6."[29] This rate had decreased further by 2011, when 600,000, or one in every four deaths in the United States was caused by coronary artery disease.[30]

The risk factors for coronary artery disease, strokes, peripheral vascular disease, and abdominal arterial disease (variants of the same disorder—atherosclerosis) are naturally similar, some of which can be controlled by behavior change and others that cannot be modified. In addition to cholesterol and lipid deposition in atherosclerosis, another substance that appears harmful is an amino acid called *homocysteine*, a byproduct of normal metabolism. Homocysteine may damage blood vessels, magnifying other cardiovascular risk factors such as smoking and hypertension, and lead to an increase in heart attacks, strokes, and peripheral vascular disease. (However, it is also possible that homocysteine is a marker of atherosclerotic vascular disease, rather than causing some of the damage.) Reducing the ingestion of meat and taking B vitamins, particularly folic acid, B6, and B12, can lower homocysteine levels and may decrease cardiovascular risk.

Inflammation of the arteries has also been discovered to play an important role in the production of atherosclerosis.[31] The exact mechanism by which this occurs is speculative, but it appears that certain infections or inflammatory processes may initiate atherosclerotic changes by damaging arterial walls and making them more receptive to the deposition of cholesterol and lipid material. Further accumulation of this material results in narrowing and finally blockage of the blood vessels, depriving the target organs of oxygen. C-reactive protein (CRP) levels can be used as a marker of inflammation.

Coronary Artery Disease

Narrowing (stenosis) or occlusion of a coronary artery by atherosclerosis causes heart attacks—MIs (myocardial infarction or death of cardiac tissue) and angina (myocardial ischemia or lack of oxygen to cardiac tissue), both of which present as chest pain. However, at times MIs can occur silently, or with pain in the neck, jaw, or upper back. An MI can kill a person or produce heart damage that results in reduced cardiac function. This can be responsible for congestive heart failure and decreased levels of activity in survivors. Injured heart muscle makes the heart less able to pump blood, particularly when demand rises, such as with exercise. If enough heart damage has occurred, patients may be chronically fatigued and short of breath, with fluid accumulating in the legs (edema) and lungs (pulmonary edema). When congestive failure is severe, the patient may become a cardiac cripple, unable to sustain minimal exertion.

If medical care is given rapidly after an acute heart attack, permanent damage to the heart muscle can often be prevented through the use of "antifibrinolytic agents" (clot-busters). As used for strokes, these can lyse the clot in the coronary artery that is causing the heart attack. This may have to be followed by a surgical procedure called a CABG (coronary artery bypass graft) during which veins from the leg or arteries from the chest wall are used to replace the blocked coronary arteries and reestablish blood flow. Other options include angioplasty, during which the narrowed segment of the artery is dilated by a balloon catheter to improve blood flow, and stenting, using a small spring-like coil to keep the artery open. These procedures do not change the basic process of atherosclerosis, but may buy the patient time to alter his or her behavior and prevent progression of the atherosclerotic changes.

Chest pain may be noted during a heart attack, or it may be a warning sign beforehand. Various types of stress tests, coronary angiography (a catheterization study of the heart's blood vessels with X-rays after the injection of dye), and the use of radioactive isotopes may help to establish the diagnosis and direct proper therapy.

Coronary artery disease may cause alterations in heart rhythm (arrhythmias) by damaging the intrinsic electrical system that regulates cardiac contractions. By reducing blood flow to the brain and the rest of the body, this can result in dizzy spells, blackouts, or even sudden death. Arrhythmias can be treated with various medications or ablation of an aberrant heart pacemaker. But if the anatomic cardiac pacemaker is severely disrupted, an implanted permanent pacemaker may be necessary. With this hardware, those afflicted with arrhythmias may lead many more years of productive life.

Examples of people who have suffered severe heart attacks and continued an active or even stressful life afterward are legion. President Dwight Eisenhower had a significant myocardial infarction during his first term in office. In spite of that, he was elected to a second term, which he served to completion without difficulty. Lyndon B. Johnson had a major heart attack in 1955. Following that, he was able to continue functioning as majority leader of the United States Senate, then was elected vice president and president of the United States, easily handling the stress of his jobs. He died in retirement some years later. Dick Cheney, vice president 2001–2009, had several heart attacks and cardiac arrhythmias, and had an implantable defibrillator in place. Yet he was able to meet the demands of his office and manage an extremely hectic schedule. (In March of 2012, Cheney had a heart transplant performed.)

Alteration of lifestyle is essential in the treatment of coronary artery disease and other forms of atherosclerosis. This includes dietary modification and medications to lower cholesterol and control blood pressure, regular exercise, and cessation of smoking. Though stopping smoking does not drop coronary disease risk to zero immediately, a gradual decline makes the elimination of cigarettes at any age worthwhile. The use of aspirin prophylactically to prevent clots from forming is also of great benefit. Cholesterol lowering drugs, such as statins, have been shown to reduce coronary artery disease, as well as atherosclerosis in general.

Some individuals with or without heart pathology, develop cardiac neuroses, concerned that exertion may cause a heart attack and perhaps kill them. In those with minimal or no cardiac abnormalities, fear directs their lives, rather than the disease itself. And some who have suffered cardiac damage and may be restricted in certain ways, become depressed or anxious, feeling sorry for themselves and unwilling to work to try to restore their previous physical state. Of course, the key to what people are able to do is the amount of disease present, for at times this may preclude significant effort and require a passive existence. Nevertheless, everyone should try to maximize whatever function remains.

Other Vascular Syndromes

As was previously discussed, with generalized atherosclerosis, patients may develop narrowing of the arteries leading to the brain, causing strokes. Peripheral vascular disease involving the arteries of the legs is also common, resulting in pain with walking that disappears with rest (intermittent claudication). Changes in the aorta (the main arterial trunk that leads out of the heart) can produce aortic aneurysms (weakening and dilatation of the arterial wall). Peripheral vascular disease and aortic aneurysms often require surgical repair to allow life to continue normally. Severe atherosclerosis of the intestinal arteries may also require surgical intervention.

Hypertension

Hypertension or high blood pressure is a major risk factor for atherosclerosis, strokes, and heart and kidney damage. It is estimated that about one in three adult Americans, 68 million in 2011, have high blood pressure.[32] Hereditary factors play a role in its development and it occurs more commonly in African Americans. Elevated blood pressure can also be related to a sedentary lifestyle, obesity, stress, high salt intake, and heavy alcohol use, as well as decreased ingestion of potassium and calcium. Because those with hypertension often do not have symptoms early on, it is known as a silent killer.

Two parameters are measured to obtain blood pressures, the *systolic* being the higher number (when the heart muscle contracts), and the *diastolic*, the lower one (when the heart muscle relaxes). Measurements above 140/90 are indicative of hypertension, with the higher the levels, the more dangerous it is. Experts in the field have suggested that blood pressures of 120/80 to 139/89 be considered prehypertensive and be treated aggressively, though there is controversy about this.[33] But most would agree that "the relationship between blood pressure and risk of cardiovascular disease is continuous, consistent, and independent of other risk factors."[34]

Treatment of elevated blood pressure should include lifestyle changes such as dietary modification, weight loss, increased exercise, and constraints on alcohol. Restrictions on the use of salt are quite important for someone who is hypertensive. Medications should be utilized aggressively when necessary. It is well-known that the condition is undertreated by many physicians and disregarded by many patients who do not develop symptoms until it is too late.

DISEASES OF THE RESPIRATORY SYSTEM

Chronic Obstructive Pulmonary Disease

Chronic obstructive pulmonary disease (COPD) is a major cause of disability in older people, with wheezing, shortness of breath (dyspnea), and coughing. Emphysema and chronic bronchitis are the usual perpetrators, though asthma can produce similar symptoms, generally in a younger population. COPD is invariably the result of smoking, with environmental factors and exposure to certain toxins occasionally contributing. In emphysema, the alveoli (terminal sacs) in the lungs are damaged or destroyed, making the exchange of oxygen between air and blood more difficult. In chronic bronchitis, the tubes that carry air in the lungs are inflamed and produce copious amounts of mucous (phlegm) that clog the tubes and prevent oxygen from reaching the bloodstream. The patient coughs intermittently and brings up this material, which may be infected as well. Shortness of breath hinders exertion and can be frightening at times, making patients feel as if they are suffocating. Those who have dyspnea on a chronic basis may become pulmonary cripples with difficulty performing the simplest tasks. Usually, people do not have emphysema or chronic bronchitis in isolation, but instead are afflicted with a combination of the two conditions.

Cessation of smoking is an important element in treating COPD, but the destructive process may already be advanced by the time that decision is made. A number of different medications may be used to relieve some of the shortness of breath and diminish the production of mucous. Oxygen can also be helpful and it may be necessary for patients to carry an oxygen supply with them wherever they go. Because of their lung damage and inability to clear secretions, they are very prone to pulmonary infections that should be treated early and aggressively with antibiotics.

Pneumonia

Pneumonia remains to this day a major killer of the elderly, particularly the old-old and nursing home residents. The reasons include diminished effectiveness of the immune system as we age, compromised pulmonary function, and COPD in many older people. There is also a tendency toward aspiration, or inhalation of fluids or foreign substances into the lungs, seen in people with impaired swallowing mechanisms, such as might occur following a stroke. When foreign substances enter the lungs, they produce chemical irritation, increased secretions, and a fertile medium for infection. People who are feeble, chronically ill, or bedridden, may have a suppressed cough reflex and an inability to clear secretions, which make them prime candidates for pneumonia. Treatment with antibiotics and improved pulmonary toilet (clearing secretions in the lungs) can often salvage patients with pneumonia, if their underlying problem is not too severe.

DISEASES OF THE GASTROINTESTINAL SYSTEM

While complaints relating to the GI system are common among seniors, they are usually not indicative of serious conditions. Among the more frequent GI gripes are constipation, heartburn, gas, decreased appetite, abdominal pain, problems swallowing, diarrhea, and fecal incontinence. Older people often focus on their bowels and are overly concerned when they are constipated. Lack of exercise, poor abdominal muscle tone, and diminished intake of fluids and bulky foods may all play a role, with straining at stool producing hemorrhoids. Gall bladder disease, hiatus hernias, and GERD (gastroesophogeal reflux disease), diverticulitis, and cancers of the GI tract all occur more often in older people, and structural abnormalities such as these must be sought if there are persistent symptoms. GERD can also cause chronic hoarseness, cough, or throat irritation through the reflux of acidic fluids.

DISEASES OF THE GENITOURINARY SYSTEM

Genitourinary problems are not life threatening for the most part, but can raise quality of life issues, particularly urinary incontinence. Urinary symptoms in seniors, including frequency, urgency, and difficulty voiding, may at times be helped by medication, but some older men may require surgery (TURP) to remove part of the prostate gland. An enlarged prostate, benign prostatic hyperplasia (BPH) is almost a universal accompaniment of age for men. If symptoms produced by BPH don't respond to alpha blockers or 5-alpha reductase inhibitors, surgery may be necessary.

Urinary Incontinence

Urinary incontinence occurs in about one third of the population over sixty living in the community and about 50 percent of those in nursing homes.[35] Patients in nursing homes may develop breakdown sores of their skin if the urine is not cleaned up quickly after incontinence. A number of different factors can be responsible for incontinence including neurologic dysfunction, urinary tract infections, mechanical abnormalities, shrinkage of the bladder, weakness or damage to the pelvic muscles, and inability to get to the bathroom in time because of neurologic or orthopedic problems, medications, dementia, and psychiatric disorders. Medical evaluation is important, as a significant percentage of those with this condition can be helped. If no solution is found, the use of diapers or condom catheters may allow activities to continue and make the incontinence more tolerable.

Sexual Function

Sexual dysfunction in the United States appears to be prevalent in all age groups. One study showed that 43 percent of women and 31 percent of men had sexual problems, often associated with poor physical or emotional health and impaired quality of life.[36]

Though a decreased libido (sexual drive) in older people is a normal consequence of aging, most healthy couples can achieve some degree of intimacy and pleasurable sexual activity. In addition to one's physical situation and desire, many elements play a role in deciding sexual behavior as we grow older. "The most important factor may be the presence of a willing and able partner. Social and cultural circumstances tend to reinforce the decline in sexual activity, especially for older women."[37] Interest in sexuality may be suppressed because of false beliefs this is abnormal, wrong, or even immoral. In general, those who were most active sexually when they were young are most active when they are older, even with the expected reduction in frequency. Baby Boomers, who were more open about sex when younger, continue to be so. But the presence of physical illness in a person, or his or her spouse, can severely limit sexual ardor. And psychological problems such as anxiety or depression suppress desire in both men and women.

Notwithstanding the difficulties noted, many healthy postmenopausal women have greater enjoyment of sex than when they were younger, and the desire for sexuality and intercourse still remains in most men well into their eighties. However, impotence (the inability to have and maintain an erection necessary for intercourse) is a common problem for older men. Again, many factors, both emotional and physical, may be involved. From the physical side, atherosclerosis of the arteries that supply the penis can result in impotence, as can diabetes or processes that cause a neuropathy. Impotence, as well as lack of libido, may also be a side effect of medications. In addition to generalized depression or anxiety, a fear of failure or "performance anxiety" may underlie impotence, becoming a self-fulfilling prophecy. Over the last decade, various treatment options for erectile dysfunction have become available, including testosterone, Viagra, Cialis, and so forth. Though vaginal secretions lessen with age, there are creams that eliminate dryness and make intercourse easier.

While the desire for sexual release may be reduced, older individuals still need intimacy and companionship—to be held and touched and loved by another person. With the death or incapacity of a spouse, the ability to satisfy these needs may be lost and difficult to establish with someone new. People may respond to the need for intimacy and sexual pleasure in ways that some may see as "undignified." As an example, an older woman may dress and act in a seductive manner, wearing low-cut dresses or short skirts that are sexually provocative. Some women who are widowed may use all of what they believe are their wiles in attempts to "hook a man." (In retirement communities, these women are thought of as predators that go about stalking available, and sometimes unavailable, men.)

Because there is an excess of women compared to men as the population ages, older men in general have less trouble finding women for sex or companionship. However, the more desirable women (those who are healthy, attractive, and affluent) may disparage attempts at courtship. A common saying around retirement communities regarding older single men is that they want "a nurse with a purse"[38] to take care of them.

Men may also act in ways that compromise their dignity, looking for women much younger than they are and with whom they have little in common. An example of this is when wealthy and successful middle-aged or older men divorce their spouses with whom they have shared their lives for many years, in favor of physically attractive younger women who may not be their intellectual equals. These "trophy wives" may be the subject of derision (perhaps admixed with a bit of envy) by the man's peers, who may have difficulty communicating with these women.

ENDOCRINE DISORDERS

Thyroid

Thyroid dysfunction occurs with some frequency in all age ranges. Hypothyroidism, or decreased thyroid function, with the reduced output of thyroid hormone by the thyroid gland, is most common. This can cause symptoms of fatigue, weakness, weight gain, lassitude, mental dullness and loss of memory, depression, hair loss, cold intolerance, and decreased libido. It is easily amenable to treatment with hormone replacement, resulting in marked improvement in symptoms.

Diabetes

Diabetes is caused by diminished insulin production by the islet cells of the pancreas, or by a lack of responsiveness by the body's cells to insulin. Older people predominantly have the latter kind of diabetes called *Type Two*, or non-insulin dependent diabetes. With this disease, glucose (sugar) metabolism is not well regulated and the levels of glucose in the blood and urine are elevated. Initial symptoms may include increased thirst and fluid intake, increased urine output, undue fatigue and lower levels of energy, generalized weakness, and weight loss.

As the disease progresses, various organ systems are affected to a greater degree. Diabetic retinopathy in the eyes can cause loss of vision. A peripheral neuropathy often develops with numbness and tingling in the extremities (particularly the feet) that can be quite painful. Balance and strength can be impaired, and impotence and incontinence may occur. Diabetes also appears to worsen atherosclerosis and circulatory problems. Susceptibility to infections and delayed wound healing is common. Because of the neuropathy and reduced blood flow to the legs, diabetic ulcers and gangrene may develop, necessitating amputation of the toes, feet, or legs.

Treatment consists of controlling blood sugar through dietary restrictions, oral medications, and exercise if possible. If this is not effective, then insulin may be prescribed. Blood sugar levels are checked on a regular basis to monitor adequacy of therapy. Keeping blood sugar within the normal range appears to lessen the rate of complications, though it does not eliminate them completely. If blood sugars are extremely high and the diabetes poorly controlled, diabetic coma may result. It is also critical that blood sugars not drop too low (hypoglycemia), for that can produce hypoglycemic coma and seizures. Good hygiene and diet, and avoidance of injury and infections, are salient rules for all older people, but are particularly critical for diabetics. Weight loss can reduce the need for medication, and eliminating smoking and controlling cholesterol and blood pressure in diabetics are also extremely important. Studies have shown that regular exercise can significantly reduce the incidence of diabetes. For anyone who is overweight, or with a family history of diabetes, an exercise program as part of his or her daily routine is imperative.

DISORDERS OF THE MUSCULOSKELETAL SYSTEM

Because of the loss of muscle strength, the pain and immobility of arthritis, osteoporosis, and spinal stenosis, older people move more slowly, walk more stiffly, and often have a flexed posture. Their ability to perform physical tasks may be diminished. Depression may amplify their complaints and they may be unwilling to push themselves to do things.

Deconditioning in normal seniors and midlifers, and those with minor physical problems, is an element that restricts their ability to lead fulfilling lives. Having ignored proper exercise over the years, they may discover that physical activity is difficult for them. They may be unable to travel to certain places or take certain types of vacations, and are incapable of playing various sports or even just going for a walk in a park. Despite this, it is never too late to make a commitment to recapture the strength and stamina that was allowed to dissipate. Starting a program of stretching and exercise at any age can arrest and reverse changes that have occurred in the musculoskeletal system. Scientific studies published in 2012 have even raised the possibility of growing new muscle tissue when it has been damaged and may have applications for older people in the future.[39]

Osteoporosis

Osteoporosis, usually thought of as "softening of the bones," is a loss of bone mass and density. Though a normal accompaniment of aging, when excessive, it greatly increases the chances of compression fractures of the spine and fractures of the hips or long bones. With this condition, the spine can bow out, causing a hunched-back appearance (kyphosis). Predisposing factors include reduced estrogen levels after menopause, a sedentary lifestyle, smoking, alcohol, and certain medications. A deficiency of calcium, possibly due to problems with absorption of this mineral, may be important, as may diminished vitamin D and parathyroid hormone metabolism. People with osteoporosis often develop fractures with minimal trauma.

Prevention appears to be the most efficacious way to handle osteoporosis. Increased calcium intake can compensate for reduction in age-related absorption, and regular weight-bearing exercise, such as walking, may help to strengthen bone and reduce fractures.[40] In postmenopausal women, hormone replacement therapy can also be beneficial, but can increase susceptibility to breast and ovarian cancers, as well as vascular complications. Bone densitometry testing can be used to predict the risk of fractures and the degree of osteoporosis, and can lead to more aggressive therapy when bones are thought to be fragile. A number of medications are available to reduce osteoporosis and strengthen bones, but have potential adverse effects.

Bony Fractures

Though osteoporosis is the primary condition leading to fractures in older people, other disorders (osteomalacia, cerebrovascular disease, cardiac arrhythmias, and so forth) also contribute to this problem. Compression fractures of the thoracic and lower spinal vertebrae are most common, the resulting back pain varying in severity. Fractures may develop with heavy lifting or straining, a jarring step, or a drop from a short height. Pain may necessitate bed rest and relative immobilization for a short period. Back braces to limit movement of the spine may alleviate some of the pain when walking or standing, but time (usually a few months) is necessary for healing.

Hip fractures, a major cause of disability among older people, usually result from falls. The number of hip fractures in the United States is the highest in the world, approximating 300,000 annually and estimated to go to 500,000 by 2040.[41] The severity of the fall necessary to produce a fracture depends on the degree of osteoporosis and the strength of the bone. Fractures may occur in different regions of the hip, and may be displaced (out of alignment) or non-displaced, or impacted (jammed together). Pain in the hip and groin, particularly with movement, is invariably present. If the fracture is non-displaced, or impacted, it can be stabilized surgically by the use of pins that allow the patient to be up and around quickly, eliminating complications that arise with prolonged bed rest.

Displaced hip fractures can also be stabilized in younger people who can participate in an active physical therapy program. In most cases however, hip replacement is recommended to prevent deformity and problems with healing. The use of a prosthesis allows rapid weight bearing with the aid of a walker, with physical therapy important. If a patient is bedridden in a nursing home prior to the fracture, the treating physician may elect to merely keep him or her at bed rest rather than pursuing a more aggressive approach.

Due to falls, wrist fractures are also seen frequently among seniors. For the most part, these are easily treated with casts or splinting.

Arthritis

Arthritis, the result of degenerative changes or inflammatory disease, can involve virtually any joint in the body. Osteoarthritis, a chronic degenerative condition, is the most common form of arthritis, attacking mainly the hips, knees, spine, and hands. It is felt to be a consequence of wear and tear of the joint, though the degree of the changes seen on X-rays and pathologically does not necessarily correlate with the amount of usage. Loss of cartilage that lines the joint spaces occurs first, followed by overgrowth of the ends of the bones near the joints, forming knobby protuberances called *osteophytes*. Stiffness, pain, and swelling are the usual complaints, but at times, progression can lead to total dysfunction of the joint. Aspirin, or non-steroidal anti-inflammatory drugs (NSAIDS) such as ibuprofen and naproxen can often provide relief, particularly in the early stages. Hip or knee replacements by artificial joints may be required in some patients, when pain is unrelenting or walking significantly impaired.

Involvement of the small joints of the spinal column by osteoarthritis may produce spinal stenosis. Though spinal pain does occur, more important symptoms are the result of pressure on the nerve roots and occasionally on the spinal cord itself in the cervical region (neck). The overgrowth of bone in the spinal column often in combination with degenerative disc disease causes a narrowing of the boney canals where the nerve roots are located (neuroforamina) or of the spinal canal. In addition to local discomfort, pain may be felt in the distribution of any nerve root that is compressed (radicular pain). Numbness, pins and needles, or tingling occur when a sensory nerve root is compromised, and weakness, if there is pressure on a motor nerve root. (Similar symptoms can be seen with herniated discs, which are more common in a younger population.) Spinal cord constriction in the neck may cause numbness or weakness in the legs along with balance problems and urinary and bowel dysfunction. Various medications and physical therapy can be used to reduce the pain of spinal stenosis, but in some cases, particularly if the spinal cord is involved, surgical decompression is necessary.

Rheumatoid arthritis is a generalized chronic inflammatory disease that can strike various organ systems as well as the joints. Though there is a propensity for the small joints of the hands and wrists to be affected, the process may also attack the elbows, shoulders, ankles, knees, and hips. An inflammatory reaction in the joint capsule damages all the elements (cartilage, ligaments, and tendons), eventually causing changes in the bones as well. It results in swelling of the joints, restriction of range of motion, and pain. Severe joint distortion can occur, greatly limiting activity. The mechanism is autoimmune in origin (the body produces antibodies that damage its own tissues) and affects women much more often than men. Aspirin and NSAIDS may be helpful in relieving some of the discomfort and can increase mobility. Corticosteroids are often quite effective, but high doses have serious side effects. Other immune suppressive therapies, including cytotoxic drugs, are utilized as well to control the disease. In addition, a host of "biologics" that are infused or injected and block the effect of tumor necrosis factor (TNF) have been found to be very useful and new agents are on the horizon.

Polymyalgia Rheumatica

Polymyalgia rheumatica (PMR) causes muscle pain in older people, usually proximal in the extremities. An inflammatory disease, it can be diagnosed by an elevated sedimentation rate (ESR), CRP (C-reactive protein), and muscle biopsy. Treatment with steroids is generally successful, but PMR can be associated with temporal arteritis, which causes headaches and can lead to blindness.

SKIN DISORDERS

Most skin disorders in older people, aside from cancers, are significant cosmetically and for the emotional distress they cause. Various techniques, including plastic surgery, can be utilized to destroy or remove offending lesions if patients so desire. Several conditions in a different category however, are worth mentioning.

Shingles

Shingles is caused by a virus, herpes zoster, also the agent for chicken pox. It occurs more often in older people, or in individuals with compromised immune systems. The virus produces a painful rash with blisters or vesicles, which stand out sharply from surrounding normal skin, within the distribution of a nerve root. The pain can be excruciating, with repeated sharp jolts or burning made worse by minor contact with the affected area. Though the active disease usually runs its course in four to eight weeks, with the rash drying up and fading away, pain can persist for some time afterward (postherpetic neuralgia). Antiviral agents given early often abort the process and promote healing. A number of medications, particularly anticonvulsants and antidepressants, help in controlling the pain.

Stasis Dermatitis

Stasis dermatitis results from poor circulation in the lower legs and increased venous pressure, and is manifest by discoloration, mainly darkening of the skin, shininess, and swelling. Itchiness and flaking of the skin also are seen and the involved areas are more prone to injury, skin ulcers, and infection. The use of support stockings to reduce fluid accumulation and aid in venous return may be beneficial.

Pressure Sores

Pressure sores or decubitus ulcers are areas of skin breakdown resulting from prolonged pressure on the skin from a boney prominence against another surface. These commonly occur over the heels, buttocks, elbows, or back in patients who are bedridden or wheelchair confined and whose positions are not changed frequently. However, these can occur at times even with good nursing care. They are found more often in older people with limited mobility, particularly hospitalized and nursing home patients. Predisposing factors include malnutrition, stool or urinary incontinence, inability to feel or react to discomfort (strokes, coma, neuropathy) and diabetes. These lesions can result in severe localized infections, osteomyelitis (bone infections) and septicemia (infections throughout the blood stream), which can cause death. Indeed, the presence of pressure sores in a hospitalized or nursing home patient is a predictor of increased mortality. Treatment consists of removing sources of pressure from involved areas, frequent changes of position, cutting away (debridement) of dead or infected tissue, antibiotics, and improved nutrition. The best treatment however is prevention, by greater attention and protective measures for patients at risk.

VISION

Though circulatory problems involving the eyes and diabetic retinopathy can cause visual difficulty, three major processes affect sight in older people.

Cataracts

Cataracts are opacifications of the lens of the eye caused by changes in their proteins. Exposure to ultraviolet rays of sunlight, uncontrolled diabetes, and the use of steroids all contribute to this condition. Whether there is interference with vision depends on the location and severity of the opacity. If sight is impaired, the lens can be removed surgically in a simple procedure and an artificial lens implanted simultaneously. With this technique, the vast majority of people have satisfactory restoration of vision.

Glaucoma

Glaucoma is increased pressure within the eye that can cause injury to the optic nerve and diminished acuity. The elevated pressure is the result of blockage of the pathways within the eye where fluid is resorbed. Various eye drops and oral medications can be used to lower the pressure and, by protecting the optic nerve, reduce the danger of blindness. If conservative measures don't work, surgery or laser therapy can improve the flow of fluid within the eye and reduce the pressure.

Macular Degeneration

In age-related macular degeneration (AMD), the central pigmented cells of the retina are damaged, substances are deposited in the retina, and new blood vessels, which bleed at times, grow into the tissues. This leads to decreased vision and ultimately to blindness, and is the major cause of visual loss in the elderly. There are two forms, dry and wet, the latter being more severe. Central vision is more affected than peripheral vision. It is believed the process is genetically determined and cannot be prevented or cured. Laser treatment may retard its progression, but not the ultimate outcome. Low vision aids may be helpful for a period of time. Medications that retard the growth of blood vessels in some cancers have had similar effects in macular degeneration and are of value in slowing the process. In the future, gene therapy may possibly be able to arrest the condition, or even provide a cure.

CANCER

Cancer is a special category of disease—actually many different diseases arising in every organ system in the body. Over 1,660,000 new cases were diagnosed in the United States in 2013 exclusive of skin cancers and carcinoma in situ (a very early stage).[42] Though cancers kill at any age, they are particularly prevalent and deadly among seniors. Cancer is the leading cause of death in women aged 55–74, the second leading cause among men in that age group, and second among both men and women above age 75.[43] "Persons 65 years of age and older bear the greatest burden of cancer; 55 percent of all malignancies occur in this age group,"[44] with two thirds of all cancer deaths. These statistics are even more impressive as this segment constituted only 13 percent of the United States population during this survey.

Cancer rates rise steadily with age. The annual age-specific cancer incidence rate per 100,000 for persons forty-five to forty-nine is approximately 300.[45] This more than doubles to 750 for those ten years older. For persons sixty-five to sixty-nine, the rate is 1,400 per 100,000, rising to 2,200 for those seventy-five to seventy-nine years of age, then peaking at 2,500 in those eighty to eighty-four.

Though the word *cancer* conjures up visions, not just of dying, but of a horrible death, cancer is not the overwhelming killer it once was. In the past, a diagnosis of cancer often came with a hopeless prognosis. Now, with early detection, improvements in surgical techniques and radiotherapy, and new chemotherapeutic agents and other treatment modalities, a large percentage of patients with cancer can be cured, while others can coexist with their disease and lead productive lives for years.

There are many different types of cancers and many different etiologies (causes). These include environmental toxins, genetic factors, viruses, tobacco, diet, radiation, and so forth. Whatever the etiology or etiologies for specific cancers, a change takes place in the mechanism that controls cell growth and division, allowing the neoplastic (cancer) cells to reproduce in an unlimited fashion. As previously mentioned, the usual check on cell division resides in the end section of the chromosomes called a *telomere*, which gets shorter each time a cell divides until it is gone and no further divisions can occur. However, cancer cells produce a substance called *telomerase* that keeps the telomere at the same length, allowing the cells to divide indefinitely. And the immune system, which would ordinarily destroy abnormal cells, does not function adequately in patients with malignancies. Thus, without intervention, the cancer continues to grow until it kills its host, by eroding a blood vessel, compromising a vital organ, or interfering with nutrition.

The most common cancers affecting older people originate in the lungs, breast, prostate, and colon. In 2011, there were 221,000 new lung cancers, 232,000 new breast cancers, and 240,000 from the prostate.[46] Other neoplasms seen frequently include bladder, ovarian, other GI sites (stomach, pancreas, gall bladder), lymphoid tissue and bone marrow (lymphomas, leukemias, myeloma), head and neck cancers, and brain tumors. Though squamous cell and basal cell carcinomas of the skin are ubiquitous, they rarely kill people, since they are very slow growing, are discovered early, and can be treated effectively. Malignant melanoma, however, which also arises in the skin, is quite dangerous, and if not treated aggressively and at an early stage, will metastasize and kill.

The key to cancer control is prevention and early detection. Avoiding agents known to be carcinogenic (producing cancer) is important. This includes not smoking cigarettes or using other tobacco products, limiting exposure to sunlight, eating a diet low in red meats and saturated fats, and averting environmental carcinogens and radiation. If cancer occurs, survival may depend on finding it and instituting treatment while it is localized and liable to be more responsive to therapy. However, some scientists believe that whether or not a cancer is aggressive and liable to spread depends more on its genetic makeup than its size.

Various screening tests can help in discovering cancer at an early stage.

Women should do self-examination of the breasts periodically, with physician's exams and mammography every one to two years. The upper age limit for routine mammography, however, is a matter of debate, with its value after age seventy-five uncertain. Similarly, since

2010, guidelines have challenged the routine use of mammography be-fore age fifty and suggest it should be done every two years, unless a patient has a family history or other risk factors.[47]

In screening for colon cancer, stool should be examined for blood at least annually. For patients at risk for colon cancer, a colonoscopy should be done every one to three years, depending on the degree of risk (strong family history, previous polyps or colon cancer, and so on). As for the general population, there is no consensus, but every five years is probably reasonable. (Colonoscopy is a procedure where a long, flexible tube with a fiber-optic system is passed through the colon after it has been thoroughly cleaned.)

Prostate cancer can often be picked up by a blood test—prostate specific antigen (PSA)—followed by a prostate biopsy. The value of PSA testing, however, remains controversial. Very early, small cancers may be found and then excised surgically, which usually is curative. Radiation therapy, either external beam or seed implantations, is an-other option with good results. But the expected course of these early cancers is unknown and treatment, particularly surgery, may result in impotence and incontinence. Since the early years of this century, stud-ies have suggested that watchful waiting may often be preferable to intervention with its potential impact on quality of life. Digital palpation of the prostate gland through the rectum should be done every year to help uncover any larger cancers, whether or not PSA tests are being done.

Yearly gynecological examinations are also warranted to look for can-cers and other abnormalities. As part of the exam, a pap smear can aid in finding early cervical and uterine malignancies, though its efficacy in women over sixty-five who have had previously normal studies is ques-tionable.

Genetic screening tests to delineate cancer risk are available for breast, ovarian, and colonic cancers. There has not been complete agreement about proper use of these tests, including the ethical prob-lems they raise and what to do if they are positive. Some women with strong family histories and positive genetic testing have opted to have bilateral mastectomies to eliminate the threat of breast cancer. In gen-eral, the tests seem more valuable in women prior to age fifty, to give them an idea of what the future holds. Positive testing allows those at high risk to be watched more carefully.

Cancer treatment must be individualized, taking into consideration the tissue of origin, stage of involvement, and age and condition of the patient. For most cancers, a single lesion without evidence of spread (metastasis) is removed surgically. At times, if a tumor cannot be excised completely, as much of it as possible may be cut out (debulking) to make radiation and chemotherapy more effective. With cancers that are multicentric in origin (starting in many places) such as lymphoma or myeloma, or with generalized spread, radiation and chemotherapy may be the only options for treatment. And in some instances, this type of regimen can effect a cure. Hormonal therapy may also be utilized in certain types of responsive cancers (breast, ovary, prostate). New classes of agents that target genes or enzymes in particular types of cancers, or immunotherapy against cancer cells, show great promise. There are also drugs being tested that attack a genetic abnormality, common to many cancers, which allow the cells to proliferate.[48]

Palliative therapy is also important in treating cancer patients. This aims at eliminating pain and suffering, and making patients as comfortable as possible, rather than working for a cure. It is utilized when the cancer is widespread and likelihood of cure is remote. To reduce anxiety, patients must know that even if the cancer is going to kill them, medications and techniques are available to treat their pain, and that their suffering will be minimal.

An element of anger is present at the outset of being diagnosed with cancer, with the question being asked, Why me? But as treatment is given and time passes, the apprehension and dread diminishes in many patients, particularly if the prognosis appears favorable. Many therapies now available can cure specific cancers or arrest progression of the disease, so that it becomes a chronic illness that people can live with and derive pleasure from life. A 2013 report from England notes that 43 percent of men and 56 percent of women with various cancers survive more than five years, the vast majority being cured.[49]

MALNUTRITION

Malnutrition among the elderly may produce deficiency diseases, weakness, and weight loss. Problems with swallowing from mechanical factors or strokes, diminished senses of taste and smell, decreased appetite, and problems with absorption of food can all be responsible. Disinterest in food may be present in patients with cancer or chronic infections. Medications, alcohol abuse, and dental problems may also play a role. People who are demented or depressed (especially those living alone) must be watched carefully by family and social agencies, or their nutritional intake may be inadequate. Those who are disabled from various conditions and unable to shop for themselves or prepare food, must also be monitored, particularly since some may be too proud to seek assistance.

PSYCHIATRIC DISORDERS

Depression, anxiety, and alcoholism are all common in midlife and older people. Hallucinations and confusional states, which might suggest psychosis in a younger group, are usually the result of organic processes, such as dementia, cerebrovascular disease, reactions to medications, and metabolic disturbances.

Depression

Major depression affects 1–5 percent of older people living independently in the community, with a higher percentage in those who need some sort of assistance.[50] Subsyndromal or minor depression is believed present in five million older people who do not manifest the full diagnostic criteria for major depression. These percentages are significantly higher than in the midlife population. Of suicide deaths in the United States, 16 percent occur in individuals sixty-five and older who account for 12 percent of the citizenry.[51]

Depressive symptoms and depressed mood may interfere with daily activities and lead to physical decline.[52] Depression can result from situational factors that induce sadness such as the loss of a loved one (reactive depression), or can arise without a specific precipitant (endogenous depression). Genetic vulnerabilities may play a role, and depression earlier in life makes older people more susceptible. As we age, many events and losses (illnesses, physical disabilities, death of a spouse, and so forth) make us unhappy. These losses are usually dealt with through the normal process of grieving which can last weeks to months. But sometimes, grief can evolve into depression and compromise functioning. Some older people with a previous history of depression and/or periods of inappropriate euphoria or manic behavior, or agitation and irritability, may have what is known as bipolar disorder (manic-depressive illness).

Questions may arise in older people as to where normal sadness ends and depression begins. And how aggressively should sadness or depression be treated when it seems to be a logical response to life's adversities? Should we expect people in their eighties or nineties to be happy if they are alone after the death of a spouse or other loved ones, limited by chronic illnesses, and unable to care for themselves? Should they be given medication or psychotherapy to try to lift them from the depths of despair that might be expected with the cumulative losses they have suffered? There are no easy answers. Higher educational levels and socioeconomic status, stimulating interests and activities, socialization, religious or spiritual connections, and regular exercise, appear to provide some protection against implacable depression.

The severity of the depression in older individuals determines how disabling this condition will be. In mild depressions people may appear fairly normal to most observers, but feel sad, with a diminished zest for life and a general absence of enthusiasm. Friends may be abandoned and family obligations met grudgingly, or ignored. There is less initiative and an aura of apathy—a willingness to sit around much of the time doing nothing. Appetite is usually poor and libido is absent or considerably decreased. Often there are complaints of difficulty sleeping at night, though the patient may fall asleep during the day. He or she may grouse about a lack of energy and a feeling of fatigue. Emotional responses generally seem flat.

In those whose depression is more pronounced, the symptoms mentioned above are accentuated. Unable to concentrate on any tasks, individuals become completely unproductive, unwilling to begin any activity, or finish any project. Feelings of despair, dejection, and inadequacy are more manifest and people become increasingly withdrawn. They have no interest in things going on around them, even events of personal significance. Indifferent as well to their own condition, they do not take care of themselves, neglecting to eat and bathe properly, and disregarding medications and other health needs. Spouses, family members, or close friends have to manage every aspect of their lives to be certain they do not develop serious physical problems. Sometimes, if the depression is bad enough, there may be paranoid or guilty delusions, or a suicide attempt may occur. Psychiatric hospitalization may be necessary in intractable cases, with outpatient follow-up. Behavioral therapy, psychodynamic therapy for brief periods, and various medications can all be helpful in the treatment of depression once it is established, and if pursued vigorously, may lift the person from the depths of despair.

For family and friends, the most frustrating aspect of major depressions is that the affected individuals cannot be motivated to try to pull themselves out of this terrible state. They may resist professional treatment and, no matter how much they are cajoled or exhorted, refuse to get moving and take responsibility for themselves. Perhaps the frustration is also there for the depressed people themselves, but it is impossible to tell because of their apathy and lack of emotional reaction.

Anxiety

Symptoms of anxiety in midlifers and older people can be due to real problems (serious illnesses, financial worries) and may be appropriate, or may be inappropriate. Sometimes, there may not be a specific focus for the anxiety and it may be free-floating or generalized. Multiple stressors in a person's life, some of which he or she may be aware of and others that are hidden, may induce a generalized anxiety disorder. Physical illnesses may often be present. The symptoms of anxiety include jitteriness or nervousness, tremulousness of the extremities, tension in the muscles, rapid breathing, shortness of breath, palpitations, rapid heartbeat, dizzy spells, lightheadedness, abdominal cramps, nausea, diarrhea, difficulty sleeping, inability to concentrate, sweatiness, tremulousness, and trouble swallowing. Full-blown panic attacks occur as well in some individuals with anxiety.

Depending on how oppressive the anxiety is, it can be a major obstacle that will not allow people to lead a placid existence and as disabling as depression or physical illnesses. This is particularly true of those with panic attacks, severe symptoms of anxiety that appear suddenly and are incapacitating. The one aspect of anxiety common to all patients, no matter what the external manifestations may be, is fear, which may be overt or denied by the individual. As with people with severe depression and because of their affliction, those with relentless anxiety also have trouble relating to friends and relatives. Minor tranquilizers like Valium, Xanax, and similar compounds are often successful in treating anxiety. Psychotherapy and various relaxation techniques may also be beneficial.

Alcoholism and Drug Abuse

Alcoholism is seen in older men and women of all social classes. Some experts consider it a hidden epidemic, since older people often drink alone and keep their drinking concealed from others.[53] It was once believed that single men were most at risk, but a report in 1998 noted that 1.8 million women sixty and older abused alcohol and 2.8 million women abused prescription drugs.[54] Middle-aged people are equally prone to alcohol abuse. The pattern may begin early in life and continue into the later years, or may arise when a person is older, possibly in reaction to the problems that must be faced with aging. Not infrequently, alcoholism is symptomatic of other psychiatric illnesses such as depression or anxiety. Alcohol is less well tolerated as people age because of changes in metabolism, with a greater effect on the brain and central nervous system. Malnutrition may occur with severe alcohol abuse, causing permanent brain damage, liver damage, or peripheral neuropathies, producing confusion, impaired balance, numbness, tingling, and weakness of the legs. In addition, alcohol can interact with many medications with potentially dangerous outcomes.

Though the use of street drugs is relatively uncommon in midlifers and the older population, prescription drugs such as sedatives and minor tranquilizers including Valium, barbiturates, sleeping pills, and similar compounds are generally available and can be addicting. Because of their potential for abuse, these drugs must be monitored carefully by the treating physician and family members. Besides dependency, the drugs can be responsible for accidents and injuries that can kill or disable both users and innocent bystanders. Marijuana is still used recreationally by many Baby Boomers and some older people, and to help medically with symptoms of cancer and chemotherapy, and other conditions.

COMPRESSION OF MORBIDITY

Given the fact that older people are predisposed to develop different diseases, one would think that as individuals age, they would be less healthy, with a greater number of disabilities and medical bills. In actuality, this is true only for the middle-aged and young-old, but then changes. People who die in their fifties, sixties, and early seventies are more likely to have had multiple chronic illnesses (diabetes, hypertension, coronary artery disease, COPD, strokes—which are preventable to a large degree) with disabilities and high medical bills, than those who die in their eighties and nineties. Those in the latter group are generally in better shape (until their final illness supervenes) and spend less annually on medical care, than those who die when they are younger. In addition, total cumulative medical spending for healthy people at age seventy who have greater longevity is similar to those whose health is poorer and who die earlier.[55] This phenomenon is known as "compression of morbidity with aging." Thus, many people who live to a ripe old age have a good quality of life. "The payments (for medical care) associated with an additional year of life and the average annual payments over an enrollee's lifetime (from Medicare) both decreased as the age at death increased." [56]

Of further interest, a number of medical studies have shown that a reduction in old age disability has been occurring over the last two decades. The improvement in disability rates not only suggests that a better quality of life for seniors is emerging, but is also happy news for the Medicare program as it might reduce expenditures. Care of a disabled older person costs three times as much on average as for someone who is not disabled. The reason for the decrease in disability is uncertain, but may be related to less tobacco use, increased educational level among seniors, and perhaps the perception of self-efficacy—that older individuals are able to do something for themselves to improve their own health.[57] Whether this will continue given the increase in obesity in America is uncertain.

FACTORS THAT ACCELERATE AGING

Some people age faster than others for a number of reasons. They may be genetically programmed to do so, they may have been ravaged by illnesses, they may have worked in a hostile environment, or other external influences may have acted upon them. Though certain changes in our bodies are inevitable as we grow older, other factors we can control appear to accelerate the aging process, either in a general fashion or by damaging certain critical systems.

Smoking

As is well known, smoking is a major contributor to human mortality, causing lung cancer, pulmonary diseases, coronary artery disease, peripheral vascular disease, and strokes. Smokers also have a greater incidence of cataracts and facial wrinkles.

Alcohol Abuse

While moderate amounts of daily alcohol intake (one to two drinks a day) appear to reduce coronary artery disease and other vascular problems, excessive drinking can increase mortality and impair quality of life.

Obesity

In 2009–2010, 35.7 percent of American adults were deemed obese (body-mass index equal to or greater than 30), almost 40 percent of those who were sixty or older.[58] This did not include a large percentage of the population that was merely overweight. The increase in obesity in adults is seen at every income level, though is less prominent in affluent than low-income women. Excessive weight gain can result from lack of activity, overeating, or metabolic dysfunction. Whatever the reason, it is a major factor in high blood pressure, diabetes, coronary artery disease, and generalized atherosclerosis, as well as arthritis in weight-bearing joints, disc problems, and lower back pain. Greater cumulative disability occurs in people who are obese when present with other risk factors.[59]

Sedentary Lifestyle

In addition to contributing to vascular disease and atherosclerosis, lack of exercise leads to a loss of muscle mass, weakness, and reduced stamina. Over the last decade, it has also been shown to be a major factor in cognitive decline. It is also of importance in the development of osteoporosis, spine, hip, and long-bone fractures.

Poor Nutrition

Lack of adequate and proper food intake can cause deficiency syndromes, with brain damage, peripheral nerve damage, muscle loss, and osteoporosis.

CONCLUSION

Though the diseases and disorders associated with aging can obviously disrupt our lives in major ways, all is not hopeless. Those individuals who take care of their bodies have the potential to avoid debilitating illnesses and enjoy life even as they grow older. Just as aging is accelerated by the factors noted in the last section, it is possible to retard the aging process and the diseases that accompany aging by behaving in certain ways. Not smoking, not using drugs, and not drinking excessively do not delay aging but do allow us to grow old in a normal fashion, as does control of blood pressure in those who are hypertensive. On the other hand, regular and sustained exercise as a substitute for a sedentary existence is an important weapon in defending ourselves against time's assault. In fact, it is probably the most important weapon in our armamentarium. (How much and what type of exercise will be discussed in chapter 8.) Physical activity is even helpful for those who are overweight, though keeping one's weight down is also important in extending life and improving quality of life. Proper nutrition, including limiting the intake of fats and simple carbohydrates, eating a well-balanced diet with sufficient amounts of vegetables, fruits, and grains, can also aid us in our battle. In addition, having a positive attitude will assist us immeasurably as we enter into combat with age.

Mortality, behold and fear,
What a change of flesh is here!
—Francis Beaumont, "On the Tombs in Westminster Abby"[60]

6

LOSS: AGING'S COMPANION

We grudge life moving on
But we have no redress.
I would become as those
Firm rocks that see no change.
But I am a man in time
And time must have no stop.
—Yamanoue Okura, "The Impermanence of Human Life"[1]

Growing older entails accommodation to a succession of losses. The psychic and physical damage starts early in life and accelerates as we age, a continuum of loss accompanying life that is present at every stage. We lose people who are close to us and whom we love: our parents, peers, siblings, friends, colleagues, and acquaintances. We lose our skills, proficiencies, power, drive, and initiative. We lose our muscle strength, coordination, mobility, balance, bladder control, memory, and abstract reasoning. Also, as we age, many of us lose our autonomy, self-image, and unique identity—what makes us who we are. This is what we must fight to retain.

Being older and having lost various functions, we may need support from others in order to manage our lives. This may necessitate a minor or major effort from these people (spouses, children, relatives, friends), depending on our requirements. Whether this support is forthcoming and the way in which it is provided may have a lot to do with our ability to preserve our self-esteem. And it is up to us to manage as best we can given our circumstances—to enhance our life situations at each stage and derive the most satisfaction from whatever time we have left.

LOSS OF INDEPENDENCE

For some older people, living alone or with a spouse of the same age may present a series of challenges that must be overcome on a daily basis, the result of physical limitations, cognitive compromise, or psychological problems. These can be due to the normal aging process, or to various disorders. While many may be able to carry on their lives without significant hardship, others may have difficulties performing even mundane activities and may need assistance of one sort or another.

There are four types of support older people may require. The first is help with physical tasks. The second is administrative assistance in running their lives. The third is emotional support. And the fourth is financial aid that may be necessary to solve an immediate dilemma, or on an ongoing basis owing to inadequate resources.

Evolution of the Loss of Independence

For most of us, the period when we are completely free and independent is quite brief, from our postadolescent years through early adulthood. Before that, we are under the wings of our parents and after that time we are usually answerable to spouses, children, coworkers, and bosses. But even though we have certain obligations that must be met, for the most part we are still in control of our lives, able to make decisions and execute those decisions, perhaps with input from others at times, but expressing our own free will. As some of us have physical or cognitive difficulties as we age, the freedom we once had may be threatened and it may no longer be possible for us to do everything for ourselves. Even for the majority without significant problems, an initial phase of loss of independence often occurs in middle age and may be so subtle we are not even aware anything has changed. With a bad back, we may no longer be able to shovel snow or carry something heavy and may request help from our children, friends, or neighbors, or pay someone to assist us. Or we may ask a child to program a new appliance or piece of equipment for us because of difficulty deciphering the instructions. A classic example of this is a teenager teaching his middle-aged parents how to set a digital watch or use a new computer. It is not that we cannot manage these chores, it is just that it takes us longer to absorb the new information and perhaps we are more easily frustrated by unfamiliar and perplexing directions. And even when we have been shown how to do something or have figured out the intricate steps ourselves, we may have to go over it repeatedly before we are secure in our knowledge and ability.

As time goes on, our reliance on other people to perform simple or complex tasks for us increases. The degree to which this occurs and the ages at which various functions are transferred to others are different for everyone. There are ninety-year-olds who do just fine on their own, and sixty-year-olds who need constant help with activities. Indeed, two people with identical physical problems at the same age who are cognitively intact may require totally disparate levels of support. The wild cards here are the emotional states of these individuals, their feelings of pride, how they lived previously, and how important it is to them to remain self-sufficient. There are some people whose self-respect would suffer grievously if they had to call on others for assistance in the tasks of daily living, and some who acquiesce and scarcely blink an eye.

In past generations, extended families cared for older people when they could no longer live on their own. Though family members still play a major role in furnishing aid to seniors, society has become the caregiver of last resort when relatives either cannot or will not assume responsibility for someone. A 1998 report notes that, "about 22 million families—nearly 1 in 4—are providing some form of assistance to an older relative or friend, according to the National Alliance for Caregiving."[2]

Dependency Upon a Spouse

Dependency upon a spouse is perhaps easiest to accept, as it is what society has built into marriage ("for better, or for worse, in sickness or in health"). However, if love was lacking or flawed within the marriage before the need for help occurred, problems may arise for both the recipient and caregiver. The recipient may be reluctant, bitter, hostile, or apathetic about taking the assistance offered, or may appear accepting and grateful but use his or her disability in a manipulative fashion.

Similarly, the caregiver may be quite angry at the role he or she was assigned by fate, and provide help with visible resentment, or try to punish his or her mate who needs assistance by not being properly responsive. However, even if the marriage had been strong previously, the feelings generated by dependency may not be predictable. The person aided might feel guilty about being a burden to a loved spouse, which might engender hostility toward the caregiver, driving him or her away and perhaps increasing the recipient's anger and depression. As evidence that dependency can be destructive to relationships, the Government's National Health Interview Survey in 1994 of 50,000 households found that 20.7 percent of disabled adults were divorced or separated, versus 13.1 percent of those without disabilities.[3] (This survey did not focus on older people.)

It is obvious both partners suffer when one has a chronic illness. Studies have shown that in addition to psychiatric morbidity, caring for a disabled spouse is a risk for higher mortality.[4] Spouses who were under stress in providing care had "mortality risks that were 63 percent higher than non-caregiving controls."[5]

When it is necessary to provide care for a husband or wife who is chronically ill on a long-term basis, healthy spouses react in different ways, affecting their own lives as well as those of their mates. A few examples from my practice follow.

> R. B. was a sixty-nine-year-old woman whose husband had multiple sclerosis for eighteen years before dying of pneumonia. He was wheelchair bound for the last ten years and R. B. gave up her job and devoted her life to caring for him, her only other activity being church on Sunday mornings. They survived on Social Security and disability payments in a small home. When I began seeing her husband, R. B. was a petite brunette. Over the years, as he deteriorated and her life was more restricted, she ate incessantly, reaching a point where she was morbidly obese. When her husband died, she tried to return to the workplace, but already in her sixties, was unsuccessful. According to an acquaintance of hers, she had few friends and few interests and spent her days watching TV.
>
> L. C. was an eighty-two-year-old woman when last seen, whose husband, a successful attorney, began to have shaking of his hands and problems walking in his late sixties, when she was sixty. Within five years, he was demented and hallucinating, with gait instability.

The diagnosis was felt to be Lewy body disease, a progressive form of dementia. Initially, his wife cared for him at home, with some assistance from a daughter and nurse's aide who came in to help when the task became overwhelming. Eventually, he had to be admitted to a nursing home where he died two years later. Throughout his illness, his wife managed to have a life of her own, albeit limited. She walked at the beach almost daily, went to the movies and dinner occasionally with friends, and was an insatiable reader. After his death, she pursued the same activities, and became a volunteer at the hospital, appearing reasonably content with her life.

T. T. was a working woman in her early sixties who was quite attractive and youthful. She had been married for ten years to a gentleman about five years her senior who was an advertising executive. It was a second marriage for both. They were a handsome couple and had led an active social life until four years earlier when he began to become forgetful. Alzheimer's disease was diagnosed, which progressed unusually rapidly, reaching a point in about two years where he could not care for himself. Whenever they came into the office, she would complain bitterly about the way her life had changed. I learned subsequently that she had taken her husband to visit his daughter in a town near Boston one weekend and had left him there. She had told the daughter that she could no longer look after him and would not permit him to return to their home in Connecticut.

R. T. was a forty-six-year-old physician when I first saw him, with slight weakness of his left hand. An avid runner, he had been married for thirteen years and had two sons, ages ten and eight. He and his wife had moved to a town in Connecticut from upstate New York to try to start a new life after she had been having an affair with a local builder. I diagnosed R. T. with amyotrophic lateral sclerosis, a fatal degenerative disease. Within a year, he could no longer work and was unable to walk a few months later. As his disease worsened, his wife moved out of the house and began living with her former boyfriend, leaving the two young children to care for their father with a nurse's aide. Since her husband would likely die within a year or two, I pleaded with her to remain with him and help with his care, but she refused to leave her boyfriend. With his arms growing weaker to the point where he could barely feed himself, he took an overdose of Valium, not wanting to burden his children any further. (Because R. T. was middle-aged and his children were young, his situation was different from the more common circumstances seen with older individuals and adult children.)

Assistance from Children

Having to receive assistance from one's children can be more injurious to a person's self-esteem than care from a spouse. How both parents and children deal with this issue is again contingent on the relationship that existed before the help was provided. Invariably in a cognitively intact parent, there is some element of guilt about having to enlist a child's aid. But if the assistance is given willingly and lovingly, the parent is more apt to receive it in a similar vein. On the other hand, if help is proffered grudgingly and complainingly, the recipient may refuse it and even show hostility to the child rendering the aid. Of course, the kind of assistance necessary also plays a role in determining the reactions of both parent and child. Whereas minor aid may be accepted as making life easier, major help with the tasks of daily living may be seen as more threatening to the recipient's autonomy, and may produce resentment and obstruction. These feelings may be particularly prevalent when an older person is encouraged or forced to give up his or her home to live with a child, or go into an assisted living residence or nursing home. If several children are involved in caring for a parent and share the commitment graciously, there may be more compliance on the part of the parent as it may eliminate some of the feelings he or she is a burden. For many children, the day-to-day demands of raising their own children complicates the efforts to take care of older parents—a particular dilemma for the so-called sandwich generation that finds itself in the middle of these two competing calls.[6]

Sometimes pride gets in the way of older individuals allowing children to manage their affairs as they stubbornly guard their independence. This can have various consequences. A retired pharmacist who was a patient of mine had accumulated a fair amount of wealth through prudent investments after selling his business. In his eighties, he began to suffer from macular degeneration and mild cognitive impairment. His wife had been disabled by a severe stroke some years earlier and required full-time care from a live-in aide. Two children—a son and a daughter—were very attentive, yet the patient refused to turn over management of his finances to them or even explain what he was doing.

When he died suddenly of a heart attack, his records were indecipherable, leading to difficulties getting his estate in order. This caused problems in caring for his wife, as well as considerable tax losses, as his will had not been updated for twenty years.

Assistance from Other Family Members

Other family members (nieces, nephews, cousins) may also be called upon to assume responsibility for older relatives when there is no spouse or child. Even friends may play this role if no one else is available. As always, the prior bonds that existed, the attitude of the caregiver, and the level of care necessary determine whether the new arrangements will be successful. But no matter how close the helpmate and recipient were before the need for help arose, it is even more difficult for someone who is not a spouse or child to furnish support on a continuing basis. A study has demonstrated a significant economic cost to caregivers of older relatives who are still working.[7] Wages, benefits, and promotions all had to be sacrificed for them to be able to provide care.

The Extended Family

Because fewer children are being born to each couple, and with higher rates of divorce and greater mobility than in the past, the extended family has been slowly disappearing. Previously, within the milieu of the extended family, older people (usually women) served valuable functions that enhanced their feelings of self-worth, helping to care for young children, preparing meals, and assisting with housework. Then, if a time came when these older people themselves required care, the family as a whole contributed to their support in whatever ways were necessary. Indeed, older parents living with married children and grandchildren, with brothers and sisters, or with nieces and nephews nearby was considered a normal scenario. A change in this pattern came about as the extended family began to disintegrate and children, being more protective of their own privacy and freedom, became more resistant to having parents sharing their space. There was also a greater reluctance on the part of parents to being under their children's thumbs. With older people living longer, as well as being more vigorous and independent, they wanted to maintain their own lifestyle without the constraints imposed by living with children or relatives.

Though the environment of the extended family no longer exists for most of our populace, there are some cultural groups where it is still seen to varying degrees. Strong feelings of respect exist for those who are older and the desire to assume responsibility for one's parents. It is particularly prevalent among peoples of Mediterranean origin (Spanish, Italian, Greek, and so forth), Asians (Japanese, Chinese, Koreans, and so forth), and African Americans. A report from the AARP in 2001 showed that Asian Americans furnished the most care for older family members; white Americans, the least.[8] Of Asian Americans, 42 percent provided care or financial support for older family members; white Americans, less than 20 percent; African Americans, 28 percent; and Hispanic Americans, 42 percent. Interestingly, those who were the most caring also felt the most guilt about not doing enough for their parents. Another study for the National Institute of Aging noted that "older blacks were twice as likely as whites to receive care from family members when their health declined."[9] Providing this care has long been a tradition in African American families, perhaps born of necessity, with poverty rates higher and other resources not as likely to be available. New immigrant groups from all countries also generally care for older family members, following the traditions of their homelands.

In the United States in 1997, fewer than 20 percent of adults over sixty-five lived with their children, compared to 55 percent in Japan.[10] However, as evidence of change occurring in Japan, as recently as 1970, 80 percent of older Japanese were part of their children's households.

Help within the Home Setting

Depending on the level of functioning, minor aid may be all that is necessary to keep an individual living at home, provided by children, a spouse, or outside agencies. Sometimes, if a person is homebound, the delivery of one or two meals a day may be needed. Social contact can be maintained if arrangements can be made to transport this individual to senior day care for a day or half day several times a week. This is important if the person confined to his or her home is cognitively intact or minimally impaired, as social interactions are essential.

The more affluent families are, the less likely they are to provide direct physical support and care for their spouses, parents, or relatives. However, they are more willing (and able) to give financial assistance. Among the upper-middle and wealthy classes, caregivers are usually hired to dispense hands-on help, whether it is paid for by the parents themselves or their children. Thus, home health aides and nurse's aides, instead of the spouse, child, or others, may assist with the tasks of daily living that the older person cannot handle adequately alone. In some cases, round-the-clock home care from these aides may be required when severe impairment is present.

For those individuals who have suffered blackouts, dizzy spells, strokes, or cardiac problems, electronic monitoring with instant communication may be helpful. Wearing a small cellular transmitter allows assistance to be summoned if necessary, giving some measure of security to both the older person and his or her family.

Other Options

At some point with older people living alone at home, issues of safety may become paramount and decisions may have to be made about the proper environment for those individuals. One option might be moving in with a child who can provide some help and hire aides for whatever else is needed. Another might be remaining at home with twenty-four-hour supervision. An assisted living complex might be another alternative, with or without special aides. And eventually, a nursing home might become a necessary choice. All of these possibilities entail major loss of autonomy for older people whose independence had been steadily shrinking previously. Not able to realistically assess their own situations, individuals may resist these changes. Though ultimately the older person may be forced to surrender to the will of the family, there should be an effort made to accommodate to his or her wishes if it is feasible. Even without full insight into their own limitations, they still have their pride and know the way they want to live.

Society's Role

There are times that spouses, children, or other family members may not be part of the equation in determining the assistance older individuals require. Someone who never married or had children may have no relatives. Or the person may, unfortunately, have outlived children and other relatives. And in some instances, the individual who needs help may refuse to call upon children or other relatives. The stumbling block may be ego, or there may be hostility and anger toward family members, the result of real or imagined slights that occurred in the past. (Over his or her objections, if the person is cognitively impaired, the physician, a visiting nurse, a social worker, or another professional may contact the family.) Where there is no family, or the family is out of the loop, society has to assume responsibility for care through various governmental agencies or private charitable organizations that have been given this assignment. Home health care organizations and visiting nurses' services may be able to provide care within the home setting, or a nursing home may be required.

Hired Caregivers

Assistance by hired caregivers presents different problems for the recipient than dealing with family members. Without the emotional baggage of past relationships, it may be easier to accept help, but in some ways it is more difficult. Though there is no love, hate, guilt, or anger toward the caregiver, and no manipulative behavior or power struggle with this unknown person (at least initially), issues of pride and self-esteem should still be considered. The type of care given and the level of comprehension and insight of the recipient are important elements. Most people get quite upset having a stranger bathe and assist them with hygiene, prepare meals, and feed them. Or shopping for them and managing their finances. Or dressing them and dispensing medications. Even without the assistance, just having another person in their home may cause resentment or anxiety. (The more cognitively compromised the individual is, the easier it may be to willingly accept the assistance.)

Over a period of time, recipients generally become accustomed to the care being given and the intrusion in their personal space. However, this is contingent to a large degree on the temperament and compassion shown by the caregiver. If this person is condescending, arrogant, overly critical, or insulting, time may increase hostility and resistance rather than assent. On the other hand, if the caregiver is kind, understanding, and patient, he or she may be able to establish a positive relationship with the recipient—a situation that makes it more comfortable for both of them.

Unfortunately, public agencies may not be able to furnish caregivers with the right demeanor and emotional state to deal with people who have different disabilities. These organizations may not have the time or funds to adequately educate caregivers about their roles, not only delineating the services they will have to provide, but also instructing about how to interact and respond to older people, especially those who require a higher level of care. Usually, professionals such as nurses or social workers are more cognizant of the problems of older people and are able to manage them better. Home health aides and nurses' aides, who are generally paid poorly and have less training, but provide more of the hands-on care, may not be as respectful or forbearing as their professional colleagues. ("Home health aide" has been one of the fastest growing job categories in the United States.)

Quite often an older client is treated as a child by a caregiver, who orders him or her about without explaining matters, even berating or scolding them when things do not go as expected. In addition, there may be cultural differences or language problems that make communication difficult, or make a caregiver less sympathetic to the person being cared for and less willing to extend him- or herself. Of course, it can be frustrating dealing with older people who do not hear or see well, move slowly because of strokes or arthritis, or have cognitive problems and don't fully grasp what is being asked of them. However, caregivers without patience and compassion often rob their impaired charges of the few remaining shreds of dignity they have left. These older people have limited power or no power at all, and are completely at the mercy of the strangers who enter their homes to care for them.

Assisted Living Residences

Even with family participation, visiting nurses, and home health aides, at some point it may become too difficult for a person to remain in his or her home. Depending on the individual's needs, various options can be considered. If the person is able to take care of him- or herself to a certain degree, assisted living residences may be the answer. These developments come in different sizes and shapes, and may be found in urban, suburban, and rural areas.[11] According to the AARP, about 1 million Americans currently reside in assisted living facilities.[12] This is projected to double by 2030. There are about 30,000 assisted living facilities in the United States at present, many of these constructed and operated by large corporations. For the most part, they are for-profit ventures that do not give anything away for free. (A small number, run by charitable organizations, focus more on lower income people.) Based on how the project is structured financially, the units may be rented by an older person, or purchased as a condominium, with additional services included for an annual fee, or paid for as required.

The services offered can vary greatly from complex to complex, or even to different people within the same complex. Usually the facility provides one, two, or three meals a day in a common dining area or in the person's own apartment if she or he cannot get out for meals. Maid service cleans the apartment, changes the linen, washes the clothes, and so on, as frequently as needed. Transportation is often furnished for shopping, with arrangements made to take residents for doctor's visits or other appointments. A nurse may be on call to help with minor problems and sometimes there are also doctor's offices on the grounds. Larger complexes may have sections where people can reside to obtain skilled nursing care, either temporarily for an acute illness or on a longer-term basis. (At times, a nursing home may be tied into the assisted living residence and be run by the same management.) It may also be possible to arrange for home health aides to assist the person in his or her own apartment for a short interval or an extended period. The best developments are light years removed from the "old age homes" of the past, having everything an older person needs, though the prices paid for various amenities can be steep.

When assisted living is chosen voluntarily by a senior, the transition may be quite satisfactory and not demeaning to the individual. But when people are forced into assisted living by family members, the move can be devastating, as it signifies they are no longer autonomous and in control of their lives.

Nursing Homes

For people who are too impaired physically or cognitively to live by themselves even with major assistance, nursing homes are a flawed though necessary solution. When there is no hope an individual will be able to resume a functional existence in the future, he or she can be sent to reside in these warehouses of chronic illness and disability, where people are sequestered to await death in the company of others in similar situations. (Patients with temporary disabilities may also utilize nursing homes for short stays to help them recuperate after hospitalizations.) Unlike a hospice setting, the patients in these institutions do not have a terminal condition with a limited life expectancy and death may not visit them for some time. So they linger in limbo, neither dead nor fully alive, sitting, eating, and excreting, with no dreams and no expectations of a better existence. No matter how dedicated the staff and how modern the physical plant may be, the conditions in these homes are generally repellent and dehumanizing.

As noted in a *New York Times* editorial in 1999,

> It is thought that as many as half of all women over 65 in the United States and a third of all men will spend some of their remaining time in a nursing home. . . . [N]ursing homes have acquired the sickest and most dependent of the old. . . . [L]ess than 8 percent can bathe, dress, go to the bathroom, move about and feed themselves without help. . . . [A]s every study for decades has shown, great numbers of the old, many as helpless as babies, continue to be neglected and abused. Some die of accidents, malnutrition, dehydration, untreated urinary infections and bedsores that turn into toxic, flesh-eating wounds.[13]

In 1985, there were 19,100 nursing homes in the United States, with a total of about 1.6 million beds.[14] That same year, 5 percent of the 28.5 million people over age sixty-five resided in these institutions, 1.3 million people. However, 21.6 percent of those eighty-five and over were in nursing homes, one third of all nursing home occupants, though they were less than 1 percent of the population.[15] Proprietary nursing homes comprised 75 percent of the total, most of them in large chains for efficiency and economy of scale.[16] About 20 percent were run by hospitals or voluntary organizations and 5 percent by government. For the most part, nursing home facilities were small, averaging 85 beds, with public units averaging 132 beds.

By 1997, the number of nursing homes was down 13 percent, though total beds were up 9 percent.[17] Interestingly, nursing home residents increased only 4 percent from 1985 to 1995, despite the fact the population over sixty-five shot up 18 percent. (From these figures we can assume that either older people were healthier in 1995 than 1985, and less in need of nursing homes, or that other methods of care were being utilized instead of nursing homes—that is, home care.) By 2011, there were 16,100 nursing homes in the United States with 1.7 million beds and an occupancy rate of 86 percent.[18] About 90 percent of patients in nursing homes were sixty-five or over, 35 percent eighty-five or over. Whites comprised 88 percent of the residents, and 72 percent were female.

Whether nursing homes are run by corporations whose goal is to make a profit, voluntary agencies whose aim is to provide a needed service, hospitals, or governmental bodies, there are certain common elements to their operations that make it inevitable that residents' dignity will be compromised. First is the sheer mass of physically and cognitively deteriorated patients requiring care. Second is the difficulty in attracting good personnel to work in a nursing home environment. Third is the fact that in order for these institutions to work efficiently, they must function like factories for the care of their charges, with fairly rigid time schedules for the tasks being performed and specific assignments for workers.

The vast majority of nursing home residents have significant cognitive deficiencies. This means that besides being unable to care for themselves, they cannot follow directions or retain admonitions regarding safety. Thus, they will get out of a chair or bed, or fall and injure themselves if not properly restrained or observed every moment. They will also neglect to ask for bedpans or urinals, or help in getting to the bathroom, instead defecating or urinating when the urge occurs. Because of this, they must be cleaned frequently to avoid bedsores and infections, or a urinary catheter may be utilized to prevent them from wetting themselves. They may also constantly demand things from caregivers, having forgotten that someone had recently provided it. And as they become more demented and confused, they may cry out or call repeatedly for no reason, disturbing everyone around them. Eventually, it may be necessary to sedate them to provide care and to allow the other patients and staff some peace.

The physical problems ubiquitous in the nursing home population also complicate their care. They are literally, as well as figuratively, on their last legs. Virtually all have multiple medical problems, needing constant attention and assistance with the tasks of daily living, such as feeding, dressing, personal hygiene, medications, and so on. For some of them simply to survive necessitates an almost heroic effort by their caregivers on an ongoing basis. The various physical disorders, in addition to cognitive impairment, continuously tax the patience and skills of the caregivers who work in these institutions. And at times, the staff may ignore patients in pain who need medication for relief.[19]

Recruiting decent personnel to work in a nursing home environment is a major concern for administrators. Because of this, standards may be compromised and the elderly residents may suffer. The best nurses and aides want to be in acute-care hospitals, busy medical offices, public health units, and the like, where there are more challenges and more intellectual stimulation. They want to feel their work means something and that the patients they treat may possibly improve, and, if in a hospital, go home. In these other venues, communication between patient and staff can also be emotionally satisfying for the caregivers. Nursing home work, on the other hand, is drudgery and unpleasant to boot, consisting of feeding, dressing and undressing patients, and cleaning up urine and feces. There is no excitement in caring for these patients, no creative energy unleashed, and little emotional interaction. And the staff has little to look forward to in terms of the care they are rendering. None of their patients are going to get better and leave the nursing home. The only way out for them is to die.

Virtually all the day-to-day care in the nursing homes is done by aides rather than nurses. The latter serve primarily in a supervisory capacity and dispense medications, rather than attending directly to patients. In general, the people who opt to work in nursing homes are not as ambitious as their hospital colleagues in terms of personal development. Education and training of the staff in these institutions is also not as comprehensive as at most hospitals, even in areas related to their specific patient populations and chronic illnesses. This is in spite of the fact that caring for nursing home residents is more demanding in a number of ways than for hospital patients. (In fact, for nurses' aides in nursing homes, "there is often less required training than for a manicurist at a beauty parlor, and they may be paid less than a beginning caretaker at the zoo."[20])

It is important to remember that in most nursing homes, the bottom line is the major determinant of the services that can be given and of what can be spent on personnel. To make a decent profit for their corporations and to boost stock prices if they are public, executives who run nursing homes want to get the biggest bang for their buck, trying to get the most done with the least number of people and the lowest expenses. These executives are out to provide adequate rather than top-notch care. They want to meet minimum standards so the regulatory agencies will not crack down and lift their licenses, but do not want to spend extra money to obtain more and better personnel. This translates into lower salaries for their nurses and aides.

The bottom line is also the reason that nursing homes tend to operate as factories for care of the disabled elderly. With limits on the number of nurses and aides that can be hired, the staff must be organized in a way that will maximize its ability to deliver services. This means assigning staff members to tasks that are tightly scheduled and must be performed within particular time constraints. Unfortunately, it is not always possible to allot definite time slots in caring for cognitively and physically damaged human beings, as problems often arise that require special attention and extra moments (incontinence, falls, pain, shortness of breath, anxiety, and so forth). And not infrequently, a depressed or anxious patient may need verbal reassurance, or hand-holding, which may also take additional time. However, if a caregiver is behind in his or her schedule and feels pressured to move on and complete his or her work, he or she may shortchange patients and not give the physical care or emotional support they require.

Because of the aforementioned problems, nursing homes should be a solution of last resort, reserved for those who have major cognitive deficiencies and are unable to comprehend the degrading conditions to which they are being subjected.

LOSS OF CONTROL WITH VARIOUS TYPES OF LIFE SUPPORT

A number of diseases in older people can damage or destroy critical organs, altering the metabolic or physiologic parameters necessary to sustain life. Before the modern era of medicine, this always resulted in death. Currently however, with the use of drugs, tubes, and electronic and mechanical devices, people can be kept alive, even after vital systems have failed. But when artificial support mechanisms are used to preserve life, the recipients may wind up losing control of the decision-making processes and be sustained in states they would not have voluntarily chosen. The type of support I am alluding to includes assistance with cardiovascular and pulmonary function, nutritional maintenance through feeding tubes, renal dialysis to forestall kidney failure, catheters for urinary drainage, and ostomies for bowel and urinary diversion. When life is extended and the quality of life is not significantly diminished, there is little controversy about the use of these aids. We can cite cardiac pacemakers or artificial valves as examples.

The use of ostomies to prolong life is usually straightforward when there is a curable, life threatening disorder that can be circumvented, or for palliative reasons when survival is extended. (Ostomies are shunts in the intestines or ureters that direct feces or urine to the surface of the abdomen where they can be collected in special pouches when the normal passages are blocked.) Their use is more questionable if survival will be short term or of poor quality, even with these techniques. Urinary catheters are generally not objectionable when incontinence or urinary retention is a persistent problem that cannot be solved in any other manner (though they do cause frequent infections). Renal dialysis, used to forestall kidney failure resulting from various disorders, can be continued for many years, unless a renal transplant can be performed to restore kidney function. Since it is an expensive, laborious process, in other industrialized countries, dialysis is rationed, with an age cut-off after which a person can no longer receive it.

In determining whether or not to utilize any of the above-mentioned techniques, increased survival should not be the critical factor, but rather the quality of the person's survival. (The process of dying, when procedures should be used or withheld, and necessary preparations for dying will be discussed in depth in chapter 11.)

LOSS OF DRIVER'S LICENSE

The loss of a driver's license and the ability to drive is a development dreaded by many older people, imperiling their self-sufficiency. In 1995, there were 24 million drivers over the age of seventy,[21] expected to increase to 40 million by the year 2020. Accident rates per miles driven rise after age seventy-five, and even more significantly after eighty-five.[22] And the use of medication can particularly compromise safety in older drivers.[23]

Though licenses may be surrendered voluntarily, often family members, physicians, or the legal system take them away. The reasons include cognitive decline, diminished visual acuity, and various physical disabilities. But the end result for those deprived of their licenses is the same: a loss of freedom and control over their lives. And if the deprivation is involuntary, the shock of the loss is heightened. When driving privileges are removed, older people become aware they have reached a new stage in their lives and from that point on must rely on others to get around. These circumstances for many are almost the inverse of their situations as youths, when they eagerly anticipated the granting of driver's licenses to affirm their status as adults. Instead, the elderly await the forfeiture of their licenses with apprehension, seeing it as affirmation of their passage into senescence. Perhaps reflecting on their masculinity, the loss appears to be even more devastating for men than for women.

Most people in the United States take their ability to drive for granted since it is so much a part of their everyday lives. Indeed, in areas lacking reliable public transportation, driving is an absolute necessity for people to function. It is only when that power is taken away that we realize its importance, as we are forced to seek rides like children in order to visit someone, go shopping, or perform simple chores. In many senior communities, a person who drives and has a car has special standing, being envied by his or her peers, because he or she has the freedom that others lack, and can also provide a valuable service. It is reminiscent of teenagers who bestow an elevated status on their friends with cars. In some older people, the ability to drive is tied to pride and self-esteem, and relinquishing that privilege may result in depression.

> A male patient of mine, a former physician who was ninety years old, refused to give up driving even though he had a budding dementia, and poor balance and coordination due to a number of strokes. He insisted he was capable and could not carry on his day-to-day existence without his car. After going through stop signs and red lights on several occasions and having near accidents, the local police took his license away pending medical clearance. Being quite affluent and extremely stubborn, he was accustomed to having his way and con-

tinued driving without a license, a manifestation of his poor judgment.

In granting driver's licenses, governmental authorities want to protect other members of society from those who have insufficient skills or acumen to operate vehicles and protect the deficient drivers from harming themselves. However, it is also vital for society to help people maintain their independence and autonomy, and so, in withdrawing privileges, must balance competing mandates. Many disabled, older drivers who lose their licenses may still be able to drive safely in certain circumstances: at low speeds, in daylight, and in local, familiar territory. Though their reaction time may be slowed, these drivers also tend to be very cautious and take fewer risks. Some states have started moving toward providing restricted licenses to seniors and disabled people, with repeated testing to renew privileges. Even more effort should be made to issue multiple categories of licenses, taking into account people's particular needs and functional abilities.

LOSS OF LOVED ONES

Sadly, as we age, we have fewer relatives and friends to accompany us on our journey through the years, as our coterie of contemporaries dwindles, producing periods of mourning and adjustment. Those who survive with us become remnants of our generation: individuals who have had the same experiences and have lived through the same times we have. Too often, it is difficult for us to communicate with people who were not there as our universe evolved, and for them to understand our lives.

When we are older, the way we deal with our losses is a factor in our ability to maintain vitality and functionality. If we are unsuccessful in this task, as our peers die, we can wind up grieving for long intervals, covered by a mantle of depression and unable to carry on with normal living. This is the expected path in some cultures, particularly when a husband dies. In many Mediterranean countries, wives dress in black and may spend the rest of their lives so attired, forever mourning their spouses. Perhaps they see themselves as figures of nobility and rectitude, though others view them as objects of pity. In Hindu cultures, suttee was a traditional practice among the upper classes. When a husband died, since the woman's life was essentially over, she would throw herself on the funeral pyre to die with him. But in modern, Western societies, all of us are encouraged to maximize our potential and live our lives to the fullest after coming to appropriate terms with the loss of loved ones. This can only be done if we don't drape ourselves in black and allow grief to overwhelm us.

Accommodating to the deaths of relatives and close friends occurs at different times for each of us, the impact depending on the strength of the relationships (and the geographical proximity) that previously existed. The deaths of people within our households, or those with whom we interacted on a daily basis, affect us the most in terms of altering our routine, but the internal consequences are determined by the bonds that had been present. In a common pattern, grandparents might die while we are teenagers or young adults, with parents dying when we are middle-aged. At least this is the anticipated sequence and, though painful, is felt to be the natural order of things. Then later in middle age, our peers begin dying, with more of them disappearing from our world as we continue to grow older.

At some point we also lose our spouses and are forced to change the way we conduct our lives. Aside from the love and comfort that is now missing, the loss of a spouse interferes most with our usual activities. Habits must be reshaped and divided responsibilities must be totally assumed by the surviving member of the couple. And one must acclimate to being alone, with no companion in the home and no one with whom to share one's thoughts. Living with someone for thirty, forty, or fifty years, a person becomes complacent, believing this is the way it will always be, even though he or she realizes at some level that change is inevitable. Then, after the loss, the survivor is immersed in a sea of depression and apathy that must be battled constantly. Sometimes, he or she, particularly the very old, simply gives up on life, and often dies soon after their spouse.

Unfortunately, children sometimes die before their parents, which can be emotionally devastating for anyone, but is perhaps less well tolerated by seniors. Severe depression and withdrawal often results, and recovery, if it occurs, may take many years.

The deaths of our peers move us in a number of ways, whether these were friends, acquaintances, or simply people who existed in our lives.

First of all, they bring home our own vulnerability and make us examine the possibility of our own mortality. Secondly, the death of someone else our age sometimes gives rise to feelings of guilt about our survival. Thirdly, as more and more familiar faces vanish and are replaced by those of strangers with whom we have no connection, our situation heightens and extends our sense of isolation. And as our friends leave us, the emotional support system we have constructed over the years begins to crumble and often cannot be replaced.

LOSS OF IDENTITY AND SELF-IMAGE

Many of us deal with a loss of identity and self-image as we age. Mired in the quicksand of minor cognitive problems and/or physical disabilities, we tend to forget who we are, what we stand for, and what is important. Looking in the mirror, we see old people who cannot be us, disregarding the possibility that what we see may merely be a veneer; an external surface that has aged, while the energy, dreams, and passions inside have remained youthful. But without knowing who we are, we may find it difficult to accept the fact we are old and have limitations, while still carrying on and relishing our lives. Instead of concentrating on the strengths still there, we obsess over what has been surrendered to the onslaught of the years and become listless and indifferent to ourselves. We forget that being older does not mean that life is over.

A number of other factors also contribute to the loss of identity in older people. For some who have previously worked, retirement itself can be destructive. Whether voluntary or forced, the loss of one's job, with its status and demands, can cause significant pain while puncturing the balloon of one's ego. During most of our adult lives, our sense of identity is closely connected to our occupation. We are known as so and so the banker, the plumber, the attorney, the cabinetmaker, and so forth. Upon retirement, the bond between our identity and our occupation is severed and we become disassociated from what we had used as our credentials. In addition to that, the entire pattern of our lives is transformed. No longer do we go to work daily and adhere to a specific schedule. And no longer do we have to be concerned with productivity and our ability to get things done. We are now called upon to establish new identities—to play new roles with different goals and objectives. In short, we are asked to reinvent ourselves, a task for which many of us are unprepared and which we are unable to perform—at least not to the degree that makes us content with who we have had to become.

Similar situations arise with women who have stayed home to raise children and run households. As the children grow up and leave home, mom no longer has the same responsibilities and the same jobs. Living now in an "empty nest," she has time on her hands and has lost her previous identity as a mother. No longer needed in the same way by her children, she must also find a new uniform to wear and redefine who she is.

The diminished income that can come with retirement may also affect people's self-image, particularly if their feelings of self-worth were tied to their financial state. With less money available, they may have to restrict their spending and "conspicuous consumption." Less extravagant clothes, travel, recreation, and dining out may be necessary, along with a less expensive car and more affordable living quarters. Moving into a smaller home and perhaps keeping a car for a longer period may seem like common sense to most people, but for others it connotes a step down on the social ladder and a loss of self-esteem.

There are those as well whose self-image may be damaged when they perceive themselves as no longer being productive members of society and not functioning in ways they consider important. Doing something, or making something, or selling something, or whatever, was significant to them and has now been taken away, with nothing comparable to replace it. Fixating on this loss instead of trying to find a new focus for themselves may lead to depression, and they may be unable to move forward with their lives after retirement.

This period may also bring forth a great deal of introspection and self-analysis in some individuals. Having reached the end of the productive road, they may feel as if they did not do anything of value during their years of working and perhaps their lives were wasted. Or they may be reminded that they did not realize the dreams of their youth, and now there will be no more opportunities for them. Of course, the situation had been like that for years, but retirement brings the reality home. Whatever they have already achieved, or not achieved—that is it forever. Most can accept this, but some see themselves as failures for not having accomplished more with their lives. For many others, however, this is not even an issue to be debated.

LOSS OF INITIATIVE

For the majority of people, aging is associated with a loss of initiative and a loss of drive, which can be upsetting for those who previously thrived on activity. In general, this is not a time for new ventures, starting new businesses, or building new homes. Some of this may be based on physical and cognitive changes, and a drop in levels of certain hormones. And in some people, depression may play a role. Many people also feel burned out, perhaps having been in the same position, or having done the same thing for years. A fatigue also sets in after decades of conflict and stress. But whatever the cause, a dwindling of energy is often evident.

It is true as well that the familiar feels good to us as we age, and being in a comfortable and predictable environment is reassuring. No longer do we lust for excitement and take risks in the way we conduct our lives. For many of us, this conservatism goes along with support of the status quo in our personal worlds and society at large. We are often unwilling to consider new ideas and new ways of doing things. However, those who are self-assured and unafraid of the future are more disposed to contemplate change, more open to new methods and new patterns of behavior, and also more amenable to new adventures.

LOSS OF MEANING

Many of us are aware of a void in our lives in our later years, as if something is missing, over and above our previous jobs and lifestyles. Although we might not be able to articulate what this is, perhaps what is missing is meaning on a spiritual level, as many of us have a yearning to understand what life is all about, including some comprehension of our role in the universe. This is different from the meaning that comes with working, with its focus on productivity and the goals intrinsic to a job. It also supersedes the need to establish a new identity and new goals that are part of retirement. During the years of employment, trying to do our work and earn a living, or manage the household and bring up the kids, we may have been too busy to ruminate about the purpose of life. Only after retirement do these questions bob to the surface, nagging at us and demanding our attention.

In the past, religion gave most of us answers to our questions, or negated the need to ask. Since survival was an issue in antecedent societies, people worked until they died and did not wonder as much about life's meaning. If they did, religion was there for them and without the constant bombardment of information that raises questions for us. Even today, for those of us who are believers, there may be no emptiness and absence of meaning, but serenity instead. And among the faithful, an acceptance of what has been and what will be, will more likely make questions unnecessary.

Existence was also less complex in earlier times as we all had a place in an extended family, with defined roles at every stage of our lives. In addition, we had an attachment to the communities where we had spent our lives, usually remaining in the same town from birth to death. We knew our neighbors and shared the good and bad times with them, watching as the kids down the street grew up, married, and had babies. All of us felt we were a part of something greater than ourselves: our families, our communities, and our nation. This changed with the mobility that became a hallmark of the last half of the twentieth century. People went wherever their corporations sent them, or wherever they thought there was work. Or they wanted a town with better schools for their kids, or nicer homes, or a better climate, or more recreational facilities. Always moving and seeking new vistas. The price paid was a rootlessness and anonymity, with strangers for neighbors. Then our kids became adults and moved away, leaving us alone to chart a new course for ourselves. And with this came an existential angst, an emptiness that is difficult to describe. Thomas Cole notes in *The Journey of Life* that "in our century, vastly improved medical and economic conditions for older people have been accompanied by cultural disenfranchisement— a loss of meaning and vital social roles."[24]

CONCLUSION

The clock cannot be turned back to assist us in our search for meaning, or for older people to regain the defined positions they once held. Instead, we must look elsewhere within the context of our own time to give our lives purpose. We must empower ourselves. We must deal with our losses and carry on. And to do so, it is necessary that we have objectives we can pursue with passion, which give us a reason to awaken each morning, while blunting some of the pain that comes with living. (I will discuss some options in chapters 9 and 10.) At the same time, we must continue to guard our autonomy and control of our lives however we can. It is important as well that we remain connected to our family and friends, and aware of what is happening in our local towns, our country, and the world. And to maintain positive feelings about ourselves, we must also find ways we can give something back to our communities.

7

AGEISM—MARGINALIZING OLDER PEOPLE

This policy and reverence of age makes the world bitter to the best of our times; keeps our fortunes from us till our oldness cannot relish them. I begin to find an idle and fond bondage in the oppression of aged tyranny.

—William Shakespeare, *King Lear*[1]

Many societies are biased against less powerful segments, or those with different values than the majority, and work to suppress them with various measures. This prejudice may be manifest as racism, sexism, or discrimination against ethnic or religious groups. In America, there is a bias against seniors that has been called *ageism*, expressed in a number of ways.

Betty Friedan noted in her book *The Fountain of Age*,

The blackout of images of women or men visibly over sixty-five, engaged in any vital or productive adult activity, and their replacement by the "problem" of age, is our society's very definition of age. . . . An observer from another planet might deduce from these images that Americans who can no longer "pass" as young have been removed from places of work, study, entertainment, sports—segregated in senior citizens' "retirement villages" or nursing homes from which, like concentration camps, they will never return.[2]

AGEISM

Ageism may be based on an undercurrent of resentment toward older people in our society. Its origins date back several centuries. During colonial times, Protestant churches espoused the ideal of a hierarchical structure in the family, with the younger members serving and venerating the elderly.[3] However, the ideal was not always practiced. There was also a belief that the debility and decrepitude of old age was punishment for sinning earlier in life and that those who appeared healthy in old age, were the ones who were morally upright. This of course led to a detrimental view of older individuals, since the majority of them were impaired in different ways. Though abuse of alcohol, tobacco, slothfulness, and sexual debauchery could cause disease and decay, most older people were simply the victims of normal aging and the illnesses of later life.

In the late nineteenth century, an American physician, George Miller Beard, propounded the idea that man's productivity was maximal by age forty and that there was a rapid decline afterward due to deterioration of the brain. He contended that the economic power concentrated in the hands of old men was misplaced, as they were incapable of managing it properly. Beard chastised society for venerating older people, whom he felt were unworthy of respect.[4] Other prominent figures in America, including Dr. William Osler, supported some of these beliefs regarding older people, and by the turn of the century, they had gained a degree of general acceptance. Since the mid-twentieth century, science has uncovered many of the mechanisms of aging and its associated diseases, showing that the previous characterizations were rubbish. However, some of the misperceptions persist, though they are frequently unspoken.

The embers of hostility toward older people are fanned by the fact that for the most part, they are the least productive members of society (in terms of having paying jobs) and have to be supported by its working members. In addition to individual responsibilities in caring for parents and grandparents, workers contribute to keep Social Security and Medicare solvent, which primarily serves older people. And since the inception of Social Security in the 1930s, the ratio of workers to retirees has steadily declined, resulting in an increased financial burden for each worker and more money extracted from his or her paycheck. "In 1950, there were 16 workers for each Social Security beneficiary. [In 1999, there were] slightly more than three."[5] By 2020, when most baby boomers will have retired, there will only be two workers for each person receiving benefits. And because of the lack of political will in Washington, Social Security has not been placed on a sound financial footing, this problem passed along to future generations.

Envy of the lifestyle of some retirees, who are seen boating, golfing, playing cards, and so forth, may also be an issue for younger people. Not only does the rest of society have to pay to assist seniors, but there is a belief that the group as a whole is fairly affluent and could afford to do more for themselves. While it is true the grinding poverty once endemic among seniors has been reduced by Social Security and Medicare, older people in general are far from wealthy and usually live in a moderate fashion. Medical expenses not covered by Medicare also decimate the finances of many older persons. The young and middle-aged may be prone to forget that in the future, they themselves will require support from those who will then be working.

Because of the care they provide, some children also harbor controlled anger toward their parents, as may other family members who consider themselves obligated to older relatives. These feelings may be repressed to some degree, but linger below the surface. It may not even be the money they are sacrificing, but the time and type of tasks required, with seniors seen as physical and emotional burdens, causing stress and aggravation. Many younger people may not even realize a role reversal has occurred and that they are now functioning as the adults in the relationships with their parents. They just know they have responsibilities they would rather do without—directing various aspects of their parents' lives. This may contribute to the resentment, which they communicate to their peers, that they have toward all seniors.

Another element that fuels society's antagonism toward older people is a belief that much of the money the government spends on them is unnecessary or wasted and could be returned to taxpayers, or spent on programs of more generalized benefit. The elderly are perceived by some as being only a step away from death with their lives essentially over. Why should funds be disbursed on programs designated specifically for them? Do they deserve it when they are unproductive? What value are they to society? These ideas may not be generally discussed and may be held by only a few, but may influence how the population as a whole views seniors.

A dramatic example of Western society's indifference toward and devaluation of older people was evident in the summer of 2003 in France.[6] The continent had been scorched by an extraordinarily severe heat wave continuing into August. Traditionally for the French, August is the month for vacations, when individuals and families leave the sweltering cities for the seashore or countryside. As the French departed for their usual vacation sojourns, many elderly parents and other relatives remained behind in the heat, with no air conditioning and no concern for their well-being. Unaware of the need to consume large amounts of fluids, or unable to do so, thousands of older people, alone and completely unattended in their oven-like apartments, died of heat stroke or dehydration. Often constrained by pride, perhaps depressed by their situation, or unable to comprehend the danger, many did not ask for help. Only the stench of decomposing bodies alerted neighbors that something was wrong. Even after being informed that elderly relatives had died, some of those on vacation were unwilling to return home early to claim the bodies and the morgues were overwhelmed. It was estimated that 10,000 to 11,000 older people died prematurely in France because of the heat and absence of precautionary measures, an indictment of the families as well as the whole social order. After the fact, the government proposed measures to prevent a recurrence of this catastrophic event. This example merely reinforces the esteem in which "modern" nations hold the aged.

MARGINALIZATION OF OLDER PEOPLE

Whether younger individuals are hostile, neutral, or understanding in their attitudes toward seniors, they still tend to disregard their elders and ignore their opinions, marginalizing them with respect to their place in society. An eighty-seven-year-old patient of mine who was intellectually intact and quite bright expressed it to me in this fashion: "The worst thing about growing old is that nobody listens to you anymore, even when you have something important to say. Everybody's either too busy or doesn't care and most of your old friends have died." Some of the elderly even visit physician's offices with minor problems just to be able to speak to the doctor and his or her staff and have someone who will listen.

An unexpected factor contributing to the marginalization of seniors has been the technological revolution, with the important role that computers, smart phones, tablets, the Internet, and social networks play in people's lives. Some seniors are not skilled in the use of these tools, not having grown up with them and never having had the opportunity to learn about them. (However, there are many seniors who can utilize all the new technology.) In today's world, unfamiliarity with computers and the Internet puts a person at a distinct disadvantage. The vast majority of our households now have PCs, Macs, and/or smart phones and tablets. These are used for communication, to buy things online, to search for information and acquire knowledge, for entertainment, for education, and to participate in social media. Indeed, it is rare for a middle-class person not to send and receive e-mails, tweets, and texts and utilize their computers for various tasks. Seventy percent of United States households used the Internet at home in 2009.[7] That some older people have not mastered current technologies makes them less relevant in other people's eyes and is another negative they must overcome.

Certain aphorisms that have circulated in our society for generations attest to the fact that ageism is not a recent development and that marginalization of the elderly occurred in the past. One example is the saying, "There's no fool like an old fool," which suggests that old people appear even more foolish than the young when their actions are outside of accepted boundaries. This can apply to any type of behavior that does not conform to what is expected for seniors. It is almost as if society has set different standards for older individuals.

Another maxim is "You can't teach an old dog new tricks," which implies that old people are fixed in their ways and unable to adapt to new developments. Thus, as the world evolves and changes, they are left behind, existing in the past. If this were correct, it certainly could be cited as a rationale for marginalization of seniors, who could not function successfully in new environments. But though this adage has been around for ages, that does not make it true. In reality, older individuals can learn and retain new information—even how to use computers. It just takes them longer. And although they may be more resistant to change and conservative in their outlook, this tendency serves a useful purpose in a society all too willing to discard old ideas and values that previously worked well. Older people function as a repository for these ideas and values and insure that they will be considered carefully before change takes place. And seniors can transform their mind-set when it becomes necessary and act appropriately in any new circumstances that emerge.

JOB DISCRIMINATION

Older employees are not appropriately respected in the workplace. Though the Federal and many state governments have passed laws prohibiting age discrimination in employment, it is difficult to enforce and there is an obvious bias related to age. This is evident in forced retirement and buyouts of older workers, and the desire of many corporations to have a younger workforce. Whenever there is downsizing, it usually involves a disproportionate number of older employees, both blue collar and lower level executives, particularly those past fifty. There are several reasons for this. With seniority, older workers have higher salaries and hourly wages than their younger peers, though they may be performing the same or similar tasks. It is always cheaper to replace them with younger people making less money. There is also a perception that younger workers are faster and more efficient than older ones, and it is believed that older individuals are more difficult to train for new jobs and to use new technology. Because of this bias, older workers are often not afforded the chance to compete with younger people, to determine whether or not they can perform.

Various unwritten job restrictions are also placed on many employees who have reached their late forties or fifties and have not attained upper echelons of management. They are no longer provided with the same opportunities for advancement as their younger colleagues and are not promoted to higher positions, though many of them may be quite competent. Once a particular age is reached and employees are at a certain level, they are seen as not being able to go further on their career paths and may be relegated to dead-end work. Thus, it is easier to lay them off in any restructuring, as they were not perceived as being important.

And once they have been laid off, it may be even more difficult for these people to find jobs because of ageist bias, though placement of older job seekers is dependent on the state of the economy. (If unemployment is low and workers are in demand, older individuals can get jobs more easily.) However, employment agencies and corporations that are hiring usually show no interest in older workers to fill positions similar to those they previously held, wanting to utilize them instead at lower levels with less pay. Trying to find a different type of work or a new career may be equally frustrating, as there is a reluctance to retrain older people. Many of these individuals have to become self-employed if they want to continue working, going into business for themselves as consultants, freelancers, entrepreneurs, franchise holders, small shop keepers, and so forth. This may entail investing some of their own money to get started and may also mean having to forego benefits like health insurance and pension plans.

Of course, the situation is different for top executives or CEOs of large public companies. Not only are they retained after fifty, but their remuneration continues to escalate as they grow older. And they receive greater responsibilities with challenging tasks and vital roles to play. Still, with many corporations, sixty-five remains the end point, after which retirement is mandatory. Only under special circumstances (such as partial ownership, or control of the board of directors) will an individual be allowed to continue working.

The story regarding age also changes if a person owns a business, or has a major interest in it. Then he or she can continue working as long as desired, occasionally into his or her eighties or nineties. These people are able to set their own schedules, working as hard as they want and tailoring their hours to meet their needs. The viability of this kind of arrangement is affirmed by the fact that these businesses continue to be successful when run by older people, as age does not preclude the possibilities of hard work, innovation, and success. The same outcome is seen in both small and large businesses, retail outlets, and in the professions—law, medicine, accountancy, and so on. And in the arts, numerous writers, artists, composers, performers, actors, and the like, remain productive in their sixties, seventies, and beyond. As examples, Arthur Miller was writing plays in his eighties; Toscanini was conducting; and Picasso was painting at that same age.

Because of bias against older workers, not enough weight is given to the positive aspects of their performance in deciding whether to advance them, keep them when corporate restructuring occurs, or hire them when they are seeking new jobs. The work records of older employees generally show less absenteeism and more reliability than those who are younger—and a greater loyalty to their companies.[8] They are usually more willing to go out of their way to help when a crisis develops, for example, by working longer hours or overtime. In addition, being less confrontational and more compassionate, understanding, and respectful, they are better able to deal with people than their younger counterparts. This is important in any position where they have to interface with the public, consumers, or other workers. Experience counts and should not be overlooked.

With the Baby Boomers beginning to retire, there will be a shrinking workforce, without enough younger workers, administrators, and managers. Corporations will have to turn to retirees and older workers to fill positions in order to maintain growth and profitability.[9] Companies perceived to have had an ageist bias may not be successful in their attempts to retain or attract seniors.

Rather than pushing them into retirement, corporations should value older workers and change the way they use them. Besides shifting them to positions less physically demanding and where they seem to function better, more flexibility could be built into work schedules, according to the needs of the companies and the employees. This could lead to less time spent commuting and part-time work when desired.

Though forced retirement may be detrimental to the individuals involved, the question arises whether it benefits society in certain circumstances. For instance, there are a limited number of tenured university positions. If these are held by professors past a retirement age, it does not allow junior people to develop and reach their full potential, and new ideas may not get as vigorous a hearing. A turnover of those at the top tends to stir up intellectual ferment and is worthwhile for academic disciplines. Younger people have to know that opportunities will be there for them to move up the ladder. Similarly, corporations need to be invigorated periodically by new blood and new ideas. And that may entail appointing younger people to leadership positions, sometimes bypassing older employees. However, it is important for all to recognize that advancement will be on the basis of merit, and not because of either seniority or youth. Older workers must feel that opportunities are there for them if they are up to the task.

In politics at least, age does not appear to be as much of a liability as in other fields. Many politicians in their sixties, seventies, and eighties are elected to office. Rarely, some even play a role in their nineties, as did Strom Thurmond and Robert Byrd in the Senate. Actually, most older politicians are reelected, rather than elected for the first time. It seems that in legislative positions, where seniority is a determinant of power, the public is more willing to support older incumbent candidates. This is true in state and local governments as well as on a federal level. In the executive branch of the government, many cabinet members serve and have served in their sixties and seventies, with their expertise overcoming qualms about their ages.

Senator John Glenn is an example of what older people are capable of doing if they have the proper drive and attitude. In addition to being involved in the day-to-day business of the United States government in his seventy-seventh year, he became an astronaut again and was launched into space with the younger members of his team.[10] He was excited by the challenge of doing what no one else had done before, but also felt it was important to learn what effect space flight and weightlessness had on the physiology and bodily processes of an older person.[11]

With the devastating recession in 2007 and 2008, many older workers did not want to retire because of the financial losses they had sustained. And many chose to keep working because they enjoyed their jobs and found satisfaction in what they were doing. They were almost equally divided as to the above reasons, and some may have kept working for both reasons or had other motivations. As of May 2012, 7.2 million Americans sixty-five and older were working, a record number, double that of fifteen years earlier.[12] Many of these people were professionals or in managerial positions, some worked in retail or sales, and some were entrepreneurs who started businesses. Though fewer people (compared to other age groups) in their fifties and older were laid off due to the recession, those who lost their jobs had more difficulty finding new ones.

GHETTOIZATION

Another way ageism manifests itself is through the ghettoization of seniors. While it is true the desire of older individuals for separate housing has advanced this trend, it is at least partially because they are not made comfortable living with younger people, who are likewise ill at ease with those older. Thus, both segments of society are responsible for segregating people on the basis of age and both segments lose out because of this. Some might say there is nothing wrong with ghettoization since it is mostly voluntary, but it reduces the diversity in communities and does not allow for enough discourse and interplay between generations. This leads to a lack of understanding of the hopes and needs of each group, and a tendency for each to stereotype and denigrate the other. Conflict thus becomes inevitable and more difficult to resolve.

By ghettoization, I am talking mainly about the huge retirement villages that have sprouted up in various areas, not the smaller complexes for older people who remain a part of the general community in cities and towns for older people. Retirement villages contain hundreds or even thousands of homes or condominiums catering exclusively to seniors. Because older people seem drawn to warmer climates, these are particularly prevalent in the Sunbelt (Florida, and the rest of the Deep South, Arizona, Southern California), though they can be found everywhere. Their common characteristic is that younger people cannot live there. The usual cut off age is fifty-five, though some may raise the bar even higher. (A younger spouse is acceptable, as long as one half of the couple meets the age requirement.) While adult children of residents may also be allowed to live in these developments, younger children are prohibited. As an example of the ultimate in segregation by age, in March of 1999, the residents of the Leisure World retirement community in California voted to turn their gated community into an incorporated city, with its own mayor and city council.[13] This city of 18,000, called "Laguna Woods," had an average age of seventy-seven, with more than 90 percent of the population over fifty-five.

The majority of the residents of these retirement villages are white and middle-class, usually without any overt discrimination on the part of management. However, some do try to attract specific ethnic groups, or people from particular areas of the country, believing their clients will be more comfortable with other people having similar backgrounds. Some complexes are also geared mainly to the affluent, offering more luxurious homes or condominiums with special amenities and pricing their products higher to insure economic selectivity. Some developments also try to recruit retired professionals like teachers, administrators, and the like, who may not be wealthy, but want to live in a nice community in a warm climate and are willing to forego some of the frills.

The actual physical and financial structure of these complexes varies. Living units may be in apartment houses, detached homes, or attached townhouses of one or two stories. Though the apartment houses have elevators, the two story developments may contain walk-up units on the second floor (a potential problem as retirees get older).[14] Many of these communities are gated and have guards. Residents may be required to purchase their units and then pay monthly maintenance charges, or may have to rent the units, though other arrangements also exist. The corporations that have built these retirement havens are out to make a profit and generally charge whatever the market will bear. However, with the glut of housing after the last recession, many older people were unable to sell their homes at the prices they expected and the retirement complexes had to lower prices to attract residents.

The facilities in each community differ widely. Many have swimming pools and tennis courts, while some of the larger and more expensive ones have private golf courses. Shuffleboard, bocci, and other similar games may be provided. A community center on the grounds is usually included as well, with meeting rooms, card rooms, and game rooms. In addition, small medical offices with a nurse and occasionally a doctor may be available, either around the clock or at specific hours. Lectures, movies, and concerts, may be scheduled by the management or under the direction of an elected council of residents. Some of the larger complexes have stores on the premises, or there may be shopping nearby that can be reached by car or private bus. With everything that is provided, many of these developments are self-contained to a great degree, so that residents rarely have to venture into the outside world. This isolation translates into little interaction with other age groups, or social segments.

One may ask why these retirement villages entice older people, when the atmosphere appears to be so constricting. Notwithstanding the negative aspects, there are a number of reasons for their success. First of all warm climates attract many seniors. Moving to an unfamiliar part of the country, they are reassured by being in an environment with other individuals in the same circumstances. And as people age, they become less tolerant of chaos, noise, traffic, and so on, whose absence make the retirement communities more desirable. The protection offered by gating and security guards is also important for some seniors, with the recreational facilities and breadth of activities serving as additional lures. Given the demise of the extended family and the fact that parents no longer live with or near their children, retirement communities offer reasonable alternatives. Here, people can form instant friendships with others their own age with similar interests. And the ubiquity of modern transportation also makes communities in different areas of the country acceptable choices for seniors. If they want to visit children, relatives, or old friends, they can hop on a plane and be anywhere in a few hours, or even drive to many regions of the country.

Though retirement villages are appealing to late middle-aged people and the young-old, the luster may be lost as these individuals age further.[15] Some of the communities are really planned for healthy residents, and as people become infirm, they may find it difficult to live in this milieu. Climbing stairs, which was not an issue ten years earlier, may become a problem. There may be great distances between parts of the complex, and when a person can no longer drive, it may not be easy to get around. Also the draw of golf, tennis, and other activities disappears when chronic illnesses and disabilities occur—when vision fades, arthritis limits movement, and balance is impaired by cerebrovascular disease or neuropathies. In addition, when a person can't manage alone, adequate assistance may not be provided for the tasks of daily living. Many of the old-old move out of these retirement communities in their later years, returning to their hometowns where help may be more readily available, or they end up living near their adult children who can lend a hand when it is necessary.

Numerous seniors never consider retirement communities in the first place, but remain in their own homes. It is often the most affordable option for them, as well as a familiar, comfortable environment. Augmenting their decision, their home is usually close to family and friends, and the support apparatus they have built up over the years. Many are also unwilling to endure the process of moving, with all the hassles that entails. And a significant percentage of older people want to remain part of the general community, rather than being segregated by age in a huge complex.

Perhaps more desirable than the major retirement villages are the smaller developments designed for seniors, with ten to perhaps a hundred residents. Being modest in scale and located within conventional cities and towns, they are not meant to be separate from the surrounding communities, and their residents are not as isolated from the rest of the populace. Shopping, recreation, and entertainment occur off the premises and there is communication with different social groups and individuals of every age. In these smaller facilities, older people get to live with others who have similar needs and problems, which can be addressed by the management and staff, yet they are not sequestered from the outside world in age-based ghettos. Both seniors and society win in this type of arrangement.

A type of retirement community that has been overlooked by many people though it meets the needs of seniors and society at large is the so-called NORC (naturally occurring retirement community).[16] These are mostly large developments or apartment houses built decades ago as affordable housing in urban settings, where the population has remained in place as it aged. Now, a considerable proportion of the residents are older and retired, many with special needs. Programs that provide various services have been devised in some of these complexes to meet those needs. These programs include those in community centers with recreational facilities, help with transportation, nurses, Meals on Wheels, and social services. Remaining in familiar, comfortable settings, people can go from youth to middle age to old age in these NORCs, with appropriate care as they grow older.

There are many suburban towns, particularly affluent ones, with policies destined to drive seniors away. Older people who have lived in these towns for decades, often with mortgages paid off, have been seeing their taxes rise astronomically to pay for the rise in education budgets because of additional children in families who are recent arrivals. These seniors on fixed incomes subsidize the school systems with their taxes, with education frequently the preponderant part of the town's expenditures. Even those older people who are moderately well off may have difficulty handling the onerous financial burdens. Thus, they wind up selling their homes and moving to condominiums or homes in less expensive areas. In their stead, more new families with children move in, pushing more older people out. But the majority of townspeople seem indifferent to this pattern.

On the other hand, some suburban towns with the opposite philosophy have been trying to enjoin seniors from moving away by reducing their taxes and providing free or discounted public transportation, medical screening, senior centers, and so on.[17] The administrators of these towns realize that seniors are an asset to their communities and it is important to have age diversity in their populations. But the major reason for trying to retain older people is economic. These towns understand that the cost of tax abatement and services to seniors is cheaper than having additional children in the school system.

THE MEDIA AND OLDER PEOPLE

The media has reinforced ageism at times by portraying seniors in an unfairly deprecatory manner. A blatant example:

> In 1988, the image of the "Greedy Geezer" was born. Depicted on the cover of *The New Republic* magazine, the advancing army of angry-faced older persons wielding garden trowels, fishing poles, and golf clubs looked menacing, poised to assault America. The essay inside by Henry Fairlie described what the cover expressed visually: Older people are selfish and drain the country of resources that might otherwise be channeled elsewhere, especially to children. There have been other similar negative attacks on older people in this country.[18]

The media reflects society's bias against older people and contributes to the perpetuation of offensive stereotypes reinforcing this bias. Aside from celebrities, or special achievements by seniors (including just living to a very old age), the news media, both in print and on television, tends to focus on the problems of seniors, depicting them as feeble, demented, and unable to manage their own lives. Older people are rarely shown in a favorable light and there are few stories about older individuals who have dealt successfully with aging. News reports may describe scandalous conditions in nursing homes, where helpless elderly patients are mistreated. Or may present details about an injudicious older person who was a victim of a scam. Or show old people who died of dehydration during a heat wave. Or a senior who had an auto accident because the wrong pedal was pressed. Or a new treatment for Alzheimer's or Parkinson's disease that may help the afflicted, with images of these patients tottering about. All these reports show older people as pitiful, helpless, or foolish, and certainly not worthy of respect, or admiration. And there are few salutary tales to counteract these characterizations.

Until the beginning of this century, there were also scarcely any films or television programs made for or about older people.[19] (This is starting to change with the realization that a large and affluent group is being neglected.) If an older person was seen in a film it was generally in a peripheral role and not as a central character. Whereas young children, teenagers, adults, or even animals were depicted performing heroic acts in the movies or on television, seniors were almost never presented in this fashion. In fact, when seen, they were often fools, or comic figures, or out of touch and not understanding the situation at hand, or even evil schemers, again reinforcing society's biased view. The target audience for movies and television are teenagers and young adults, and the content of these productions is what media executives believe this audience likes. Thus, action and violence, sex, and visual effects are pushed, over the coherent stories older persons prefer. Part of the problem may be that people who make the movies and television shows, and those who control the purse strings, are rarely in their sixties and seventies, with the sensibilities and perceptions common to this age group.

Older people will go to the movies more frequently and be more interested in television programs if the offerings have themes more appealing to them, perhaps even about some of them and the lives they lead. They will also be more likely to respond to media advertising promoting fashionable clothes if older models are used instead of the characteristic, unblemished bodies of the young. Some leaders in the fashion industry are beginning to understand this and have been displaying their clothes on senior models, receiving favorable publicity for their "innovative" stances.[20] And given the large demographic wave of the Baby Boomers who are middle aged and older, since at least 2000, there have been more movies and television offerings aimed at this segment, with advertising focusing on them. These are prominent on many of the cable channels and PBS, with programs like *Mad Men* and *Downton Abbey*, and movies with Diane Keaton or Meryl Streep, Jack Nicholson or Tommy Lee Jones. The Silent Generation and the Baby Boomers were accustomed to going to the movies regularly when they were younger, and can boost box office receipts if the films are right.[21]

Unfortunately, advertising agencies now target older people more. Watching television, we have to sit through ubiquitous ads regarding treatments for erectile dysfunction and osteoporosis, or to reduce the symptoms of menopause, or to relieve constipation, which can seem humorous to younger audience members.

CRIME AND SENIORS

The prevalence of crimes against vulnerable seniors is a further sign of the insensitivity, lack of respect, and lack of caring by the rest of society toward older people. Because some of them are disabled in various ways and slow to react to unexpected attacks, or not as discerning as they once were and, thus, more trusting of strangers, the younger criminal element views them as "easy pickings." The old-old are the ones most often targeted, and because of society's ageist bias, the predators can almost rationalize their behavior, seeing their victims as not needing their money or possessions because they are old.

Crimes directed against seniors can be physical in nature, or fraudulent and "white collar." The usual physical crimes the general public encounters, such as robbery, burglary, muggings, and the like, also involve older people, perhaps occurring with even greater frequency in this population. The felon knows seniors generally will not fight back and does not view them as any threat, knowing they are fearful of even minor trauma. Two types of physical crimes are visited more often on seniors than the public at large and usually occur in urban settings. The first are purse snatchings where the thief will rip a purse from his prey and run away, sometimes disappearing into a crowd. The thief realizes that once he is out of sight he is home free, since an old woman cannot give chase. This ordinarily does not result in any harm to the victim unless she offers resistance or will not give up the purse. At times however, the victim can be thrown to the ground as the purse is wrestled away and this can cause a serious injury. The second type of crime is designated as "push-ins." In this kind of assault, the perpetrator follows an older person home, usually into an apartment building or walk-up. As soon as the victim takes out the key and opens the door to his or her apartment, the felon pushes him or her inside and follows, closing the door behind them. The victim is terrified as he or she is threatened with physical force, a knife or gun, as cash and valuables are demanded. With just the fall from the initial push-in, a hip, wrist, or ribs may be broken, but the person may be beaten as well, even if he or she complies with the demands. This is the most cowardly of acts and robs people not only of valuables, but also of any feelings of security they might have had in their homes and neighborhoods.

Fraud and scams directed at seniors take a number of different forms, with the realization by the criminal that many older people are not knowledgeable regarding economic matters. Because seniors are trusting and unable to analyze financial claims, Ponzi schemes and con games are frequently accepted at face value when pitched at older people. Some have given away part or all of their life savings to strangers in response to promises of impossible returns. Worthless penny stocks and phony home improvement schemes have also been used to flimflam them, and sweepstakes companies and telemarketing pitches offering extravagant prizes have preyed on the aged for years, bilking some individuals out of thousands of dollars.[22] The devastation wrought by these unscrupulous criminals on seniors is immeasurable, since these people no longer have opportunities to recoup their losses, and it is usually the less affluent and unsophisticated who suffer the most. And irrespective of their own feelings of inadequacy and stupidity, they are also made to feel foolish by others around them for what they have done. In addition, they may not know what steps to take to seek redress, making it more likely the criminal will go unpunished.

Whether the crime is physical or white collar, it takes a tremendous emotional toll on the victims, stripping away people's dignity and self-esteem. And society does not take the necessary measures to deter these types of incidents and offer older people sufficient protection.

AGEIST JOKES

Social attitudes toward older people and the bias endemic in our culture is reflected in the ageist jokes delivered by stand-up comedians, imparted in the movies and on television sitcoms, passed from person to person, and circulated on the Internet. These anecdotes generally denigrate and ridicule seniors and their infirmities, focusing on the problems inherent in growing old. Characteristics are exaggerated and the incongruity of the situation makes it seem funny, but it is also an attack on the dignity of older people. This distasteful humor is similar to racist, ethnic, or sexist jokes and is hurtful to those who are the butt of the jokes. However, since aging is a universal condition and everyone will pass through the same stages of life (unless they die prematurely), young people should consider that they too will have the same infirmities at some point and think twice about disparaging seniors with their jokes. On the other hand, if an older person tells a joke about aging, it should not be discouraged. Joking about one's problems is a way to deal with pain, and it is good to be able to laugh at yourself and be self-deprecating.

Many ageist jokes focus on the sexual difficulties of the elderly, or their bowel or urinary problems, hearing loss, or memory and cognitive decline. Though many books could be filled with these jokes, a few examples will be illuminating.

> Jack and Lucy have been dating at their assisted living residence and Jack thinks it's time to make a move. "Lucy, why don't we go upstairs and have some sex," he asks her at dinner one day.
> "Jack, at my age we can only do one or the other."

> Young child pointing to old gray-haired woman approaching her and her playmate.
> "Here comes my grandma."
> Second child. "She can't be your grandma. Grandmas are blond."

> An elderly man is at home in bed dying. He smells his favorite chocolate chip cookies being baked and wants one last cookie before he dies. Falling out of bed, he crawls to the landing, rolls down the stairs and crawls into the kitchen where his wife is baking. With waning strength, he is barely able to lift his arm to the cookie sheet. As he

grasps a warm, moist chocolate chip cookie, his wife suddenly whacks his hand with a spatula.

"Why?" he whispers as he drops the cookie. "Why did you do that?"

"Those're for the funeral."

An older couple is playing golf in the club championship. They are in a playoff and the wife has to make a six-inch putt. Trembling, she takes her stance, putts, and misses, and they lose the match. On the way home in the car, her husband is fuming.

"I can't believe you missed that putt," he snarls. "It was no longer than my willy."

His wife looks over at him and smiles. "Yes, dear," she says. "But it was much harder."

Acquainting himself with an elderly woman who is a patient in the hospital, the young doctor asks, "How long have you been bedridden?"

The woman looks confused and flustered. "Why not for twenty-five years when my husband was alive," she answers.

Perhaps there is an element of denial in the people who tell these ageist jokes, with the belief that if they laugh about these situations, it won't happen to them. However, age and its problems are inescapable, and whistling in the dark offers no protection. On the other hand, a positive attitude and actions can make a difference.

8

THE QUEST: STRATEGIES FOR CONTROL

Chase after money and security
and your heart will never unclench.
Care about other people's approval
and you will be their prisoner.
—Lao-Tzu, *Tao Te Ching*[1]

Keeping our independence, vitality, and dignity as we age may not be easy given the multitude of factors arrayed to destroy self-esteem, self-respect, and strength in older people, tearing down the protective walls constructed by us brick by brick over the years. Nonetheless, most midlifers and seniors can retain control over their lives if they are willing to work to develop the proper mind set and physical status. To make success more likely, there are issues that need to be understood and steps that should be taken.

ACCEPTANCE OF THE AGING PROCESS

On some level, each of us tries to deny our own aging, thinking that somehow it will be different for us, while knowing it will not be. An essential element that can help us maintain poise and self-confidence is to accept the aging process as inevitable—not doing things that make us seem foolish as we attempt to ward off the hands of time. That does not mean we should remain passive and allow age to conquer us without resistance. Instead, we should choose our battles selectively, in places where the terrain is favorable for us and we have some advantages. We should also have realistic goals and, preferably, act in ways consonant with nature.

In our society where youth is inordinately favored and age stigmatized, it is little wonder people will go to great lengths and spend large sums of money to look young. On television, radio, and in the print media, pitchmen (usually handsome or beautiful specimens) constantly bombard us and tell us to buy this or that product—vitamins, dietary supplements, exercise machines, skin care oils, creams, items of clothing—that will help us appear and feel young. Advertising agencies know there is a strong market for merchandise claiming to help people remain youthful. Since the mid-1990s, we have also seen numerous advertisements advocating different types of cosmetic surgery and special procedures, like BOTOX and collagen injections to eliminate wrinkles, to reverse the aging process. What are reasonable steps for us to take in the pursuit of youth and where do we step over the line and invite ridicule? The decisions must be personal depending on each man and woman's insecurities and needs, and there is no right or wrong path. But sometimes we make choices that cause others to question our actions and that we ourselves may question later on.

In general, it is important for each of us to look as good as we can, for that promotes healthy feelings of pride and self-worth. And our looks are our introduction to other people, even before we speak. While the substance of a person is not necessarily reflected in what we see superficially, dress and appearance do tell us something about that individual and we do make judgments on that basis. Both for ourselves and others, we should be clean and neat and dress well. However, we should not go to extreme lengths in an attempt to seem younger than we are. Looking good does not necessarily mean looking young. Ideally, it means being as physically fit as we can be; with our weight within a moderate range, neither too obese nor too thin; with appropriate hair styles and dress for our ages. The question then arises: What is appropriate dress or hair style in relation to age? The answer is that we should adhere to no specific mode or fashion, but rather a range of dress in terms of what seems right from an esthetic standpoint. For example, a woman of seventy with wrinkled skin and prominent veins in her legs should not wear short skirts like a twenty-year-old, but could buy pants that might also appeal to a younger person.

Though one should not be a slave to fashion, there is nothing wrong with being stylish if you enjoy it. It is also okay to have your own unique style and make a statement about who you are, as long as you do not take it too seriously and denigrate others who are less stylish. And it is not necessary to spend huge amounts of money on clothes in an attempt to be fashionable, as style is merely putting things together in a way that makes people look interesting. Of course it is more of a challenge to cultivate style when you have less money, when creativity and innovation become critical. (I had a woman in my practice in her seventies who barely got by on Social Security, but always looked like she just stepped out of the pages of *Vogue*, with chic haircuts and creative ensembles.) Numerous women over sixty, or even much older, are interested in dressing well but bemoan the lack of options available to them, as designers seem to ignore this demographic group.[2] There are millions of women in this market, many of them affluent and willing to spend if they find clothing that appeals to them.

In general, men are less interested in fashion than women and pay less attention to the latest styles. But it is still important for them to look clean and neat in the way they dress, particularly when they interact socially after retirement. If they are sloppy and unkempt, people will tend to disregard them and their opinions.

The use of makeup by women is also a subjective choice, including whether to use it, what type, how much, and where. Unfortunately, makeup is not always applied properly. Excessive facial powder in some circumstances accentuates wrinkles rather than hiding them, bringing about the opposite effect of what was intended. Older women may also have vision problems that result in difficulties utilizing makeup. Lipstick and eye shadow may be smeared or wander onto adjoining areas of the face, which can become unsightly.

Most measures promoted to retard the effects of aging, such as special skin creams, oils, or nutritional supplements, have not been shown to be of particular value. However, the application of retinoic acid to the skin does seem to reverse some of the changes of photoaging, though it also can produce an inflammation that usually improves over time. Other compounds are available as well that appear encouraging in counteracting the consequences of aging upon the skin, but all need to be used under a physician's supervision.

No exercise machines have been proven to have special merit in reducing abdominal paunches, heavy thighs, and so forth. However, any aerobic exercise in itself is worthwhile. In addition, there are no pills that promise "girth control" that do not also have unacceptable side effects.

Cosmetic Surgery

As techniques improve and the downside risks lessen, cosmetic surgery is being enlisted as an ally by more and more seniors (and younger people) in the battle against aging. Asking the question again of what is sensible, again it must be answered on an individual basis, influenced by desires and expectations. The procedures offered include face lifts to erase wrinkles, removal of redundant skin in the eyelids and around the eyes, removal of excess skin underneath the chin, cutting away skin and fat in the abdomen and thighs, removal of age spots or other blemishes, liposuction to reduce fatty tissue, stripping away varicose veins from the legs, and hair transplants. BOTOX injections and collagen injections can also eliminate wrinkles, but must be repeated periodically. Chemical peels, dermabrasion, and laser surgery can be employed as well to improve the skin's appearance.

There is little criticism of procedures that remove a disfiguring blemish, but others that attempt to reverse the tide of aging, where vanity alone may be the motivation, are more controversial. However, for people who relate self-esteem to their physical facade and who suffer greatly when they look in the mirror and see the ravages of time, cosmetic surgery may provide relief. Some may argue that the positive effects of the procedures are only transient and that the advances of age are inexorable. So why go through these operations when age will ultimately eradicate the results and possibly even make things worse? Then a second or even third operation may be necessary, with the outcome a bit less satisfactory each time. And even the initial procedure may not produce the anticipated results, leaving facial features that seem artificial and skin stretched too tight. But it may be worth it for those who are emotionally distraught over the consequences of aging and willing to take the risks. Another caveat is whether or not the person can afford the procedure, for the exorbitant cost is another aspect of cosmetic surgery that must be factored into the equation. In addition, the fees must be paid out of pocket, as health insurance will not cover these types of operations. However, some people will borrow thousands of dollars to have one of these procedures hoping it will make them look younger. There are even loan companies who specialize in this type of financing, if adequate collateral is available.

Inappropriate Behavior

Our actions may also indicate whether or not we have come to terms with growing older. Again, a range of behavior at various ages is considered acceptable and if one wanders too far out of that range, eyebrows may be raised, snickers may be heard, and one may look ridiculous. Age is not, however, the sole determinant of behavior; geographic region, urban or rural locale, educational status, and ethnic background are among other factors that help set the norm.

The area of greatest conflict in terms of behavior as we age revolves around sexuality. (This subject will be discussed further later in this chapter.) To a large degree, society expects its older members to be asexual and when they act in ways that would be sanctioned in younger people, they may be castigated. If a single older man and woman connect and become a couple, the rest of society sees them as "cute" when they hold hands or hug each other, even though this perfectly natural activity wouldn't warrant a second look if they were in their twenties or thirties.

While sexual indiscretions and affairs are common patterns of behavior in the young, they occur as well in the older population, more frequently among middle-aged single and married men and women, and rarely in the elderly. For some, it is a last fling; an attempt to affirm youth, sexual attractiveness, and virility. But it is not only about sexuality and youthfulness. Some men also see it as a validation of their power, and proof they have "made it" and are successful. Depending on the circumstances, the affairs may be a passing need during a particular period that a strong marriage can weather, or they may lead to separation and divorce. Even if the marriage survives, strains in the relationship, including a lack of trust, inevitably result and may persist for years.

Some young people are surprised when they see older couples dancing, particularly when they are doing a fast number, or they sensuously move their bodies during a slow piece. Society's vision is still of old people who are feeble and infirm, and don't participate in "youthful" activities. But many seniors find dancing a lot of fun and liberating in some ways. Ballroom dancing, square dancing, and even competitive dancing are increasing in popularity and gaining more and more adherents among the older crowd.

Exercise or competitive sports by older people may also be derided by those younger, who may be unsettled by sagging bodies in shorts and tank tops, and who don't see it as normal behavior for seniors. Not only is it healthy for older people to be active physically, but being fit enhances their pride and self-esteem, and should be encouraged. (This will also be discussed later.)

Alcohol and Drugs

Abuse of alcohol by middle-aged and older people is a potential recipe for disaster. Often, the intemperate use of alcohol began earlier in life and continues with aging. Older individuals may drink in secret and keep their addiction hidden, may drink openly and deny their dependence, or may not care about society's reprobation. For some, excessive drinking may be a sign of depression and a general unhappiness with life. It may also help the drinker escape feelings of inadequacy and failure—the realization that life has not turned out as he or she had hoped. In addition, it allows him or her to escape dealing with various problems. But once a person is addicted to alcohol, there are two problems to solve instead of one: changing the reality he or she tried to escape and coping with the addiction itself. Some seniors who were not problem drinkers, become so after the loss of a mate, when they literally try to drown their sorrows. Other changes in life situations, such as retirement or children moving away, may increase drinking as well.

Many older alcoholics have difficulties bonding with people and are unable to express their feelings or get close to others. Drinking alienates them from their families and friends, allowing them to avoid the intimacy that is part of normal relationships. While alcoholism is often blamed for the breakup of marriages and the end of relationships, at times it may be a symptom of preexisting problems, rather than the cause itself.

Drinking wine or other alcoholic beverages in moderation can be pleasurable and is beneficial in terms of overall health.[3] It is the abuse of alcohol, not social drinking, that is dangerous. However, older people must be vigilant even when drinking moderately if they take medications, as harmful interactions may occur.

As previously mentioned, the misuse of prescription drugs, particularly sedatives and minor tranquilizers, occurs not infrequently among seniors. Many of those who take excessive amounts of these drugs deny their addiction, though some are quite aware of what they are doing. The reasons for their drug abuse are the same as those for alcohol.

Detoxification and rehabilitation for alcohol or drugs is usually quite difficult for older people (as well as for those who are younger). Special medications may be necessary during withdrawal to prevent seizures and DTs (delirium tremens). To be successful in the long run, individual and group therapy is important, including support groups such as Alcoholics Anonymous. Families must also learn how to deal effectively with this condition and organizations such as Al-Anon may be helpful in this regard. However, a person must be properly motivated and truly want to stop in order to achieve abstinence.

Marijuana, although illegal in most states, is used by many Boomers and seniors. It helps people relax, improves socialization, and can heighten sexual pleasure. If tried occasionally, it appears to be safe, though intemperate use may affect memory and can also lead to pulmonary problems. The legalization of marijuana by Colorado and Washington in the 2012 elections shows we are moving toward approval for recreational use, though it remains a crime under federal statutes.

Inappropriate behavior by those who are cognitively impaired or psychotic and also abusing alcohol or drugs presents a different type of dilemma than in intact individuals. Substance abuse in these people may be even more refractory to treatment.

PHYSICAL FITNESS AND HEALTH

Achieving and maintaining a decent level of physical fitness and remaining as healthy as we can be are extremely important in preserving vitality and functionality as we age.

Exercise

The evidence supporting the value of exercise in reducing various diseases, improving cognitive function and overall mortality is overwhelming to the point that people who avoid physical activity do so at their own peril.[4] Exercise greatly decreases the chances of becoming diabetic as well as developing atherosclerotic vascular disease and hypertension. And not only does exercise enhance survival, but disability rates also are lessened and overall quality of life is improved. While any level of exercise is beneficial, a graded inverse relationship has been shown to exist between physical activity and all-cause mortality. That is, the more a person exercises, the lower his or her death rate.[5]

Everyone's capabilities vary as far as exercise is concerned, depending on genetic predisposition as well as past illnesses, accidents, and so forth. But within the constraints imposed upon us, we should all try to be physically fit. By this I do not mean training to become world-class athletes in seniors or masters competition, but rather seeing to it that we stay in shape aerobically and do not have limitations in our daily activities because of neglect and indifference. Exercise and sports are used by many older people in an attempt to improve their appearance, but the benefits are far greater than that. Exercise should be part of everyone's daily regimen. The actual routine followed can be individualized and changed at will, but should never be omitted.

I advise my patients to engage in aerobic activity for a minimum of thirty minutes each day, though an hour, or even more, is preferable. In fact, the guideline issued by the Institute of Medicine is for everyone to exercise at least an hour every day[6], the benefits confirmed by multiple medical studies. Of course, for those who are working, time can be a major hindrance. Repetitive, mindless exercise is the desirable mode, where one doesn't have to think about what is being done. (Competitive sports, while enjoyable, serve somewhat different purposes, and if desired, should be done in addition to aerobic exercise, dispensing with the latter on the days one competes in athletic contests.) Weight training or musculoskeletal resistance training is also beneficial in terms of improving strength, balance and coordination, and reducing osteoporosis, but does not negate the need for aerobic workouts.[7] When initiating any type of exercise program at an older age, it is a good idea to have a medical check-up first to be sure there are no contraindications. It is also prudent to begin any activities slowly, gradually advancing both distance and speed until reaching the targeted maintenance level.

Exercise equals empowerment for all of us. It gives us an opportunity to exert some control over our lives and our health—doing something we recognize as good for us. Knowing that many people are incapable of willing themselves to work out regularly as we are doing generates feelings of pride and self-worth when we exercise.

Brisk walking is an excellent exercise for most individuals. The potential for injury is minimal, as there is little impact and feet barely leave the ground. The speed at which you should walk depends upon your overall physical condition and not your chronological age. Walking a mile in fifteen to seventeen minutes is excellent, but any rate is beneficial. (Some seniors are able to cover a mile in twelve minutes while others may take twenty or more.) It is helpful to find a course that interests you and measure it with your car's odometer or a pedometer. You can go in a circle, or return on your original route to get back to your starting point. Some people like to walk the same course every day, while others constantly change their itinerary. Four miles daily is a worthwhile goal, but not feasible for everyone. If you have the time and discipline to do more, so much the better. The key word is discipline.

Running or jogging is also a good aerobic activity, though it results in more injuries than walking. Many people who were runners when younger switch to walking as they get older because of musculoskeletal problems. The main advantage of running is that you can achieve the benefits of walking in less time. The same amount of calories is burned per mile and the cardiovascular protection is the same. (A 154-pound person will expend about 110 calories for every mile traveled, walking or running, no matter the speed at which the distance is covered.) As with walking, when running, it is helpful to find a route or routes you like. Some people prefer to utilize a treadmill indoors, either at home or at a gym, for their workouts, watching television or listening to music or books on tape. (Socializing around exercise at the gym is an excellent motivator.) Others use a treadmill only when the weather precludes outdoor activity. It makes no difference where the exercise is done, as long as it is done regularly.

I personally prefer walking outside, unless the weather is really miserable. Being outside in the fresh air is invigorating, with the changing environment stimulating the senses. I love to watch the evolution of the seasons and the transformation of the trees and vegetation, as they are clothed and unclothed, going from green to pastel colors to bare, then starting the cycle over again. I also like the early morning, before the day begins for most of the world, when I am part of the cold darkness in the winter and the sunrises that come earlier and earlier until the heat of summer, when they recede again. Being outside also provides an opportunity for brief interactions with other people, as you pass one another on the road, comrades-in-arms fighting the same good fight. Finding a partner who will share the time with you also makes the miles pass more quickly.

Bike riding is another form of exercise that meets the necessary criteria. This also can be done outdoors, indoors, or both. (Biking three miles is roughly equivalent to one mile walking or running.) Other types of mindless, repetitive activity include swimming, jumping rope, rowing, and cross-country skiing. Fitness instructors have also developed different routines that provide an aerobic workout and various machines have been devised to enhance cardiovascular fitness and burn calories.

Many exercise physiologists suggest resting one day each week, but cutting down on mileage or slowing your speed for a day may also be restorative. Cross-training, that is, trying different exercises on a regular basis, such as walking four days a week and bike riding three days a week, may also be worthwhile in terms of utilizing different muscle groups and limiting injuries.

To derive the most benefit from an exercise regimen it is necessary to have an ongoing commitment and be disciplined. Without these elements, success will be elusive. Having a hard-and-fast schedule followed fairly rigorously is a significant step forward. If you exercise at the same time every day, it becomes easier after a while and eventually becomes almost automatic. For a number of reasons, I believe early morning is best. You are less likely to be fatigued since you are just awakening and other tasks are less likely to interfere. Later in the day, obstacles frequently arise. In addition, the brain produces endorphin in response to sustained physical activity and the levels of this chemical remain elevated for a number of hours afterward. Thus, by exercising earlier in the day, we reap the benefits of endorphins while we are awake.

Another way to improve conditioning is to do small amounts of exercise whenever possible. This has been called integrative exercise, when it is integrated into one's usual routine, such as walking up the stairs, if it is feasible, instead of taking the elevator, or walking or riding a bike to do errands instead of using a car. If you play golf, walk and carry or pull your golf clubs rather than riding in a cart. In addition, stopping work or other sedentary activities and walking briskly for ten minutes three times daily has been shown to be beneficial.[8] All of these add up to improved physical fitness. Minimalist, high-intensity workouts have also been suggested, but are potentially dangerous for middle-aged or older people.[9]

You may still ask the questions, what do I get by including exercise in my daily routine? Is it worth my commitment? The answer is a resounding *yes* for every moment devoted to physical activity for the reasons I will discuss.

From the standpoint of health, cardiovascular disease is significantly diminished by regular exercise, which can lower blood pressure and cholesterol, as well as control or prevent diabetes in some people. A sedentary lifestyle and obesity are risk factors for heart attacks, strokes, and peripheral vascular disease.[10] Osteoporosis is also delayed or prevented in individuals who do weight-bearing exercise and immune function may be enhanced. Interestingly, some evidence suggests that various types of orthopedic problems are lessened by frequent exercise, though one would expect the opposite to be true. Numerous reports also find the risk of dementia is markedly reduced or may even be prevented by exercise.[11] People who are fit in midlife have been shown to have a lower incidence of dementia later in life.[12] Significant evidence indicates as well that aerobic exercise can enhance memory.[13] A report in 2012 also notes that resistance training may delay the onset of dementia.[14]

Emotional health is improved by exercise. The endorphins generated act as natural tranquilizers, painkillers, and possibly antidepressants. Because of this, stress and anxiety can be lessened by aerobic activity, which may be similar to meditation in terms of its relaxant effect. Studies have also shown that mild to moderate depression can be alleviated by exercise, with response rates comparable to or better than psychotherapy or medication.

Weight training should supplement aerobic activity in all older people, with free weights or resistance machines. "The Surgeon General recommends the following strength training routine for people over the age of fifty:

- 8 to 12 exercises engaging the major muscle groups;
- 8 to 15 repetitions performed to fatigue or a level perceived as comfortably hard;
- 1 set;
- 2 times per week" [15]

Strength and stamina can be built up over a short period of time and the program should only require twenty minutes or so twice a week, a good investment in maintaining health. There are other exercises aimed at improving posture and balance that can also be performed regularly, with directions available from physicians, physical therapists, and the like. By working out in a gym or fitness center, both aerobic exercise and weight training can be opportunities for communication and companionship, and for some, can make the process more enjoyable.

Exercise helps older people improve their ability to care for themselves, allowing them to remain independent longer. And contrary to what many people believe, it is never too late to begin a conditioning program, no matter how old you are and how sedentary you have been. In an interesting research study, frail nursing home residents with an average age of 87.9 years were started on a schedule of strength training for an eight-week period. There was a dramatic improvement in strength, walking, and functional ability by the end of the program. [16]

People who are physically active look better than their peers and generally feel better about themselves. The burning of extra calories helps keep their weight down and allows them to enjoy eating without guilt. With more discretionary time available to us after retirement, it is certainly possible for each of us to devote an hour daily to our bodies for physical fitness. While still working in midlife, time may be at a premium, but finding a period for exercise will pay off in the future as well as showing immediate returns. Though it may be harder to exercise as we get older if we have not done it before, it is vitally important for all of us.

Master's competitions are only for those fanatical about their training regimen and those who enjoy competition. If it adds excitement to someone's life and is not dangerous, there is no reason not to do it. (Medical clearance is particularly important for seniors who push themselves in competitive events.) Aside from the various racquet sports, track and field events, and swimming have regular master's competitions. The training for these events ensures a high level of fitness and is even more important than the competition itself. While many people feel golf is also a sport, conditioning and aerobic training play no role in performance on the golf course and so it is really more of a game than a sport. This is not to negate the skill involved and the pleasure derived by those who love golf, but it is not a substitute for physical exercise.

Nutrition

As people get older, some neglect their diets, eating haphazardly and not always adhering to an adequate, balanced food intake. This occurs more often when a person lives alone and either does not want to be bothered with shopping and cooking, or is simply unable to manage it because of physical, cognitive, or emotional problems. Sometimes, older people get by with cereal, candy, or snack foods for every meal, which requires no preparation and alleviates hunger, but does not provide essential nutrients. Whatever the reason, if dietary depletion is severe enough, it can result in malnutrition and damage to various organs as well as greater susceptibility to different diseases. This is why Meals on Wheels and similar programs that cater to the homebound elderly are necessary for the recipients' wellbeing. (Though a number of studies have suggested that overall caloric restriction may enhance longevity, a study published in 2012 contested that concept.[17])

As the converse of dietary deficiency, overeating and obesity are major health hazards in America, where a high percentage of the population is overweight.[18] The increasing popularity of fast foods and greater intake of foods with high fat and carbohydrate content play a major role. Because many people reduce levels of activity as they age, vulnerability to obesity becomes greater with the same caloric intake. And obesity is a major risk factor for diabetes, atherosclerosis, and some cancers, reducing life expectancy significantly.[19] In addition to heightened risk for illnesses, obesity also exacts an emotional toll through poor self-image and loss of self-confidence. It also causes greater difficulties for people who may already have impaired balance, lack of energy, and stamina. People can shed pounds in only two ways: either reduce caloric intake by eating less or burn up more calories through increased exercise.

Since the mid-1990s, dietary supplements purporting to provide energy and vitality for those fatigued or weak have become increasingly popular for older people. There are also formulas to enhance sexual performance, cognitive ability, or just about any function that declines normally as part of aging. Some of the supplements are food substitutes, others are herbal mixtures, special vitamins, vegetable derivatives, and other types of nutritional additives. No persuasive evidence shows that these are of any value for those who eat a well-balanced diet. Though taking a multiple vitamin, vitamin D, and perhaps folic acid may be worthwhile, their value is also controversial. (In theory, vitamin E and other antioxidants have been thought to be beneficial by retarding the development of atherosclerosis, some types of cancer, Alzheimer's disease, Parkinson's disease, and the effects of aging, but studies have not proven their worth.) However, those with osteoporosis may require vitamin D and calcium. While the medically supervised taking of food supplements can help individuals whose nutritional intake is deficient, it does not appear to be necessary for the population at large.

For decades it has been known that a healthy diet entails frequently eating fish, along with fruits and vegetables daily. Minimizing the intake of fast foods, lunch meats, and red meats were also believed to be of value in lowering obesity and atherosclerosis. However, an article in *The New England Journal of Medicine* featured on the front page of the *New York Times* quantitates the role that diet can play in promoting health and longevity.[20] The Mediterranean diet was shown in a large study to reduce strokes and heart attacks by about 30 percent in people at high risk. The reduction occurred independent of factors such as obesity, diabetes, hypertension, elevated cholesterol, or smoking in the 7,447 people who participated in the study. Indeed, because the effects of the diet were so prominent, the study was ended early after five years. (The Mediterranean diet has also been shown to reduce the risk of dementia.[21])

In the study, those on the Mediterranean diet were told to eat three servings of fruits and two servings of vegetables daily, with fish at least three times weekly as well as legumes (peas, beans, lentils) at least three times weekly. Red meat was to be avoided in favor of white meat and seven glasses of wine weekly with meals was recommended. At least four tablespoons of extra-virgin olive oil were to be ingested daily and an unlimited amount of nuts, even though they were high in calories. Commercially made cookies, cakes, and pastries were out-of-bounds, and intake of dairy products and processed meats was restricted. Of all the various diets that have been recommended over the years to cut down on coronary artery disease and strokes, and promote healthy living, the Mediterranean diet appears to be the best and probably the easiest to adhere to. Eating other foods on occasion that do not fit within the parameters of the Mediterranean diet are certainly permissible and will not decrease the benefits of the diet itself. Another study published in 2013 has shown that consumption of nuts reduces all-cause mortality as well as deaths due to cancer, heart disease, and pulmonary disease.[22] This is an inverse association: the more eaten, the lower the mortality.

Medical Care

Medical checkups with appropriate treatment and follow-up for illnesses aids in maintaining health and fitness as we grow older. The utility of a routine physical examination is controversial, but there are some important elements. These include measuring blood pressure, lipid and cholesterol profiles, blood sugar, and hemoglobin levels on an annual basis, along with a digital rectal exam for men. PSA (prostate specific antigen) testing has raised questions of efficacy. Colonoscopy should be performed periodically in both sexes in addition to mammography in women, though the frequency of these procedures remains unclear. The need for pap smears in older women is also a matter of debate. A flu shot should be obtained by seniors every year prior to flu season, as influenza is a significant cause of death in those sixty-five and older.[23]

Another aspect of the regular physical is establishing a relationship with a physician. You must be certain you are comfortable with your doctor and can discuss the intimate details of your problems with this person. If you are uneasy in any way, you should try someone else, since this individual is going to be responsible for critical decisions involving your life. Your physician should also be familiar with your wishes about death and dying, and should possess your advance directives. You must have confidence in your physician's intelligence and knowledge, respecting the way his or her practice is conducted. Once you are ill and under his or her care, like changing horses in midstream, it is much more troublesome to make a switch.

Aside from well care, your physician is there to investigate and treat your illnesses, perhaps with the assistance of specialists in particular areas. He or she may order tests and then initiate therapy when a diagnosis has been made. Dealing with any disorder entails a continuous dialogue between doctor and patient, with the latter detailing the symptoms of the disease, the response to medications, and any side effects that develop. Too often difficulties occur because of denial of illness by an individual, or noncompliance with the regimen prescribed. To maximize any doctor's effectiveness, the dialogue must go on and if the patient doesn't follow instructions, he or she must discuss that failure with the physician. Lying to the doctor or ignoring the problem with the hope it will go away are not acceptable alternatives. If communication is not there, or a person is unwilling to engage in a frank exchange with his or her physician, there is no point in wasting the doctor's time and that person's money.

SEXUALITY

That older people have sexual needs and desires is not an issue our society is willing to address openly, though some scientific work in this area is starting to disseminate to the lay public. For the most part, religions ignore this subject, while emphasizing the prohibition against adultery and sex outside of marriage. Hollywood and the entertainment media do not generally feature stories about romantic love between septuagenarians, nor do they show older men and women engaged in any type of sexual activity. Unlike the sexual habits of younger people (particularly celebrities), it is not something programs on television want to feature and is not a frequent topic of discourse at dinner parties. However, the introduction of Viagra has made the news media at least look at sexuality among older people and has made it more acceptable for discussion sans snickering. Indeed, advertisements for medications for erectile dysfunction, as well as for women's problems with "intimacy," are commonplace on television and radio. Society is beginning to understand that many older adults are interested in sexual gratification, even if they are believed by some to be "too old" for that sort of thing.

Being old does not mean you should not be having sex. There is nothing dirty about it at any age and nothing wrong in doing something enjoyable and healthy. Sex is a normal part of life, though how sexual drives are fulfilled is an individual matter or something for each couple to decide. In itself, sex should be fun, perhaps even more so once the time of reproduction has passed and the possibility of pregnancy is no longer a concern. Interest in sex is also a reason for people to take care of themselves, to remain physically fit and to try and look as good as they can.

What individuals expect in terms of sexual gratification is as varied among the old as it is among the young. For some, hugging and kissing may suffice. For others intercourse and orgasm are necessary. If intercourse is desired, the frequency can run from once a year to daily. And the type of foreplay and positions used are different for every couple. The delight of intimacy between two people is also a part of sexual relations: touching, caressing, and just lying together. How people meet these needs as they age can affect their feelings of self-esteem and dignity. Being married and having a partner certainly makes it easier, if both partners love and respect each other.

A 1999 survey on sexuality in seniors conducted by AARP revealed that "more than 70 percent of men and women who have regular partners are sexually active enough to have intercourse at least once or twice a month," the frequency decreasing with age. "About half of 45-through 59-year-olds have sex at least once a week, but among 60-through 74-year-olds, the proportion drops to 30 percent for men and 24 percent for women." Confirming that frequency was not the most important factor in gratification, "about two thirds of those polled were extremely or very satisfied with their physical relationships." The survey suggested that the younger cohort of Baby Boomers (age forty-five to fifty-nine) may well have more active sex lives as they age than those currently over sixty, espousing a more liberal attitude toward sex between unmarried partners, and engaging in oral sex and masturbation.

They were also more likely to disagree with the statement that "sex is only for younger people."[24]

Studies have shown that a vigorous sex life may have health benefits. Men who have frequent intercourse appear to have a reduced incidence of heart attacks and both men and women who have regular sex appear to have less depression. However, the lower rate of heart attacks may have merely confirmed that these men were in better shape and more physically fit to begin with, which allowed them to engage in sex more often. Also men and women more interested in sex tend to have better relationships and fewer emotional problems than others in their age group and may have been less depressed initially. But whether improved health results, and whether it is cause or effect, most geriatricians would agree that older people who are sexually active are better off both physically and emotionally, and have a better quality of life.[25]

One of the reasons for marriage is the formation of a sexual alliance and that is valid later in life as well as when we are younger. To have a satisfying sex life at any age requires a caring partner, perhaps even more so as we grow older, when various infirmities may interfere. These may be relatively minor, or serious, but have to be addressed if the inclination is still there. Included are musculoskeletal disorders like arthritis or back problems, cardiac or pulmonary conditions that restrict exertion, weakness from strokes or injuries, and so forth. Because of these difficulties, different positions and more restrained movement may be necessary. With age, men may also have trouble achieving or sustaining an erection and may be too embarrassed to talk about this with their partners or physicians, instead simply refraining from sexual contact. And women as they age after menopause may experience vaginal dryness.

Both men and women should be able to discuss sex with their mates, and if there are any problems, with their physicians as well. Many people avoid this area and may not have broached it during decades of marriage. But if their needs, desires, and possible impediments to success are not shared with their partners, they are less likely to have their needs met. Any discourse, however, should occur during a dispassionate time, neither related to an immediate goal of sexual satisfaction, nor just after advances have been rebuffed and there is an aura of tension about. Frank exchanges should occur about any physical limitations and any activities that produce discomfort, and ways should be explored to eliminate these obstacles. Discussions about what increases excitement and maximizes pleasure should also take place. Because sexual reactivity is reduced with aging, greater effort may be necessary to attain responses. This may include heightened foreplay and increased manual or oral stimulation of the genitals. Excitement may also be augmented by approaching sex differently at times and changing scenery. Using different rooms in the house and different times of the day may be helpful, or going to a hotel or motel. Sometimes pornography may also enhance excitement. Whatever works should be used as long as it is acceptable to the other person and does not cause physical or emotional injury.

Physicians should be consulted when there are difficulties that cannot be managed by the individuals themselves. Medical solutions exist for many of these problems and it is at least worthwhile to know what is available. In a large percentage of older men, erectile dysfunction can be treated quite successfully with anti-impotence drugs, Viagra, Cialis, Levitra (or their generic equivalents).[26] New compounds are also being developed for this condition and various mechanical aids are available. Testosterone (the male sexual hormone) therapy and other options may be useful in selected cases. If there are no medical contraindications, women as well may be helped by hormone therapy to combat vaginal atrophy and increase lubrication. In addition, many women find artificial lubricants may be beneficial. When a couple has sexual problems, their going for counseling with either a religious or lay therapist may help, as some people need guidance to prevent this issue from becoming a festering sore that can infect their marriages.

Having a good sexual relationship within a marriage is merely part of the total relationship and requires both partners to love and care for each other. If a marriage is devoid of love and affection, there cannot be satisfactory sex. However, when there is apparent love and one partner is not interested in sexual activity though physically able, and it is important to the other partner, the situation can be a source of conflict. If there is a disability or medical reasons for an individual to avoid sex, his or her partner may be more understanding, but the situation still may engender hostility. In general, clashes involving sexuality are more prevalent among midlifers and are seen less among the old-old whose drives are considerably diminished. Sometimes the professed sexual interest may be more for psychological reasons than physical need, but still has to be addressed.

It may seem strange to those still young that older people remain concerned with sex, but it is a force to contend with, even in later life. Many older men with various conditions or none at all have asked me for medications to help them with erectile dysfunction. Yet a large percentage of them would only discuss their problem with me when their wives or partners were not present, finding it difficult to communicate with them about this issue. But communication would have made the situation much easier for them and it was not something for them to be embarrassed about. Anyway, it would have been more productive if the problem were addressed as a couple, since vaginal dryness could also have been contributing to the difficulty.

At times, because the predicament seems so intractable for a couple, one partner will suppress sexual desires for the sake of peace. But there are several options available to the person unwilling to accept the status quo and wishing to continue sexual activity. One is to attain release through masturbation. Though this is not a satisfactory alternative for everyone, it does leave the structure of the marriage intact and may be the least traumatic way of dealing with the problem. Another possibility is to find a different partner for sex. This can mean having an affair with someone while remaining married, or getting divorced and marrying another person. For some people, it is simpler to see a prostitute or gigolo occasionally and pay for sex, though this is illegal and can lead to AIDS and other sexually transmitted diseases. (There was a report around 2004 detailing an outbreak of AIDS and syphilis among a group of elderly men in a retirement community in Florida who had been going to prostitutes, many of whom were intravenous drug users.) What a person does may depend on the intensity of his or her sexual drive and the moral considerations of his or her choice. Again, counseling may be helpful.

Single older people without partners face similar problems in seeking sexual outlets. For those who have been single all their lives, it is usually easier, as they have dealt with this dilemma over the years. But for those who have been widowed, it may be more difficult to devise a solution. (Of course, sex itself may not be an important issue, as they may be more concerned with companionship, or merely learning how to survive and thrive on their own.) The options for sexual release for single people are the same as those listed above. However, when and if a new partner is found and a relationship of any sort is established, at some point when both people are comfortable, it is good to discuss sexual needs and expectations to avoid future disappointments, particularly if marriage is contemplated.

The negative stereotype of older people with an interest in sex is that of "the dirty old man" who leers at younger women or makes overtures to them. As mentioned before, there is nothing dirty about an older man with sexual needs, even if he is drawn to someone younger. For a number of reasons, it may be inappropriate for a seventy-year-old man to pursue a twenty-five-year-old woman. But there is nothing illegal or immoral about it, if it is done within the constraints of accepted behavior. Two consenting adults can act as they please. However, there are circumstances in which an older person is cognitively impaired or disinhibited and his or her actions in terms of sexuality may be outside the bounds of acceptability. Though this occurs infrequently, these people may need to be medicated and watched carefully, particularly if children have been approached.

RELEVANCE

To preserve our status as we age, we should be knowledgeable about the world around us, and both intellectually and socially relevant. Past events and the cultural milieu that flourished in our youth may be important to us, but to be respected and connect with other people, we also have to be attuned to what is happening in the present. We can concentrate on those elements that affect us directly, but should still have a broad understanding of significant issues.

Information on current events can be gathered on the Internet, by reading newspapers and news magazines online or in hard copies, and by watching news programs on television. Newspapers provide exposure to local news in addition to national and international events, and it is essential to know what is occurring in all these areas. Having a viewpoint we can defend and discuss intelligently gives us more credibility among our peers and the general population. We must not be afraid to have opinions and express them. It becomes difficult for younger people to dismiss us if we know as much or more about what is happening than they do.

In terms of awareness from a cultural standpoint, it is impossible for anyone to encompass developments in every field. The kinds of things we should stay abreast of should be determined by our own interests and the social circles in which we move, including our friends and relatives. This may mean reading the latest books (digitally or in hard copies), going to the movies, watching television, listening to music, attending the theater, and so on, but should focus on doing what we find stimulating and enjoyable. (I am not dividing activities into pop culture and high culture, but speaking of the collective creative output of our society and the need for older people to participate and comprehend what is going on.)

Seniors do read more than the young, since this was a major source of entertainment when they were children and the habit has remained. They are also able to sit still for longer periods than younger people. If we like reading, our subject matter should depend on our personal tastes. Of course, there is no reason to confine ourselves to one sector and we can try anything that kindles our curiosity, even topics that are unfamiliar. Though the primary reasons for reading are pleasure and learning, it is also valuable for us to get feedback about the books we read from other people, as that heightens our critical powers and understanding. Conversations with friends may suffice, but discussion groups and book clubs may sharpen our minds as we debate the issues that books raise.

In America, if we want to be in touch with the times, it is good to be knowledgeable about the latest films. Putting forth our views on these movies also hones our thought processes and powers of perception, and helps us to remain relevant. We should see movies that are purely entertaining, but to expose ourselves to different ideas, it is also beneficial to sit through some that are controversial or even disagreeable. With the new streaming technology, smart television, cable, and computers, we can watch films we might have missed, or that might have had a limited commercial run, but were critically acclaimed. This is less expensive than going out to the movies and permits people who are housebound to enjoy films they otherwise would not be able to see.

In some social circles, television programs are also topics of major interest. Being able to discuss the latest developments on these shows is an easy way to reach other people and always engenders lively discourse with friends and family members who watch television. We should watch whatever we find exciting or enjoyable, but should not spend an inordinate amount of time in front of television screens. Being a couch potato is not a healthy way to conduct our lives.

Going to the theater and seeing live performances helps to expand our horizons. Either the classics or contemporary plays may raise issues requiring thoughtful analysis, besides being entertaining. Musicals usually provide a shared experience with family and friends, as this is the most popular form of theater for Americans. Opportunities to attend the theater vary greatly depending on geographical location and the cost of tickets, but numerous fine regional companies and university and local community theaters around the country mount excellent productions. And many offer senior discounts, so that prices will not be prohibitive. Other cultural events that should be considered when the possibility arises are art and photography exhibits and dance, opera, and orchestral performances.

Though music is a large part of our culture, older people and midlifers may find it difficult to appreciate the sounds lauded by the young, as tastes among the generations are very different. There are not many seniors who can "get into" rap, hip-hop, heavy metal, or grunge music. But there is nothing wrong with rejecting creative work we find unpleasant or do not agree with. Instead, we should listen to music to which we can relate, whether it is pop from the 1940s and 1950s, early rock and roll, folk or folk rock, jazz, country and western, or classical. There are usually local radio stations or Sirius radio that plays the type of music we prefer. And MP3 blogs, various software we can download, iTunes, eMusic, CDs, and live concerts are other ways to keep the melodies flowing.

In terms of cultural exposure and understanding, it is important for us to pursue those things we enjoy, but also to try and broaden our experiences, whether passively or actively. At every age, we should always try to grow and learn, and be stimulated in whatever ways we can. This keeps us vital and engaged with the world around us, allows us to interact better with others, and makes our lives more interesting. This is true as much for an older person as for a young child.

Besides keeping abreast of current events and remaining attentive to cultural matters, older people should converse regularly with friends, acquaintances, and relatives. Having acquired a body of knowledge that we are constantly expanding may be good in itself, but is of greater value if it is shared with others. To maintain decent relationships, it is also essential for us to be cognizant of the latest news involving friends and relatives. Who had a grandchild recently? Whose child just finished graduate school and what is he or she doing now? Who just retired? These may seem trivial, but they are the changing facts about the people in one's life, and in order to relate well to others, it is critical to know what is happening with them. This is "being socially relevant" and is necessary if one's own voice is to be heard. Many people have a need to talk about their families and the milestones they have achieved, and it is helpful to be a good listener, showing interest in what others have to say and reacting appropriately. (Socializing has also been shown to reduce the incidence of dementia, another reason to keep interacting with other people.)

Though most midlifers are already in the game, to remain relevant in this day and age seniors should also try to be comfortable with computers and smart phones, and be capable of going online, utilizing the Internet, and doing searches to get information—perhaps even being able to text with grandchildren. Many seniors learn about computers through classes at community centers, colleges, and libraries around the country, or are taught by children or friends.[27] Though it may take a while for seniors to feel at ease using various technologies, anyone who has the patience can do it.

INDEPENDENCE

For individuals no longer working, independence is of major importance in the continuing battle to retain self-respect and remain vital, though it can be withdrawn by factors beyond one's control. The degree of autonomy possible as we age is determined by physical ailments, emotional illnesses, cognitive compromise, and our level of affluence. However, within the limits imposed upon us, we should all try to manage our lives by ourselves as best we can (or in an arrangement of mutual dependence with a spouse or partner). This is not to downplay the obstacles we might encounter, realizing that for some of us, circumstances may make autonomy impossible. But for many, like Esau who sold his patrimony to Jacob for a bowl of porridge, independence may be given away for ease of living.

If an older person has degenerative hip disease or a bad back, it is much simpler to ask someone to bring them a glass of water than to get it themselves, which may require effort and some degree of pain. With Parkinson's disease, it may be faster to have a spouse or other family member fetch the mail rather than going for it ourselves. As well, if an older person has had a heart attack and is fully recovered, he or she may allow relatives to do the shopping even though there is no reason he or she cannot handle it alone. When older people try to accomplish all they can for themselves, they affirm that they are in command of their own lives and do not need others to care for them. This may necessitate doing things more slowly, or enduring temporary pain because of a physical condition, but it is a small price to pay to maintain one's independence. Whenever feasible, disabilities should be approached as a challenge to be overcome.

I am frequently amazed the way patients of mine with multiple medical problems are able to brush them aside and lead active, rewarding lives.

> With degenerative cervical spine disease and severe neck pain, an eighty-two-year-old widow of an investment banker was alone for eighteen years, living in a large home on the Connecticut shore. She also had cerebrovascular disease, neuropathy, and ocular myasthenia (a muscle disease restricted to the eyes). A number of medications taken regularly helped these various conditions. She traveled into New York City three or four times a week with a driver, going to plays and the Metropolitan Opera. She also sat on the boards of several philanthropic organizations and was making an earnest effort to give her money away. This woman's energy and vitality considering her age and illnesses was inspiring. (Being wealthy may make it easier, but money is not required for life to be fulfilling.)

Though preserving independence should be a goal for all of us as we age, situations may require us to relinquish some of our autonomy. We should not take actions that countermand medical instructions without first discussing them with our physician and obtaining approval. There may be reasons for the restrictions we are unaware of, and injury may result from disregarding the advice we have been given. Sometimes, we may deny illness or disability, because we want to be well and function the way we had previously, and that can have disastrous consequences.

In attempting to remain independent, one should avoid activities that are potentially dangerous to oneself or to others. Sometimes one's judgment and wishes to direct one's own life and not be beholden to other people may be clouded by pride. If there is ever any question about what one has in mind, ask someone with no emotional investment in the outcome (physician, nurse, friend) for an opinion about that conduct, such as, having poor vision and driving a car, having a bad back and lifting something heavy, or having a history of dizzy spells and working on a roof. At times, medical consultations and tests may be necessary to determine whether or not various roles are prudent and safe.

Independence should also take a temporary back seat if it means inconveniencing others. The desire for autonomy should not hold any-one else back unreasonably. For instance, if a group is leaving to go somewhere and a sweater is needed from another area of the house, allow someone else to retrieve it to save everyone time if it will take a while to obtain because the person who needs it has arthritis in the knees. Or if cutting food is a laborious process because of a previous stroke and one is at a family dinner, request help so the dinner can proceed. Under these conditions, if others want to assist us, allow them to do it to accommodate the group. But do not let it become a common practice, particularly if it is just to make things easier.

Most of the issues I have discussed regarding independence involve physical problems and disabilities. However, when cognitive impair-ment or emotional illnesses are involved, the situation is different. As previously mentioned, not all memory problems are due to dementia and one should not automatically surrender independence because of minor forgetfulness that is a normal part of aging. Even people with mild cognitive impairment can often function well in terms of their daily routines. Keeping one's life organized with lists and calendars can be helpful in this regard to supplement memory, with a schedule to be followed and an established pattern. As an example, one might arise at the same hour each day, perform chores, have meals, and exercise at set times. Pocket organizers or smart phones to remind one of appoint-ments, phone numbers, and so forth, can also be utilized effectively if the technology is not threatening and can be mastered without stress.

Clouded judgment and lack of insight are usually found in people with dementia at an early stage of their disease. Although they may be incapable of full independence at that point, they can make decisions with some oversight, hopefully from a caring family member, allowing them to have some amount of freedom. Then, as the dementia progresses, the circle of their autonomy shrinks until it eventually disappears, and their lives must be completely controlled by their caregivers. When people are affected to a moderate degree, the greatest areas of conflict with family appear to be over driving and going out of the house alone.

Independence in the face of emotional illness is a more complicated matter that lacks a scripted solution, since a different approach may be required for each individual. That said, anyone who is psychotic needs to be maintained on medications and monitored carefully, and can never really be fully independent while ill. (However, this is uncommon among older people, unless a consequence of dementia.) Obsessive compulsive disorders and phobias certainly restrict the freedom of those who have these conditions, interfering with autonomy. (Phobias are irrational fears of certain situations or objects that direct behavior.) Medication and psychotherapy may help somewhat, but limitations often remain.

The two most common psychiatric problems in older people are anxiety and depression, and the amount of independence desired and sustained by those afflicted varies according to the severity of the process. Those with major anxiety or depression need medication and therapy in order to carry on their lives at a minimal level, and independence is usually not a concern. On the other hand, individuals with mild anxiety or depression are able to act in a fairly normal manner, and usually try to maintain their autonomy. However, some may use their illnesses in a manipulative fashion, employing symptoms to get people to do their bidding. This makes it hard for friends and family to know how to deal with them: whether to give them assistance or make them fend for themselves. Should they be pushed toward independence, or helped with tasks they should be able to handle?

Often combined with psychotherapy to maximize success, a number of different medications may be utilized to treat disabling anxiety or depression. These include benzodiazepines (Valium, Ativan, Xanax, Klonopin), tricyclics (Elavil, Tofranil, Sinequan), SSRIs—selective serotonin reuptake inhibitors (Prozac, Zoloft, Paxil, Lexapro), SNRIs—serotonin-norepinephrine reuptake inhibitors (Effexor, Cymbalta), atypical antidepressants (Serzone, Remeron, and so forth), and others. Older people usually require smaller doses of these medications and, at higher levels, can suffer adverse effects, such as drowsiness, impaired coordination or cognition. Relaxation techniques such as biofeedback, meditation, and exercise, along with behavior modification, may also have roles to play in treatment. And a 2013 study suggested that sleep therapy that deals with insomnia may benefit those with depression.[28]

Though we all want to maintain autonomy throughout our lives, we must also be realistic as age takes its toll. If infirmity imposes limitations that would seem reasonable to an unbiased observer, we should be willing to acquiesce. We can debate these restrictions with family, friends, and physicians, but if they are in agreement, and we believe they have our best interests at heart, we should go along with their recommendations. There are times, however, when the issue of autonomy may be so important, that an older person may be willing to risk injury to remain in control, and his or her family and physicians may have to give in. This was brought home to me by an incident involving my mother several years prior to her death.

> My mother, who was then eighty-nine years old, was brought into the hospital with a broken and dislocated hip. As recovery progressed, she was sent to a rehabilitation unit and began walking. Some mild problems with balance were noted and her doctors felt she should permanently relinquish her slippers (scuffs with low heels and no backs) because they made her too unstable. She refused, saying she had worn these all of her life and they were fine for her. After arguing to no avail, my sister and I took them away against her wishes, telling her she would have to wear flat slippers. But as soon as she left the hospital, she bought another pair of her old scuffs, which she wore around her apartment. She wanted to be in control and would not let anyone else dictate to her what she could or could not wear.

It may also be possible to have a degree of independence even if a person has physical impairments, if one is willing to develop and accept "shared dependency" with people other than a spouse. By this I mean a group of older people who help each other out when necessary. It is preferable to establish this support network even before disabilities occurs, a group of individuals who live close to one another, are concerned about one another, and perhaps have common interests. Couples, widows, widowers, and singles could all be included. Perhaps one person has poor vision and needs to be taken shopping as he or she cannot drive. Another person might have severe arthritis and needs to be assisted with household chores. Someone else needs help with bookkeeping. These are just examples of how the network could function and allow people to live semi-independently with certain disabilities. In many communities, these types of arrangements are already utilized informally, usually by siblings or groups of old friends who live in close proximity. In other instances, a group of friends may buy a large residence or several adjacent homes and move in together for support and socializing, with the availability of mutual assistance if it is needed.

FRANKNESS ABOUT SHORTCOMINGS

Being candid about disabilities and acknowledging problems resulting from illness or aging are important if one wishes to maintain pride and self-respect, although these issues are rarely discussed in public. Rather than being embarrassed and trying to hide flaws, one should make an effort to speak about them openly, when and where it is appropriate, understanding that these matters are beyond one's control and do not mean one is lazy, unintelligent, or offensive in any way. Most often, impediments are obvious to casual observers anyway and one looks foolish when attempting to conceal them or deny their existence.

As examples, an individual with Parkinson's or other types of tremor may hold onto one hand with the other to prevent it from shaking, or keep it hidden behind his or her back, rather than admitting the illness. Once one has told others about the disease, there is no need to feel ashamed and the shaking may actually be reduced because of less anxiety. Another example might be a person who has had a mild stroke and has slightly slurred speech. He or she is very self-conscious about it and does not converse in social situations. It may be even worse if there is drooling in addition to the slurred speech. The affected person may become withdrawn and isolated, resulting in an impact on his or her quality of life disproportionate to the physical problem. Another example might be someone who will not reveal a visual impairment that does not permit driving at night. Or someone who's afraid to go out alone because of dizzy spells, but will not tell anyone. Or a man who has chest pain with physical activity but will not acknowledge it to his golfing buddies.

It may also be hard for older individuals to concede any minor problems with memory and the slowed reaction time that are accompaniments of aging. Too often, people feel they will be disregarded if they are cognitively compromised in any way and will be shunned by others if they are suspected of having Alzheimer's. So they may try to cover up deficiencies involving memory without realizing they are not unique and that many older individuals have similar impairments. If they do not remember a face, name, or situation, they should say so without an extensive apology. (Perhaps they can also joke about it and say they are having a "senior moment.") By telling family or friends their memory is not as good as it once was and that they cannot remember something, they will no longer have to feel ashamed and try to conceal it. This will eliminate some of the stress from social interactions and result in better communication and improved relationships.

Increased fatigue and daytime sleepiness is another area that causes embarrassment for some older people and limits activities. If medical treatment does not help, they should discuss it with those individuals with whom they have frequent social contact. Certain strategies may also be useful in prevention, such as a nap prior to any engagement, avoidance of alcoholic beverages, and changing the schedule of medications.

Dealing with bodily functions gone awry is extremely traumatic for many seniors who frequently choose to ignore these subjects. To preserve self-respect and dignity, however, the involved person should explain the situation to those close to him or her. Older adults find urinary and/or bowel incontinence to be a particularly difficult issue to confront and experience a great deal of embarrassment from it, perhaps because it is often associated with senility. However, with an increasing number of advertisements on television and in the print media since 2004 for adult diapers and medical help for incontinence, it is something that more people are aware of. If incontinence can be managed with diapers, medication, or other aids, then there may be no reason for it to be discussed publicly. Urinary frequency (having to urinate very often) is also a common occurrence in older people. Unfortunately, some seniors are so upset with these conditions that they become reclusive rather than trying to find ways to handle them.

When our bodies act in ways we cannot regulate to produce undesirable effects that are frowned upon in polite society, there is no need for us to be ashamed. Though it may be hard to accept this rebellion and our inability to keep normal physiology in check, that is the way it is and denial will not change things. Being candid and willing to speak about personal matters is not something easily done by everyone, especially those who are modest and essentially private people, unaccustomed to discussing bodily functions. It is worthwhile trying, however, for once a problem is acknowledged to others, there is less stress from trying to keep it under wraps.

APPEARANCE

As we get older, it is necessary to pay attention to our appearance. Once we are retired and do not have to go to work regularly, or do not have children around the house, it is easy to fall into a pattern of sloppiness and ignore our personal demeanor. We may think people's impression of us is no longer important and not particularly care about how we look. However, appearances do matter and we lose our dignity and self-esteem if we are slovenly in our dress. And if we seem unconcerned about ourselves, others may become unconcerned about us as well. Some of us may also allow our apartments or homes to fall into disrepair and not paint them or attend to our lawns and gardens. The interiors of our homes may become cluttered and dusty, with objects askew and infrequent cleaning. This may cause neighbors to become antagonistic and people may perceive the condition of our homes as reflective of our state of mind.

An effort should be made to be neat and clean whenever out in public, being certain that one's clothes are not stained or torn. This does not require buying new and expensive outfits, but merely taking care of what one already has. Men should be clean-shaven, or their beards neatly trimmed. Hair should be in place and not permitted to run wild. Homes should be maintained to the best of a person's ability, taking into consideration physical or financial constraints. This will make the neighbors happy and make one seem more in control of his or her environment. Keeping up the home also increases its value, so it will be worth more to one's children or heirs.

COGNITIVE VITALITY

Maximizing cognitive abilities as we grow older is essential to successful aging and maintaining autonomy and self-reliance. I have mentioned certain behavior patterns in this chapter that can contribute to cognitive vitality, such as remaining relevant and independent, and will emphasize the importance of goals and objectives in the next chapter. As I have discussed previously, with the aging brain having considerable plasticity and with learning still possible, deterioration of intellect is not inevitable. Intellectual stimulation as we grow older enhances cognitive function and protects against dementia, and cognitive training programs can be helpful.[29]

"[S]tudies suggest that lifelong learning, mental and physical exercise, continuing social engagement, stress reduction, and proper nutrition may be important factors in promoting cognitive vitality in aging. Manageable medical comorbidities, such as diabetes, hypertension, and hyperlipidemia also contribute to cognitive decline in older persons."[30] A 2013 report emphasizes that cognitive activity throughout one's life is associated with reduced cognitive decline when older, independent of pathologic conditions affecting the brain.[31] Contrariwise, smoking and excess alcohol can impair cognitive function. All of the factors mentioned are under our control to at least some degree, indicating that we can influence the changes that occur in our brains and it is up to us to make the right choices. The key is to be active, both physically and intellectually—the best treatment for aging.[32]

9

IT'S IN YOUR HANDS:
ADDITIONAL STRATEGIES

Even such is Time, which takes in trust,
Our youth, our joys, and all we have,
And pays us but with age and dust.
    —Sir Walter Raleigh, Epitaph [1]

Age is a great equalizer. We all face the same problems as we grow older—whether rich, powerful, or famous, brilliant or average in intellect, middle-class strivers or impoverished welfare recipients. Wealth offers no protection from Alzheimer's disease. Power is no shield against heart attacks. And our cells undergo the same changes, whether we are from Watts or Beverly Hills, Scarsdale or the South Bronx. Because of the universality of the aging process, one would like to imagine there might be a "brotherhood of the aged," allowing all older people to understand one another's pain and commiserate on the changes they face in common. One might also imagine there would be an absence of competition and that one-upmanship would cease, with status and income less important than in earlier years. But of course, it's not like that. The barriers that existed previously do not crumble as the years advance. People remain in the same isolated social pockets, with the same viewpoints.

Still, a brotherhood of the aged is an ideal we should all consider and there are certain measures we should take to avoid inflicting indignities on our fellow travelers on the dwindling road of life. Those who are fortunate should not flaunt their affluence in front of those who have difficulty making ends meet. Live well if you can and enjoy the benefits of wealth, but do not brag about what you have achieved or the material goods you have accumulated. Do not denigrate anyone whose life you perceive as a failure, or those less successful than you. And be compassionate to the needy and the impoverished. Remember that happiness is not predicated on material success, and that love and fulfillment do not require money. Many people who are not rich, famous, or powerful have found contentment in life others would envy, and that is the bottom line.

Baby Boomers should also keep these thoughts in mind as they pass the artificial barrier from middle age to being young-old. Though Boomers are considered by some to be narcissistic strivers, interested in status and tangible possessions, strains of spirituality and altruism run through many of them. As life begins to wind down, it may be time for them to enjoy the fruits of their striving and maybe to share some of their material and emotional wealth with others less fortunate. This does not necessarily mean giving money away, though that might be worthwhile, but giving time and effort to lift up those on the bottom rungs of the ladder, who do not have the strength or ability to climb higher by themselves.

GOALS AND OBJECTIVES

When we are young, with careers ahead of us and children to raise, we all have visions of the future, with long-term goals and aspirations. Performing well at a job, reaching a particular position, creating something important, and attaining financial independence are among the ends we set for ourselves. Overwhelmingly, these goals revolve around our jobs and our families. In addition to distant objectives, we have daily and short-term goals, which may or may not be related to our major aims, but give our lives coherence and structure. What happens when we retire and our careers are over, or our children grow up and move out of the house? Should we sit around eating, sleeping, reading, and watching television, waiting to die?

Though goals and objectives may differ from those of our youth, it is just as important for us to have them as we grow older. We do not want to get by on memories alone, existing in the past. We need to have reasons to arise every morning and look forward to each day; to plan for the future though our time may be short. We need to have some purpose in our lives, even if through a very personal vision. Since job, career, and children are gone, it is important to find new outlets for our energies and not allow them to dissipate without direction. We need to find new ways to be productive and get the most out of the time allotted to us. If we are lucky, we can even inject new fervor and excitement into our lives.

With the contentious world of business and the desire to make money now behind most of us, it is important to establish new values not tied as much to financial rewards and acquiring things. More attention needs to be paid to spiritual evolution: nurturing relationships, helping other people, becoming active in charities, developing intellectually, and unleashing creative talents. And for those who are believers, greater participation in religion may be another option.

Very often, objectives in later life emerge from interests we had before, perhaps from when we lacked enough time to cultivate them fully. Thus, fulfillment may be found in a business venture dabbled in previously, to which we had been unable to devote much attention before retirement. Or a hobby of collecting coins may become totally absorbing. Or improving a golf game may consume us. Or working to raise money for a particular charity may become a fixation. Or spending a day or two teaching inner-city children to read may provide gratification. Or studying the Bible intensively may help us understand life's contradictions. Of course, goals do not have to come from past interests but can develop from exposure to new ideas and new opportunities. And they can come at different times in midlife and during our later years, leading to one goal at a certain point and another goal at another time. There is no reason goals cannot be changed several times over the years, as one's needs and values evolve.

Focusing on one objective at a time, a single driving motivational force, may also be unnecessary. One can have goals in different areas that provide excitement to varying degrees, but in combination make one's life satisfying. Just as financial planners advise diversified investment portfolios to assure safety and success, diversified interests in life with numerous friends are more likely to make one happy (assuming good health).

In pursuing goals and objectives, we need to find things to be passionate about. This can include devotion to particular people, such as a mate, children, grandchildren, or friends; or participation in special causes: political, educational, cultural, social, religious, or health related. And games such as golf, tennis, bridge, chess, and the like can impel us to get out of bed in the morning. Or one can develop obsessions with objects of various sorts and become a collector. One may also find enjoyment in activities such as traveling, dancing, college courses, physical fitness, gardening, managing finances, a new occupation, hunting, fishing, or boating; or unleash one's creative side through painting, sculpting, writing, knitting, quilting, and so forth.

Relationships

Whether we are young or old, relationships with other people are essential in terms of emotional wellbeing and overall happiness. However, they alone are not enough to sustain an individual if he or she does not have his or her own persona. It is wonderful to have a spouse to love and a strong marriage, but spouses die and then one has to carry on alone; or a spouse can become disabled and his or her partner may have to assume the role of caregiver. That is why it is critical for each partner in a marriage to do things apart from his or her spouse, for each to have his or her own goals and interests, and be able to run his or her own life.

Many seniors, overwhelmingly women, try to live their lives through their children. They want to be involved with every aspect of their offsprings' existence, assisting with grandchildren, as was done in previous generations with the extended family. These days however, there is not the same need for physical help in raising children. Modern appliances makes doing the laundry much easier and prepared meals are readily available. And there is usually convenient day care that can be utilized. Of course, grandmothers can still be helpful with many tasks and it is nice for youngsters to have the love and warmth grandmothers can provide.

However, it is not healthy for either adult children or their parents for the latter to interject themselves into their offsprings' daily routine. Both need to let go and be independent of each other, maintaining separate identities and separate lives. At the same time, there's no reason why grandparents cannot help out periodically with their grandchildren, such as babysitting, furnishing back-up care, and playing a small role in raising them. They can even offer opinions on decisions relating to the grandchildren, but only when asked to do so by the parents and without trying to direct the process of child rearing. And certainly they can follow the progress of grandchildren from afar, be enthusiastic and proud of their accomplishments, loving them and deriving pleasure from them. It is important also to remember that children can move away from their parents, or become estranged from them for various reasons. Neither children nor grandchildren should be the central focus of older people's lives, causing them to neglect their own interests.

In addition, too close a relationship between children and parents can at times have a constraining effect upon older individuals. Some children see their parents as members of a different generation, out of touch with today's world. They may not allow their parents the freedom to be themselves, telling them they seem foolish or silly for doing things they enjoy, or even mocking them for trying to act young. In these situations, it may be difficult for parents to know when the criticism is warranted and when it comes from the children's own insecurity. In a proper relationship between parents and children, neither should interfere in the others' lives.

Currently, friends provide most of us with a support apparatus. Preserving and nurturing these relationships should be a goal for Baby Boomers and seniors. When a spouse dies or a major illness or injury afflicts someone, we often depend on friends for solace, sometimes as much or even more than families. With children and grandchildren scattered around the country or the world, and the extended family a faded photograph from the past, only friends may be available. Shared confidences, shared ideas, and shared interests all contribute to building solid friendships, but a commitment to spend time together is also necessary to foster relationships. This may entail going out to lunch or dinner, shopping, seeing a movie, attending church, and so forth. Without blood ties, friendships last because people want them to and are willing to extend themselves to strengthen the bonds.

Even if desired, making new friends when one is older can be difficult. Because they are insecure, fixed in their ways, or perhaps depressed, many people do not open themselves up to new relationships. This is unfortunate, since as one grows older, previous companions die and leave voids that cannot be easily filled. And when it is necessary to move to new surroundings, such as a smaller apartment or an assisted living residence, there is often the hope that new friends will be found to make life more enjoyable—people with whom to talk and accompany one through the good times and the bad. Even greater barriers to friendship arise if a person is disabled and lacks mobility, or has an impairment of hearing or vision. But friends remain important to everyone. In fact, studies have shown that socializing increases longevity, quality of life, and cognitive ability.[2]

> What though youth gave love and roses,
> Age still leaves us friends and wine.
> —Thomas Moore, "Spring and Autumn"[3]

Causes

Involvement in a cause may develop because of an affinity for a particular organization or particular issue. Individuals may aid a cause by giving time and energy, donating money, or both. Sometimes they can provide special administrative or creative talents, or they may simply function as foot soldiers for an organization. Volunteerism is in itself a goal for many seniors who know it keeps their minds and bodies active, even as they perform good works and help others. It is also an opportunity to get out of the house to meet and interact with others. Numerous examples exist of retired people becoming involved in organizations as volunteers and giving something back to their communities in health-related, educational, or environmental projects, or other socially beneficial programs. [4]

Politics

Older people tend to vote in greater percentages than the population at large and because of this are courted by political parties and individual candidates on both national and local levels. People sixty-five or older were more than twice as likely to vote as those from age eighteen to twenty-four, particularly in nonpresidential elections. In some states on election days, they may comprise one third or more of the electorate and are often moved by matters that affect them directly, such as Social Security, Medicare, taxes, or various local problems.

Depending on their orientation, older people may actively serve either political party, sometimes working for a candidate, sometimes championing an issue. They may also support third parties, independent candidates, nonpartisan groups (League of Women Voters), or advocacy groups for senior citizens (Gray Panthers, AARP). Some may also work for ballot initiatives or referenda on a local or statewide basis, or constitutional amendments nationally.

The *New York Times* in April of 1999 had a feature article about an eighty-nine-year-old woman walking from Pasadena, California, to Washington, DC (over 3,000 miles), to protest the failure of Congress to pass campaign finance reform, and stopping at various points to proselytize about this problem.[5] This shows that anyone can make a political statement and engender support for an issue in which he or she believes.

Social

Social causes run the gamut from charities such as the Red Cross, or United Way, to child advocacy, gun control, pro-choice, anti-abortion, women's rights, curbing drunken driving, family values, control of violence on television, and so forth, along with a multiplicity of environmental concerns. National organizations exist that espouse differing stances on all of these subjects, with regional and local chapters always seeking members. On some issues, the positions taken may encompass religious convictions, and not infrequently, supporters of these causes will cross the line into political activism to advance their views. Participation in fraternal organizations, such as the Masons, Shriners, and Eagles, or Rotary, combines social contact with social causes. These groups meet regularly for camaraderie, but also sponsor events that raise money for charities. The American Legion and Veterans of Foreign Wars might also be considered in this category, though their orientation is more political, supporting veterans' rights and a conservative agenda.

Seniors are also involved in trying to improve education, directly or indirectly. They may solicit funds for schools or educational organizations, or act as teachers' aides in the classroom, augmenting instruction. This is a wonderful opportunity for older people to interact with the young, absorbing the stimulation and energy the children generate, while performing useful tasks that are immensely satisfying. Those involved in this area are usually fervent about it, saying they get as much out of it as the children. One can also function as a mentor to a child on a one to one basis, assisting a boy or girl with poor self-esteem who perhaps comes from a broken home and lacks good role models. Some extremely affluent individuals have carried this even further, acting as mentors to entire classes of students in inner-city schools, promising to help them obtain college educations with financial aid. Another area that can be gratifying is working as a literacy volunteer with adults who have never learned to read, or teaching English as a second language.

Many health-related organizations with chapters around the country focus on distinct disease entities and have seniors participating in their operations, trying to raise money, helping to educate people about the illnesses, and providing support to patients and family members. Among these organizations are the American Cancer Society, American Heart Association, National Stroke Association, Alzheimer's Association, and the Parkinson's Disease Foundation. Though these disorders are more prevalent among seniors, older people also work on problems that do not ordinarily affect them, like AIDS, multiple sclerosis, and juvenile diabetes. They also volunteer at hospitals and have a considerable impact on patient care, being involved in administrative chores, in an educational capacity, transporting patients around the facilities, providing emotional comfort, and boosting morale by distributing flowers, newspapers, and so forth.

Some seniors enlist for assignments in third world countries, either with the Peace Corps or with private charitable organizations. They may go individually or as couples if married, and stay for months or years. Their function depends on their skills and can include teaching various subjects, working in hospitals or clinics, helping farmers, and/or working on building projects. For the most part, people who have been involved in these ventures feel they have been wonderful experiences, for what they have seen as well as for what they have done.

Cultural

Promoting favorite cultural causes are also important for some older people, with both national and local organizations benefiting from their work. Included are museums, symphony orchestras, chamber groups, theatrical organizations, and the like. Some seniors function as docents in museums. In addition, seniors are active in local library associations and historical societies, with some providing backing to the Daughters of the American Revolution and similar groups that act in both the cultural and social spheres. Again, they perform administrative chores, sponsor fund-raising events, and act as volunteers for different tasks. Some cultural institutions depend on their seniors' efforts and money for survival and actively try to recruit older people.

Religion

For many older individuals, involvement in religious worship and the traditions of their faith are essential. This may merely entail church attendance on Sundays or other times, providing financial support, and adhering to church doctrine in their daily lives—following the precepts of Judaism, Islam, Buddhism, or whatever religion they believe in. However, other older adults choose to play a greater role. They may proselytize, handle administrative or organizational functions for their local churches, work on affairs to raise money (bake sales, dances), or even teach the Bible or Sunday school. Some also join study groups or formal classes, to learn scriptures and various other aspects of their religions.

The central role religion plays in the lives of many older people cannot be overemphasized, with their faith serving to sustain them in a world that some see as threatening and where they no longer feel in control. Whether or not that faith was followed when they were younger, as they see their peers dying and are approaching death themselves, they search for meaning in their lives. Belief in God and their religion can provide that meaning for them, bringing them peace and contentment in their later years.

A scientific report suggests an added benefit of longer survival by those who attend religious services.[6] Previous studies had described that religious observance resulted in a reduced incidence of anxiety, depression, and substance abuse; fewer suicides; lower blood pressure; and fewer strokes. Greater social support for members of religious congregations was also noted. Though subjects who attended religious services frequently were healthier at baseline in a report in the *Journal of*

Gerontology in 1999, their survival was still greater than the general population, even when this was taken into consideration.[7]

Games

An obsession with various games also motivates numerous older people, with an objective of improved performance or merely frequent play (with the enjoyment it provides). Some find the competition exciting, but the social aspect is usually as significant as the game itself, if not more so. An element of physical aptitude and fitness may be necessary for tennis, and minimally for golf or bowling, but most of the games are sedentary. They include card games like bridge, pinochle, hearts, gin, and poker; and board games like chess, checkers, mahjong, and Scrabble. Bocci and dominos also have their adherents. Some people take games quite seriously, with devotees obtaining lessons, either individually, or in groups, to enhance their play. A number of games like chess, bridge, pinochle, and Scrabble are quite complex and cognitively stimulating, and their adherents believe the games help to keep them sharp. Crossword puzzles are similarly challenging for many individuals.

Many seniors, mainly men, are involved passively (though often passionately) in sports—watching football, baseball, and basketball on television, or going to ballparks to see their favorite teams. As fans, they also follow reports on their teams in the newspapers, magazines, and on television, and can argue the pros and cons of personnel moves and strategies their teams employ.

Over the last few decades, gambling has become a major form of entertainment for many older people, some of whom become addicted and impoverished.[8] "In a national survey, Harrah's casino found that 27 percent of Americans over the age of 55 visited a casino at least once last year. In Illinois, a recent survey found that 40 percent of gamblers who visit that state's 12 riverboat casinos are over the age of 55; 30 percent are retired."[9] And a large study published in the *American Journal of Geriatric Psychiatry* in 2005 found that nearly 70 percent of Americans over age 65 had gambled the previous year.[10] Of this group, 10.9 percent were labeled at-risk gamblers, betting more than they could afford to lose. For most seniors, however, gambling provides a little excitement and a way to pass the time. Initiation often starts innocuously with bingo at a church or community center. This may lead to attendance at a professional gaming establishment, where the payoffs are higher with a greater risk of losing money. Slot machines are particularly popular among older adults. In the Midwest, excursions on gambling riverboats attract many seniors, with the proliferation of casinos on Indian reservations also a big draw. Those with more money and greater interest may travel to the gambling meccas of Las Vegas and Atlantic City. Though gambling can ensnare individuals of any age group, older adults, on fixed incomes, can least afford to lose large sums of money and those who cannot control their urges should seek help through Gamblers Anonymous or counseling.

Collecting

Those with a passion for "things" or objects of any sort may become collectors, their goal being to acquire examples of the items they covet. Either, they may simply be interested in quantity, or they try to obtain objects with specific qualities. Collecting is a wonderful avocation for all ages, but may be especially appropriate and satisfying for older people who have more time on their hands. Any type of object is fair game for the collector, from "garbage" to fine art. Prices for individual items can range from pennies (or even nothing) to millions of dollars. And people do not have to be wealthy to be collectors. All they need is the interest in something and the time to pursue it. If they educate themselves about the objects they wish to collect and develop a good eye for determining quality, their collections can grow significantly in value over the years.

A middle-class couple of modest means who purchased contemporary art in New York City from the 1960s to the 1990s, amassed a collection that was eventually worth tens of millions of dollars. They had paid a small fraction of that, buying paintings they believed to be of merit by artists who were then unknown. The collection occupied every available niche in their small apartment and was finally donated to a major museum. With a discerning eye, they were able to choose outstanding works before the artists became famous. They learned about their subject by reading, going to galleries and museums, and speaking to artists and gallery owners and became well versed in the art and the artists during this period.

For most people however, collecting involves mundane objects that require minimal expenditure to accumulate, depending on how greatly they are in demand. Some collections have little or no monetary value but may still provide great pleasure to the collector and are valuable because of that. Examples of this may be different types of rocks, seashells, leaves, pressed flowers, buttons, spools, bottle caps, and matchbook covers. Other collections necessitate small outlays of money when started, but subsequently can be worth large sums if other people become interested and a market develops for resale. Baseball cards, posters, and colored bottles could be included in this category. There is almost a childlike quality about some collectors, with an innocence in the way they confer value on objects.

People collect virtually everything imaginable, whether of natural origin or man-made. Collectors clubs, newsletters, Internet websites about collecting various things, and books about these objects soon become available, covering every area. Items embraced are as diverse as marbles, various kinds of dolls and their paraphernalia, bird houses, Walt Disney memorabilia, typewriter ribbons, Bakelite jewelry, Occupied Japan pottery, vintage clothing, Coca Cola memorabilia, postcards, Depression glass, cookie jars, Victoriana, art deco items, art nouveau pieces, and books on every subject or by particular authors. The list could go on and on.

A major aspect of collecting is the "quest." For those bitten by the bug, the search for objects can generate an intense "high" and finding something special or rare can induce euphoria. While the quest can be pursued in one's local geographical region, it can also provide extra enjoyment when traveling—or even be the impetus for traveling. One must be willing to spend time—not necessarily money—to discover the objects of one's desire. For every individual, collecting can potentially furnish a goal unique to that person. It also promotes social interaction as one buys, sells, trades, and discusses one's collection with other people with the same or similar passions.

For older people, collecting may also be a subconscious reaction to the losses they have suffered. In stark contrast to losing friends, physical prowess, identity, and so on, they acquire new objects, indicating they still have some power and control. But whatever psychological needs collecting may meet, people are seduced because it is fun.

Creative Pursuits

Creative impulses that may have been suppressed by the exigencies and demands of youth may be able to blossom forth during a more leisurely time when one is older. Almost limitless ways exist to be creative and the form of self-expression may depend on past experiences, interests, and knowledge. Sometimes a mentor already working in a particular field may provide one with guidance and inspiration. Whatever we do, it is important to keep in mind that attempts at creativity do not require recognition. And this should also not be perceived as work, with a product resulting that can be marketed. While one can try to sell one's creations if so desired, this should not be the primary goal and there should be no illusions about the possibility of making money. Grandma Moses was a one in a million phenomenon.

It is also true that not everyone can be creative and one should not be discouraged if one is not so inclined. Besides the necessity for at least a modicum of talent in the area of choice, discipline is required to generate any sort of art. If a person discovers this is not meant for him or her, simply find another interest.

In many urban and suburban areas, classes or individual instruction are available if one wants to work in a specific medium. Whether one partakes of these opportunities is contingent on how intensively one wants to learn and how much one wants to spend. Adult education courses in community colleges and high schools are one resource that can be utilized, and some large senior centers also offer classes in different art forms. Art supply stores may sponsor classes as well, or be able to recommend instructors if one wants to take private lessons.

Painting is probably the most popular type of artistic expression among seniors, with work in watercolors on special paper, or in oils or acrylics on canvas or canvas boards. Sculpture is a more difficult form to master and also more expensive, depending on the material utilized. Working in pottery entails using a potter's wheel with its idiosyncrasies, a kiln, and knowing how to apply various glazes and paints. Other creative pursuits include woodworking and carpentry, knitting, crocheting, needlepoint, and quilting.

Writing allows great flexibility, since it can be done in whatever time is available and without the need to purchase expensive equipment; however, a computer and word-processing software will make life much easier. One can choose to write fiction or nonfiction, poetry or prose, short stories or novels. Music also attracts many older people who participate according to their talents and level of interest. Some start instrumental or singing lessons after retirement, others become members of local orchestras, opera companies, chamber groups, or chorales, with periodic performances. Seniors also become involved with country and western or jazz groups, or barbershop quartets. Theater furnishes a forum for creativity as well, generally through local community groups, though some senior centers also have theater companies.

ACTIVITIES

Older people enjoy numerous other activities and find them stimulating. One of these is work, a significant calling for a large percentage of seniors that will be discussed separately. Several of the activities mentioned here could be placed under other headings, as there is an overlap in some of these areas.

Travel

Traveling to different regions is an important objective for many older individuals, how and where they go encompassing a wide spectrum. Affluence is not a necessary prerequisite since people can travel inexpensively if they desire. However, some seniors don't like to travel because of illnesses or unexplained fears. Others are only interested in visiting their families, and seeing their children and grandchildren. It has been said that travel broadens an individual, and in the past, a person was not considered educated unless he or she had been to a number of foreign countries. But with television and the movies, we are able to get some feeling for other parts of the world without having gone there. Still, we cannot truly savor another country unless we have been physically present and immersed in its culture. Obviously, certain destinations and itineraries have to be avoided if travelers are not in good health, and other responsibilities (for example caring for a spouse who is ill) may also be limiting factors. Since 9/11 and the wars in Iraq and Afghanistan, the possibility of encountering terrorism in various countries has been a consideration as well. And some individuals fear flying.

Recreational vehicles (RVs) have a special allure for some seniors, who are on the road much of the year, covering the depth and breadth of the United States and Canada. The RVs allow them to enjoy a "home" of their own, while moving about and sightseeing. An entire movement has developed around RV living, with newsletters and websites. It is estimated that hundreds of thousands of people have chosen this lifestyle.

As another alternative, many older individuals journey to elder hostels in the United States and abroad, where they can stay inexpensively and are given lectures or classes on topics of interest. In 1978, Elderhostel offered a few courses at New England colleges and had 240 participants.[11] It grew so dramatically, that by 1998, there were over 10,000 courses in its catalogues, with more than 300,000 people a year attending in both traditional and more esoteric sites. This is indicative of the desire seniors have for learning and new experiences. By 2013, over 5 million had participated in the Elderhostel programs.[12]

Special tours to different parts of the world that target older people are also increasingly popular, providing opportunities to visit new places at reduced prices. Mature travelers (those over fifty-five according to the Travel Industry Association) have a penchant for high adventure, including safaris, rafting trips, treks, sea kayaking, hot air balloon travel, and horseback riding.[13] "[A] study for the A.A.R.P. found that travelers 50 and older spent more than $30 billion on vacation travel in 1994. Since then, by all accounts, their numbers, expenditures and travel options have increased sharply."[14] Many airlines, trains, and buses give senior discounts, lowering the cost of any journeys.

Some older people who love to travel have the grit and determination to carry on no matter what their circumstances might be. In September of 2003, my wife and I were on a guided tour of Italy that required considerable walking and physical exertion. Our group included an eighty-eight-year-old man who was hard of hearing and had minor problems with vision, but was otherwise in good shape. In the Sardinian port city of Alghero, he did not see a curb bathed in shadow and feel forward onto his face, breaking his fall with his outstretched hands. He received a deep gash in one hand and abrasions on his nose and chin. Downplaying his injuries, he later said that the major damage was to his pride. After having his wounds cleaned and bandaged, then resting that afternoon, he rejoined the tour the following day, with long hours of sightseeing and lectures, eager to discover new vistas and artistic treasures.

Outdoor Activities

Hunting, fishing, boating, and sailing are other recreational pursuits that invoke passion in their proponents, overwhelmingly men, though the chance to engage in these diversions depends on geographical location. Boating, sailing, and fishing can be done on the ocean or on inland waters. One can sail either locally or over great distances. And what you do in terms of powerboating depends on the craft at your disposal. Long trips along coastal waters around the United States, heading up to Canada and Alaska, or down to the Caribbean are all possible with the proper boat and expertise. Similarly, fishing can run the gamut from sitting on a pier, to fly casting, to deep sea adventures. Fishing can reduce stress, is not physically taxing, and does not have to be a budget buster. Hunting is of course limited to rural areas and usually focuses on deer, geese, or ducks. However, trekking through the woods and handling a gun are not tasks every older person is capable of doing.

Dancing

As noted, many older people enjoy dancing. Though it is easier to go dancing if you have a partner, it can be an opportunity to meet new people of the opposite sex under nonthreatening circumstances if you are single, widowed, or divorced. Dancing lessons may also be available in your community, through senior centers, YMCAs, the school systems, or privately. Some communities and churches also schedule regular dances for seniors. In addition to these, one can go dancing at nightclubs or at special affairs, or enter dance competitions, which are becoming quite popular.

Studying

Returning to school, either in pursuit of a degree, or to gain knowledge of certain subjects, is also important for some seniors and midlifers, with individuals determined to graduate from high school or college or even obtain a graduate degree. These can be acquired for a person's own feelings of self-esteem, or can be used in preparation for teaching or possibly another career. Some older adults believe that further education may also open up job opportunities. Most people however, take nonmatriculated courses because they are interested in a particular area of study. "[A]ccording to the National Center for Education Statistics, 1 in 3 Americans over 50—23 million—were engaged in some sort of adult education [in 1998], more than double the 11 million (18 percent) involved in 1990-91."[15] In 2005, the Census Bureau reported that half a million of the 17 million college students in the United States were over the age of fifty.[16]

There are many venues for senior education, both formal and informal, affiliated with educational institutions or free standing. One is the Plato Society—the Perpetual Learning and Teaching Organization—founded at UCLA in 1980. These groups have expanded dramatically since that time, as more older people want to learn. Some universities have even set up residential communities for seniors near their campuses, so they can attend courses and participate in the intellectual life of these institutions.[17] About 50 percent of older students attend community or junior colleges. Many shun programs devised specifically for seniors because they feel they are not demanding enough.

MOOCS, massive open online courses, also offer seniors learning opportunities while sitting at their computers at home, and at no cost, unless a certificate is desired. Virtually every subject can be found, and a directory of free offerings is available at www.moocs.co/. Since MOOCS only began in 2008, how they will evolve in the future is uncertain.

Conclusion: Activities

Aside from improving quality of life, social and productive activities in older people have been shown to enhance survival independent of physical fitness.[18] This was demonstrated in a large study with a thirteen-year follow-up, controlled for multiple risk factors. The way in which these activities conferred survival benefits is unclear, though all-cause mortality appeared to be reduced. (Social activities include church attendance, visits to the movies, restaurants and sporting events, day or overnight trips, card playing, games, bingo, and participation in social groups. Productive activities comprise gardening, preparing meals, shopping, unpaid community work, paid community work, and other paid employment.) This study is one of a number of research reports in gerontology emphasizing the need for social engagement and productive activity for successful aging.

Another study suggests that in addition to longevity, older individuals involved in certain leisure activities have a reduced risk of dementia.[19] These activities include six cognitive pursuits: reading newspapers or books, writing for pleasure, doing crossword puzzles, playing board games, participating in organized group discussions, and playing musical instruments. The mechanism behind the lower risks is also unclear and whether participating in these activities truly protects against dementia remains unproven.[20] However, a number of subsequent studies show protective effects for cognitive activities. But as mentioned previously, aerobic exercise is even more important in terms of preventing dementia. Though it may be difficult for younger people with the burdens of work and family to put time aside for physical activity, there is no excuse for those who are retired and they should aim for at least an hour of exercise daily.

PETS

The care of a pet or pets and the companionship they offer provide a reason for living and solace in difficult times for many older people. Dogs and/or cats are the common recipients of their affection, but some seniors may also keep unusual animals and birds. If individuals or couples do have pets in their homes, they usually limit them to one or two, but occasionally, excessive numbers can create a nuisance. No matter how many pets someone has, if he or she becomes disabled or cognitively impaired, it may be necessary for another person to assist in giving the animals adequate care. But whatever the physical or financial burden pets may entail, there is no denying the emotional benefits they bestow.

EMPLOYMENT

Many older people do not view retirement as a desirable goal and want to continue working until stopped from doing so by death or disability. This wish may be due to a lack of financial resources or a paucity of other interests, but some individuals who have been working all their lives love their jobs, with their structure and routine. Indeed, many individuals now work productively into their nineties or even beyond.[21] They may derive great pleasure and a sense of accomplishment from what they do, and have nothing outside of work that is equivalent. In addition, their sense of identity and feelings of worth may be tied to their jobs and they're unwilling to surrender these. If pressed, they may cut down on their hours, but will not give their jobs up completely, unless forced to do so.

Of course, with the decline in the stock market and housing prices due to the recession in 2007–2008, many families saw declines in their assets. This took retirement off the table for many Boomers and seniors and they were happy to still have jobs. According to a survey by Career-Builder in 2010, 72 percent of workers past the age of sixty intend to put off retirement because of financial difficulties.[22] Household debt has gone up so high with savings depleted that many older people cannot afford to retire.[23] A 2012 report notes that 56 percent of workers have less than $25,000 in retirement savings.[24] But even before the sharp drop off in savings and pension funds, many Americans had chosen to retire later.

The ability to work through one's sixties, seventies, or even older, is contingent upon one's health, the type of job one has, and the situation in the labor market. As mentioned previously, commonly in corporate America, forced layoffs and early retirement have targeted older workers in the name of cost savings in spite of the fact these workers are more reliable, take less time off, and are involved less with drugs and alcohol. In addition, they have greater people skills. A person in his or her fifties or sixties who has been laid off and wants to work, may find him- or herself having to start over at a lower wage in a new job with a new company, and in a position for which he or she is overqualified. It may be necessary for the worker to accept this situation, not just for the money, but for the benefits. However, given the demographic imperative, more companies are starting to keep skilled older workers in high-paying jobs because comparable talent is not available in a younger group.

With the population growing older, the retirement age is being pushed back (and will probably be pushed back further) to preserve Social Security. It is already rising gradually from sixty-five to sixty-seven and many economists and some politicians feel it should go to seventy to relieve financial pressures on the Social Security system.[25] As Dr. Robert Butler, the editor of *Geriatrics* states, "It does not seem reasonable and economically sustainable to have 65 million skilled and educated Baby Boomers sitting idle. When older persons remain active in the work force they contribute to a productive economy and make financial contributions to, rather than requiring payments from, Social Security trust funds."[26] American businesses need to find more ways to retain seniors to help their companies and the seniors themselves in a changing world.

A survey in the late 1990s revealed that the idea of retirement as merely a time of leisure for older Americans was already changing.[27] Older people wanted to be more engaged and more productive than past generations. Sixty-five percent of those surveyed felt that retirement is when a new chapter in life should be started with different activities and different goals. Only 28 percent thought of retirement as a time to relax and take things easy. The survey found that "40 percent are working for pay in retirement or plan to after they retire, while an equal percentage do volunteer work or plan to."[28] Of course, fulfillment of these aspirations may depend on the availability of meaningful positions.

Because of unhappiness with their jobs and searching for more satisfaction, some Baby Boomers have made career switches in midlife, many of them taking a cut in pay. This career reinvention has been called an "encore career" and there is a nonprofit group, Encore.org, which can help with transitions.[29]

FINANCIAL MANAGEMENT

Since the majority of people do not have paying jobs after age sixty-five, their income depends on pension funds, 401Ks, savings, and Social Security. Managing their money well is essential, if they are to make the most of their assets and insure long-term financial security. This is particularly true after the meltdown in the stock markets and home prices with the 2007–2008 recession. Unfortunately, many older people are not knowledgeable about investments and not aware of the differences in returns and risks of various financial instruments, often making poor choices. They may listen to friends or family members—or even strangers who sound persuasive—about where to place their money. And because some are financially naive and too trusting, at times they fall victim to scam artists. It is important to remember that if an investment seems too good to be true, it usually is and we should stay away from it. There is no easy way of making money and anything with a high rate of return involves a high level of risk. Also, we should not make snap decisions or be pressured into arrangements without adequate time for consideration and consultation. Before we hand anyone money or sign up for any "deals," we should give it plenty of thought and discuss it with other people experienced in financial matters.

To increase sophistication and general knowledge about finances, it may be worthwhile to take classes dealing with money management and investments. Courses on these topics may be found at community colleges, libraries, high school adult education sections, or senior centers. Seminars and lectures may also be advertised in the local newspapers or on the radio or TV, either free or for small fees. However, one has to be wary of these, as often the lecturer is seeking clients as a financial planner or is trying to drum up business for his or her own firm, selling stocks, annuities, insurance, or other types of investments. Always look for possible conflicts of interest before accepting that what you're being told is valid.

Many books have also been written on the subject of financial planning and investing, some of which are quite good and some of which are worthless or even dangerous. Here too, one must watch to be certain the author is not pushing a specific agenda, but rather is providing useful information about different options. Your local library or the AARP might be able to recommend the best books for you, as might a

reputable financial planner or your accountant. In addition, some financial magazines, such as *Fortune, Money, Your Money, Smart Money,
Worth*, and *Barron's* (which are also suggested reading), should be able
to assist you in picking the most salient books.

If you have significant assets, you can consider the use of a financial
planner to aid you in managing your money. However, there are pros
and cons to this. The biggest pro is that you enlist a person purportedly
objective and erudite, who should be able to help you maximize your
returns and protect your assets. The con is that these individuals are not
always what they are advertised to be and may be pushing specific types
of investments that are inappropriate for you. If you are going to use a
financial planner, find one who is certified and endorsed by your accountant or someone else whose judgment you trust. You also want a
planner who will work for a set fee rather than on a commission basis,
eliminating conflicts of interest in directing you to particular financial
instruments. In addition, you need a person with whom you can communicate well and who will be available to answer any questions that
might arise.

Very often in a marriage, one partner, generally the man, assumes
the role of handling finances and making decisions regarding investments and allocation of assets. This usually continues as the couple
ages. However, this pattern can be disastrous if the person in charge of
finances dies or becomes cognitively impaired, and the second partner
is suddenly faced with financial decisions about which he or she may be
totally ignorant. It is important in a marriage for both partners to deal
with monetary issues together and for both to understand the economic
ramifications of their choices. Also, if an older person has cognitive
problems and is widowed or single, it may be necessary for the children,
other close relatives, or the person's attorney to step in to manage his or
her money, to be certain it is not squandered on foolish schemes.

In the past, the population over age sixty-five was the most impoverished segment of society, with many seniors simply concerned with
survival and the necessities of life. Since the advent of Social Security
and Medicare, this is no longer true. Though these programs provide
significant support for older people, many have found Social Security
and Medicare do not meet their total needs. That is why pension plans
and savings, along with astute financial management are so important in
our later years. Because seniors are generally risk averse, many do not

receive an adequate return on their money. This will change only if they make a concerted effort to become more knowledgeable financially and invest whatever capital they have appropriately.

Reverse mortgages have been available for decades, becoming a popular way for some seniors to enhance their incomes over the last ten to fifteen years.[30] Companies allow homeowners to borrow against the value of their homes without repayment until they die or move elsewhere. However, these companies are out to make money and terms may not be favorable for homeowners, some of whom have lost their homes with these programs. Again, if something is too good to be true, it probably is.

PREPARATION

To maintain vitality and self-esteem as we age, early preparation is important—doing things when we are younger that will improve our lives when we are older. This is true not only in terms of financial arrangements, but also in matters of lifestyle and mental set. One should start considering the evolution of one's life early on, asking the questions, "Where am I going?" and, "What do I want to do with my life?" It is helpful to have a general schema devised in terms of how long you want to work and at what job, how much money you will need when you retire and how you intend to accumulate it, and what you want to do in retirement.

Certainly by your forties, these issues should be on your mind and you should try to be realistic about your employment situation and financial potential. If you are married, planning should be done together with your spouse, with contingencies discussed for each of your deaths. It is much easier analyzing needs and possible paths your lives might take after a partner's death when both of you are healthy and planning can be done in an orderly, logical, nonpressured manner. Concern about how a spouse will manage when you are gone is a practical sign of love and not merely morbid rumination. And living within your means, budgeting, and saving should be a continuing goal throughout your life, including putting something aside annually to prepare for the future. Even if the amount saved is small when you are young, it is a good pattern to establish and maintain until more money is available.

Also, the earlier you start, the more money will accumulate, with interest and dividends growing, and appreciation of stocks if you invest in the market. The returns are even better in IRAs (individual retirement accounts) and tax-sheltered programs. Some people hire retirement coaches to help them plan the transition, not only with finances, but also with what they will do with their lives.[31]

Physical fitness and care of your body when you are young are other areas that will pay dividends when you are older. Though one can initiate an exercise program any time, the younger you begin, the more substantial the benefits. Exercise should be a lifetime activity that continues as you age. The longer you wait to start, the harder it may be to achieve a desired level of functioning. However, for those who have been remiss, it is worthwhile beginning at any age, for you can always be better than you are. In addition to exercise, physical fitness entails watching your diet and avoiding excessive amounts of fatty foods, not smoking cigarettes, and not abusing drugs or alcohol, all of which will come back to haunt you as you grow older.

The pursuit of interests to sustain and motivate you is as essential to happiness in later years as is your physical and financial status. I have mentioned various goals and objectives people need when they are older to make life exciting and pleasurable. These passions, outside of work and families, optimally should be started when you are young, then developed over the years, accelerating when your children leave home and the time of retirement nears. If there is nothing that energizes you, you should actively seek out an interest, exploring various options, studying them carefully, and possibly making a trial run here and there if something is the least bit enticing. Then, when you retire, the seeds planted will be ready to blossom and you can expand on your early work. Preparation in this area is critical. You cannot just suddenly retire at some age and begin a new life from scratch without an inkling of what you are going to do. That path inevitably leads to boredom, restlessness, and depression.

Even without regard for the future, you should try to be intellectually and socially engaged all of your life. You should know what's going on in your community, the nation, and the rest of the world, and participate. You should be aware of social changes, current events, political matters, and cultural developments. It is also important to keep up with technological advances, so you do not feel out of touch in terms of the

Internet, social networks, and whatever else may follow. And acquiring a store of information should be a lifelong process. Though living this way will be preparation for when you are older, it is merely the right way to live at any age. In other words, the tenets for maintaining self-esteem and vitality as you age are the same as for living well when you are younger.

DEALING WITH GRIEF

Grief, intense sadness and despair as a reaction to losing someone we love, interferes with our ability to function normally. We express grief through a process called *mourning*. There cannot be grief without love or emotional involvement. Invariably, it signals a change has occurred or is going to occur in the life of the person grieving in regard to a close relationship. Individuals may also grieve because of the loss of a pet, or something significant to them, such as a house burning down, or a favorite piece of jewelry being stolen. It may occur with loss of a job, or loss of status. Grief may be exaggerated by someone who is depressed, but grief itself can also lead to depression. Though everyone's grief is different, as is the loss to which they are responding, there are certain behavior patterns that are fairly predictable. The way we deal with grief and the increasing losses we sustain as we grow older can affect every aspect of our lives.

Profound grief may also be seen in conjunction with a disabling illness or injury in someone dear to us, when that individual is impaired to the degree that he or she will never be the same person and in a way is lost to us. Grieving occurs as well when we ourselves are disabled and cannot do the things we did in the past. We may also be wrapped in a cloak of grief upon learning we have a terminal illness and are going to die, mourning our own anticipated death.

The loss of someone we love results in grief because that person, who was so dear to us, is no longer there for us physically and emotion-ally, producing an emptiness within us. An interdependency that had been there no longer exists, forcing us to reshape our lives. Though the prevailing feelings are those of overwhelming sadness, guilt is often also associated with the loss, with the belief we had not loved the other person enough, had been remiss in doing or not doing certain things, or simply that we had survived while the loved one had died. Restlessness, difficulty sleeping, physical pains, and various other health problems frequently accompany grieving. Feelings of anger that this person has been taken from us may also be directed toward the loved one, society, God, fate, or ourselves. Usually, aside from the sadness, we are not conscious of the different feelings encompassed by grieving, which makes it more difficult to come to terms with them. With the disability of a loved one however, anger may be closer to the surface, as we are regularly forced to confront this person, who is no longer the same individual we loved. The anger may be more intense if we have to take care of this person on a continuing basis, interfering with the way we lead our lives even more than his or her death would.

The most often seen and usually the most painful grief occurs with the death of a spouse. Since women on average live longer than men, they are generally the ones who survive and have to deal with this. In 1999, it was noted that nearly half of the twenty million American women past sixty-five are widows; and fewer than 10 percent of them are believed to remarry.[32] Adjustment to the death of a spouse can take as long as two to four years, though many survivors suffer longer term problems, including depression, alcohol and prescription drug abuse, and greater susceptibility to diseases.[33]

Our own loss of function or disability induces anger as well as sadness at the realization of the limitations imposed upon us. This may occur as part of the aging process, as we break down in various ways or develop illnesses associated with aging and can no longer do things that were previously automatic. If enough areas in our lives are still pleasurable, we eventually accept the losses and carry on with living, though we may still grieve to some degree. Sometimes, when the function lost was critical to our sense of self, particularly if we cannot care for ourselves adequately and feel we are a burden to others, normal grieving may evolve into depression, even to the point of wanting to end our life.

Knowing we have a terminal illness and are going to die also produces grief, which is rooted in a number of concerns. There is disappointment and sadness over leaving those we love, the things that were never accomplished, and the future that will not be shared. Perhaps as well, we feel an element of guilt about not being able to meet our responsibilities because of death. In addition, we worry about being an encumbrance—physically, emotionally, or financially—to our loved ones while we are dying. We may also be angry about our impending death, wondering why it is happening to us. The knowledge we are going to die may also make us fearful, as we are unaware of what lies ahead and do not know whether there will be pain and suffering.

I have mentioned some of the emotional components of grief, but others may appear as well at different stages of mourning. Initially when learning of the death of a loved one, we react with shock and disbelief, followed by a period of denial. Then we tend to become apathetic and depressed, perhaps withdrawing from social contact. During this time, we may be unwilling to do anything or make decisions and we seem almost in suspended animation, going through the motions of living. After this there is usually a gradual acceptance and re-entry into the world with a resumption of activities. These are not necessarily sharply delineated stages with smooth transitions, but often overlap. And many people may skip a stage or remain fixed in a particular plane from which they cannot escape. The duration of the entire process varies greatly, usually in the range of months to years. This may be determined by the individual's coping mechanisms and resiliency, his or her dependency on the deceased, age, the support apparatus available, and other factors. Even after recovery, when a person is functioning again, some residua of grief often lingers. Sometimes we overcome grief by immersing ourselves in activities or throwing ourselves into new relationships to avoid experiencing the loss.

Grief commonly elicits sympathy from family, friends, and acquaintances. However, if it is too intense, overly histrionic, or persists for an inordinate period of time, it begins to grate on people's nerves and compassion may turn to disinterest, disgust, or even worse, pity. Our inability to handle grief may thus destroy our fragile wall of dignity. What should we do to constrain our grieving and keep it within acceptable boundaries?

We must understand that though our grief is unique to us, as is our loss, other people also lose loved ones and suffer as we have suffered. We must mourn appropriately, then carry on with our lives, remembering our loved ones.

As Ernest Hemingway expressed so beautifully toward the end of *For Whom the Bell Tolls*, the people we love live on after death within us and we owe it to them to go on living as productively as we can. Robert Jordan, who has been wounded in battle and is going to die, says to his love Maria, who does not want to leave him, "Listen. We will not go to Madrid now, but I go always with thee wherever thou goest. Understand? . . . I go with thee. As long as there is one of us there is both of us."[34]

We are responsible for the memories of our loved ones and should celebrate their lives rather than focusing on their deaths. The tendency to withdraw and isolate ourselves must be fought, and we must return to living after the period of mourning. We cannot keep feeling sorry for ourselves.

Most of the evolution from a state of grief to acceptance and normalcy occurs because of adjustments and changes within ourselves that are part of the restorative process. Though we have to do the heavy lifting, help is available from many sources to ease the burden and we should use it as necessary. Family and friends are the first line of support and we should not hesitate to call upon them in whatever role we require of them. They can provide us with both physical and emotional comfort, and appropriate sympathy. In most circumstances, these people have also experienced our loss, having known our loved one who has died. This permits us to share memories and reminiscences, which are often helpful in a time of grief. They may also be able to assist us in simple tasks, like shopping, preparing food, and so on, which we might neglect while mourning.

Religion can also offer solace and, if we have faith, we should turn to God and His ministers to provide answers for us and help relieve our pain. For many, the power of faith and of prayer is a spiritual balm that can heal all wounds. This may be even more important as we age. Whether previously observant or not, death and illness are two crises that may direct us toward religion with the hope that belief in God and acceptance of His precepts will bring us peace. This assistance in the transition between life and death seems to be a universal attribute of religions.

Help can also be obtained through various support groups, some which have been formed to respond to particular illnesses, such as breast cancer, prostate cancer, Alzheimer's disease, Parkinson's, and so forth. Many hospitals, communities, and churches also have bereavement groups to guide the relatives of those who have died through the process of mourning. Bereavement counselors are available as well in some communities to assist people. Family physicians may also be valuable resources to help those who are grief-stricken understand what has happened and to alleviate fear and anxiety through brief psychotherapy. Medications to reduce anxiety and allow sleep may be beneficial on a short-term basis. The use of psychiatrists and psychologists should probably be limited to those people who have excessive difficulty in managing their grief, or when mourning has gone on too long and interferes with someone's life.

Since everyone goes through the process of mourning in his or her own way, those watching the person trying to handle the pain should not be judgmental, thinking it should have been done differently. Two examples that follow show how individuals dealt with a loved one's death:

P. R. was a ninety-year-old man in good physical shape and mentally sharp. After living in the New York metropolitan area all of their lives, he and his wife moved to an inexpensive condominium community in Florida when he had retired from an administrative job in the city, managing to get by on a small pension and Social Security. For nearly ten years, he ministered to his wife with breast cancer as she went through surgical procedures, courses of radiation, and chemotherapy. Deeply in love, he was greatly supportive of his wife during her illness, having been married to her sixty-four years when she finally died. Several hours after returning from her funeral, one of his neighbors, a woman in her eighties who had been a close friend of his wife, came over to his apartment with chicken soup and freshly baked pastries. She stayed for a while to commiserate with him and the following day brought him dinner. They were married three months later and lived together, apparently happily, for four years before he died of a massive stroke.

R. K. was an eighty-two-year-old breast-cancer survivor with cervical spine arthritis and a neuropathy. Her pain was controlled for the most part with small amounts of medication and she led an active life, playing golf and bridge, and traveling a lot, with elegant apartments in Connecticut and Florida. Married to a banker for over fifty years, she cared for him during a five-year decline and eventual death from diabetes, congestive heart failure, and prostate cancer. A year after her husband's death, she met a charming man of her age at a golf range. He started a conversation, then asked her out to dinner. Within three months, she moved into his apartment. They lived together for six years, sharing each other's lives. Because of financial considerations, they did not want to get married. When he developed kidney failure and cognitive problems, she could not manage him at home, but after he was admitted to a nursing home, she continued to visit him and take him out for dinner occasionally until he died.

There are some people who might find these relationships shameful, saying that not enough time had elapsed for proper mourning between the deaths of the long-time spouses and the new connections. But we all want love and companionship and when the opportunity knocks in the sunset years of our lives, perhaps it should be grasped. We do not have much time left and it may not happen again. It does not negate feelings for the deceased loved ones. In addition, sometimes the period of mourning starts before the death of a spouse, when the illness is long and drawn out, and death is expected.

DEALING WITH LONELINESS

Loneliness can, of course, occur at any age, but is more characteristic of older people than the young for a number of reasons. After retirement, there is no longer daily contact with others on the job and, thus, a lessening of the social intercourse which was part of their lives. Children are gone and have their own lives, and as one ages further, spouses as well as more friends and peers die off. Physical handicaps and disabilities may develop, making it difficult to get out of the house and interfering even more with socializing. Some may also have to take care of impaired spouses, which limits freedom.

It is essential that older people not allow themselves to be defeated by loneliness, which can lead to depression and surrender of the will to live. Friendship is the best weapon in this battle and one should do all he or she can not only to maintain old relationships, but to initiate new ones—not necessarily an easy task as one grows older. Physical isolation must also be fought against and older people must force themselves to get out of their houses and involved in the communities around them. Joining groups of people with similar interests or working for particular causes, and sharing activities with other individuals, such as by playing bridge or golf or exercising in an aerobics class are important for seniors' wellbeing. Religious services offer other opportunities to be with people. Though each person has to find his or her own way out of loneliness, it should be remembered that "prevention is the best cure." By not permitting oneself to fall into the chasm of loneliness, it will not be necessary to worry about climbing out.

Over the last few decades, the Internet and social networks have become new tools for older people to deal with isolation. For example, in nursing homes, the plague of loneliness infects much of the population. But some geriatric experts have found that the Internet and e-mail can revitalize nursing home residents, improving their morale and decreasing their manifestations of depression.[35] Studies have shown that large numbers of these people can be taught to use a computer and communicate by e-mail. If the institutionalized elderly can do it, certainly those on the outside can also do it, utilizing e-mail, social networks, and chat rooms to alleviate loneliness and enrich their lives. However, it is critical that older people using the Internet be aware of possible scams and misuse of information, keeping personal data out of the hands of schemers.

COUNTERACTING SOCIETY'S AGEIST BIAS

Older people have considerable power economically and politically, but do not wield their power as effectively as they might to reduce society's ageist bias. This must be accomplished to eliminate the indignities society imposes upon individuals because they are older.

People over sixty-five control a major portion of the nation's wealth, through their pension plans, other retirement vehicles, and the assets they have accumulated over their lifetimes. As stockholders in every large corporation, they should be able to force an end to age discrimination and help older employees obtain better treatment. Given their tremendous buying power, they should also be able to influence the media to depict older people more favorably, and develop more television programs and movies aimed at older audiences. Over the last few decades, a number of corporations have begun to realize a major market exists among older people who have not been served adequately and these companies are starting to address this deficiency.[36] Some have become "senior friendly" in an attempt to generate more business in this burgeoning group with a vast amount of discretionary income. Because of the financial stakes, companies can no longer afford to show indifference to seniors.

With the growing number of older people in the United States and the fact that they vote in higher proportions than any other segment of the population, seniors should be able to assert themselves even more strongly from a political standpoint, to have greater attention paid to their agenda. At their direction, legislation should be passed that further bars age discrimination, levels the playing field for senior citizens, increases low-income senior housing, and protects the core of Social Security and Medicare. (Changes will have to be made to these entitlement programs in light of America's budget deficits, and the facts that people are living longer after retirement and fewer workers are supporting the older population.)

RANDOM THOUGHTS ON AGING

Having discussed the major areas of concern in terms of maintaining one's self-respect and vitality, the following are some general precepts to keep in mind as we grow older.

- Our attitude and approach to life are important as we age. We can either perceive the glass as three-quarters empty or as one-quarter full and that view will affect the way we live. Being depressed not only makes us unhappy, but also affects all of those around us as well.
- We are who we are, both in fact and in other people's perceptions. We must try to be at peace with ourselves and accept what we have done with our lives. Whether successful in our own eyes or not, it does not benefit us to be resentful of the past, including career decisions, choices of mates, and lack of financial security. What has happened cannot be altered.
- While we are all capable of change and learning at any stage of our lives, our personalities have already been forged and our patterns of behavior are fairly fixed. If we are truly unhappy about whom we are, we can try to live differently in the time we have remaining, working at something new. Though it is possible for us to bring about change, we should be realistic. We can dream, but

that should not run our lives. It is unlikely we are going to become a scratch golfer or write the great American novel at age seventy.

- Since the past is set and we do not know what the future holds, the only period we can do anything about is the present. We should live well, for our time is short.

- We should deal with the enmities and antagonisms that have colored our lives, and come to terms with those we dislike. This can be done openly or within ourselves, but we should not let hatred fester, for it will only poison our own systems.

- Be kind to other people, forgiving them their failings and overlooking small mistakes, remembering our own imperfections. At the same time, we should not let others take advantage of us, or we will feel duped and unhappy later on.

- Self-respect entails respect for others. We should treat everyone as we ourselves would wish to be treated.

- Having survived into middle or old age, we should try to give something back to our communities, for that makes our lives more meaningful.

- Though bringing joy to other people is important, we have to live for ourselves as well. We should try to find enough pleasures of both mind and body to sustain us while we are still able to appreciate what we have.

- It is important to be productive when we are older. However, productivity can be measured differently—using our time well. This can mean reading a good book, walking five miles, or helping someone.

- Find a peaceful time every day for renewal. Whether it is through meditation, prayer, walking, or any form of conscious solitude, it is necessary to give our lives balance.

- We should not withdraw into ourselves, nor only share our lives with a single companion. We should interact with the world around us, with different people of all generations.

- We should maintain a "youthful" outlook as we age. By that I mean, remaining curious about life, with a willingness to explore and try new things.

- Age imposes limitations upon us. The older we get, the more limitations we face, though it is different for everyone. At each

stage of life, we must do the best we can within our own limitations.

- Burning the candle at both ends is not necessarily bad. Having
  many interests and activities can make our lives exciting.
- Don't gossip. This is a characteristic often attributed to older people that is demeaning. If our lives are interesting and fulfilling, we
  do not have to talk about others.

POSITIVE THINKING

Several studies have suggested that those individuals who are optimistic
about life as they age and have a positive attitude, live longer.[37] Whether this is cause or effect is uncertain, as is what people can do to develop
a positive attitude and make themselves happier. Feeling empowered,
or having some degree of control over their lives, as well as being aware
and knowledgeable about their environment, seems to increase peoples'
happiness and correlates with longevity. These people seem to be more
conscientious about the way they conduct their lives, engaging in
healthier actions and avoiding riskier behavior (smoking, eating poorly,
driving without seat belts, excessive alcohol, drug abuse, and so on).

PIRO

I have examined many factors that must be considered in the attempt to
preserve vitality, self-confidence, and self-respect as we age. However,
four of these are of primary importance in our struggle and can be
represented by the acronym PIRO.

> **P** stands for continued physical fitness and physical activity as we
> grow older.
> **I** symbolizes maximizing our independence whether we are healthy
> or disabled.
> **R** signifies remaining relevant in our interactions with other people
> and understanding the world around us.
> **0** stands for the objectives and goals we should always have—to
> provide reasons for us to continue living.

10

WHAT THE FUTURE HOLDS—AGING IN THE NEW MILLENNIUM

Trying to control the future is like
trying to take the master carpenter's place.
When you handle the master carpenter's tools,
chances are that you'll cut your hand.
—Lao-Tzu, *Tao Te Ching*[1]

During the next few decades, advances in scientific knowledge and technology will dramatically change everyone's lives, particularly those of Baby Boomers and seniors. In addition to drugs and gene therapies that will protect against diseases associated with aging, the aging process itself may be attacked and advance more slowly. This will allow more quality years of life. And machines and gadgets will be developed for those who are impaired or just want help with the tasks of everyday living. Many high-tech companies are searching for ways to tap into the expanding senior market, utilizing computer applications, communications systems, and discoveries in biotechnology.[2] In the years ahead, we can expect the living environment of older people to be significantly altered, the aging process to be modified, and society itself to undergo a metamorphosis.

CHANGES IN LIVING ENVIRONMENT

The number of nursing home beds and assisted living units will begin to decline in the near future, as older people remain independent longer in their own dwellings. This is partly because seniors will be healthier deeper into old age, while their life expectancy continues to increase. Other important factors supporting their independence will be the transformation of their living environment with so-called smart homes,[3] the use of "robotic companions,"[4] and "smart cars,"[5] allowing even many of the disabled elderly to live alone rather than being institutionalized, or having a human attendant constantly with them.

Smart Homes

As a starter, every older person's home will be equipped with a computer programmed to help it run efficiently, requiring limited attention from its occupants. This will be networked to all the appliances and devices in the home, as well as to sensors in appropriate locations. In 1999, the average American home contained 40–50 microprocessors, anticipated to increase to 280 within five years.[6] And the number of microprocessors in every home has continued to grow. Most of these are embedded in various objects, including sensors, appliances, toys, automobiles, and so forth, monitoring and controlling different functions. As better voice recognition software becomes standard in all computers, it will not be necessary for anyone to have special knowledge or training to interact with his or her electronic assistants. If the task has not already been preprogrammed, people will be able to direct their computers to alter their home environments or meet other needs simply by telling them what they want done. The devices will also communicate with people by "talking" to them, providing information such as when a task has been completed, or asking if there are new tasks to be performed, based on previous behavior patterns. (Android phones and iPhones are already doing this to some degree.)

These new "occupant friendly" houses will have motion sensors in each room, causing lights to go on and off as people enter and leave, reducing the danger of falls and injuries. (If someone does fall, appropriate responders will be alerted.) Television cameras will allow monitoring agencies to look into every room if there is a question of a resident being ill or injured. People with cognitive impairment will be verbally reminded to take their medications, eat and drink the required amounts, and perform various other tasks. The temperature in each room will be self-regulating according to the presence or absence of people, with perhaps only the bedroom and bathroom being comfortably heated at night. Oil and gas for heating will be delivered as requested by computer, without anyone's intervention.

Speakerphones will be present throughout the house allowing phone calls to be answered or made by someone simply saying a key word, with the person able to have a conversation while moving about the house or seated, hands free. At the occupant's command, the shower or bath will go on at the desired temperature and turn off when he or she is finished. When that person is ready for sleep, the bed will be warmed to the level he or she finds comfortable, by a person merely giving the order. Similarly, the stove or microwave oven will be able to make tea or coffee as directed—or even a complete meal, by reading the coded instructions on the food packages.

Ovens and burners will switch off automatically, eliminating any concern about fires. Indeed, smoke, heat, and carbon monoxide alarms will be more sophisticated, alerting occupants and firehouses, if there are any possibilities of danger. And, after their approval by voice or computer, bills and taxes will be paid by the banks electronically, the latter technology already being utilized by many people.

Televisions, radios, and CD players will also be operated by voice command, with movies or other programming from sources online. High-definition, large-screen "smart" television are already commonplace with visual quality greatly improved over past equipment. And three dimensional television is making inroads. Within a few decades, every home will have an entertainment machine. Through virtual reality, this equipment will allow individuals to become part of programs they are watching. This may occur with a bubble like screen around the viewer or with that person wearing a headset and glasses. Each of us will also be able to conjure up any kind of programming we desire, old or new, from movies, to Broadway shows, to sporting events, to news stories. In addition, through interactive television or high definition video phones, friends and relatives will always be available to us for conversation and companionship. No one will ever have to dine alone if they don't wish to do so.

Entry into our homes will no longer require keys. Our thumb print on a pad outside our doors will suffice, though retinal patterns or voice recognition may also be used, making our homes aware of our presence and starting them up. A tiny implanted chip under our skin may also be employed to activate our homes and allow computers to locate us in any area of our homes, or outside. This technology will be valuable for keeping track of people with Alzheimer's who wander; global positioning systems will always be able to find them. In July of 2003, the Intel Corporation announced that they and the Alzheimer's Association were joining together in a research initiative to try and harness computer technology in the care of Alzheimer's patients.[7] This collaboration has continued in a partnership called ETAC, Everyday Technologies for Alzheimer's Care.

The Internet

Using the Internet and software such as Skype, people who are home bound can make visual as well as auditory contact with others. This allows social interaction with the ability to have discussions, share ideas, and alleviate feelings of isolation. These activities will be enhanced in the future with faster chips, greater broad-band access, and improved digital technology. Given improved ease of computer operation, seniors can develop new online friends and become members of online communities. People can already play various games with their Internet companions, travel to different places for virtual tours, shop at various websites, and so forth. In addition to downloading e-books, if they have problems with vision they can use audiobooks or have their computers read books to them. And shopping for everything can be done over the Internet, permitting people to buy whatever they desire without stepping out of their homes. (It seems unlikely, however, that the Internet will be able to provide us with online hugs.)

Working at home in the twenty-first century is already a common practice and will be further facilitated by new technologies. This will allow many older people to continue to work and perform various functions without commuting. In a virtual office, they can now communicate face to face with coworkers, and participate in conferences on television or computer screens.

Smart Cars

In the years ahead, older people will be less reclusive even if disabled, because their cars will be able to operate without drivers, providing them with more freedom. These so-called smart cars are already being tested on the roads in California and will likely be available by the middle of the 2020s or even earlier.[8] Again they will be activated by voice pattern, thumb print, or other identifying characteristics, rather than keys. Instead of people climbing behind the wheel to drive these vehicles, they will tell them where they want to go, sit back and relax. The car's computer will enable the transport of the occupant to his or her destination, using the global positioning system to move the car to the required site, where it will be given instructions which driveway to enter, or where to park. Various sensors and detection systems inside and outside the automobile will feed information into the car's computer to help it maneuver through traffic, avoiding other vehicles, pedestrians, and hazards. Computers in different cars will be in contact with each other, allowing traffic to move smoothly. With these improvements, older people who cannot drive because of poor vision or other limitations will be able to visit friends or family, go shopping, go out to dinner or the movies, or even go on dates without imposing on others to drive them. Further in the future, smart cars may be aided by smart roads—highways imbedded with sensors that feedback information to a main computer that assumes control of the vehicles. Control can be transferred back to the cars on the secondary roads.

Robotic Companions

Robotic companions (RCs) will make life easier and safer for older people, permitting them to do things not otherwise possible.[9] These robots will be particularly helpful for those who are disabled or have problems with balance, but valuable as well for those physically and cognitively intact. The RCs will "live" with seniors in their homes, acting as companions and assisting them with the tasks of daily living. They will respond to their friend/master's verbal instructions, both with actions and verbal acknowledgment. The RCs will have to be fairly large, possibly human size, in order to perform the required work. They will each have their own computer and operating system, programmed according to the needs of their individual friend/master and will be able to communicate electronically with the smart home, smart car, and other computer systems. They will also be equipped with various sensors to "see" and "hear" what is going on about them and know what is happening in their environment. Their shape, the number and form of their limbs, and other extensions, will depend on what functions they might be required to accomplish, and the addition of new limbs, or removal of old limbs might be necessary with different tasks. Ideally, the RCs will be endowed with some anthropomorphic qualities that might help older people to more readily identify with them. Each one will be named by its friend/master who will summon it when needed.

As programmed or by specific command, the RC will execute household chores, relieving its master of those responsibilities. It will clean the house regularly, dusting, vacuuming, and washing, using appropriate cleansers and detergents. Removing dirty bed linens, towels, and clothes, it will wash and dry all the laundry, fold and stack the pieces, and put them away. It will make the bed with fresh linens and put out new towels. Though these tasks and their frequency might be programmed in, its master could order the bed to be changed or a new wash to be done, if he or she had been incontinent or there had been other problems. (Older people are mortified having soiled bed sheets or clothes, but may find it too demanding to wash and clean everything. An RC will eliminate this concern.) Cooking and shopping will also be handled by the RC. It could provide meals either by following instructions from its master, or could be programmed by a family member or visiting nurse to prepare and serve particular meals if its master were incapable of instructions. Programming could occur from distant locations, so visits will not be necessary each time the meal content or schedule was changed. RCs could be directed to cook meals for special diets, for example, low salt, low fat, and diabetic, and gourmet dishes or ethnic foods to suit individual tastes.

For older people unable to feed themselves, the robotic companion could take over that role as well, making certain their charges ingested adequate amounts of food and fluids. Meals could be pureed when needed, or mixed with thickeners, and even if feeding were laborious, the RC will show infinite patience spooning out nutrients to its friend/ master. The RC could also check food stocks regularly with its scanner and order provisions from a delivery service at the local supermarket when items in the pantry or refrigerator were running low. When the food was delivered, the RC will put everything away. Being cared for by their robotic companions, older people will no longer be afflicted by malnutrition or dehydration.

Substituting for home health aides, RCs could also render help with other tasks of daily living such as bathing, washing, and general hygiene when necessary. If the person were disabled enough, it could perform the job completely, changing underwear or diapers if its friend/master was incontinent. (Again, these tasks could be preprogrammed, if its master could not furnish directions.) The RC could also dress its charge and get him or her up in a wheelchair if it were required, placing him or her in front of the television or offering other forms of entertainment. If its friend/master were able and interested, the companion could play cards, checkers, chess, or other games. It could engage in conversation, relate the latest news, or be a general source of information. Perhaps it could even provide words of comfort and support if programmed properly, like a friend available at all times. If guests came to visit, it could hang up their clothes and serve them drinks, snacks, or meals.

In addition to acting as a home health aide, maid, and companion for many older people, the robotic companion could serve as a nurse and physical therapist for those who are housebound. As programmed to do so by the patient's physician or actual nurse, it could supervise and administer medications; take blood pressure, pulse, and temperature; and measure blood sugars, oxygen levels, and other important parameters. This information could be forwarded to the nurse or physician, who could then adjust medications or change other orders. Constant attendance and monitoring of the patient will allow for frequent corrections in the patient's regimen, resulting in superior care. In its role as physical therapist, the RC will regularly put its master through range of motion or other appropriate exercises, as well as helping him or her with ambulation. The RC will also serve as a transporter for any disabled person, taking him or her by car for doctor's appointments or other important meetings outside the home. In all of its functions, the RC will be ready for action twenty-four hours a day, at its friend/master's beck and call, needing no sleep and performing the most menial and repellent tasks without complaining.

Smart bedrooms have already been developed that use microchips to monitor people's temperatures, metabolic rates, cardiograms, and blood sugars; and smart toilets can now measure weight, fat content of stools, and urine sugars. This data can be transmitted to the person's physician who can utilize it in patient management. A robot is also presently available that does vacuuming and cleaning in the home, using onboard sensors to avoid obstacles.[10] Lawn mowing robots can be currently purchased as well and snow shoveling robots should be on the market shortly. Not only are many different types of robots for sale that perform household tasks, the prices of these aides are also dropping steadily.[11]

THE AGING PROCESS AND DISEASES OF THE ELDERLY

Though scientific progress will transform the aging process in the next few decades, people currently middle-aged or older may not reap much benefit from these modifications. However, their children and grandchildren will. Baby Boomers or the generation following may be the last to die prematurely from heart disease, strokes, and cancer, with life expectancies in the Western, industrialized countries increased from 80 to about 120 years, or more. And not only will people survive longer, but they will be healthier and more active, and able to enjoy their later years to a greater extent than is true today. Our generation is already living longer than that of our parents, and our children will live longer still. However, we also feel healthier, younger, and more vibrant than our parents' generation as we are aging. We considered our parents old at fifty or sixty and they also thought of themselves as over the hill. At fifty, sixty, or seventy today, many of us are still rearing to go, looking forward to the challenges ahead. Age categories will also have to be redefined as average life expectancy increase. If people live to 120, middle age might be from 50 to 85, with old age from 85 to 120.

Preventive maintenance will be the catchphrase for medical personnel in the future. Their goal will be to prevent illnesses, rather than to treat them once they arise. However, checkups and diagnostic evaluations of patients may be mainly automated. A person will come to a "health station" (or physician's office) periodically where he or she will have all physiologic parameters measured, including blood pressure, pulse, temperature, EKG, urine composition, and blood chemistries. Blood will not have to be drawn, but instead will be surveyed by spectrophotometry through the skin. On a routine basis, total body scans (without radiation) will be performed to search for evidence of cancer and other diseases, or various structural changes, with more specific testing of organ systems when indicated. Of course, if a person does become sick, rapid diagnosis using the above techniques will aid in treatment, and new therapeutic modalities will be available to maximize patient recovery and restoration of function.

Genetic profiles will be a standard part of everyone's assessment, used to determine an individual's susceptibility to illnesses. This will be of particular value in determining the risk of different types of cancers and hereditary diseases. Even today, women with or without certain cancer suppressor genes can discover whether they have a predisposition to developing breast or ovarian cancer. Soon, this will be true for many other cancers as well as other diseases. Another aspect of genetic profiling will be to match cancers to the pharmaceutical agents people will receive, to be sure the most effective drugs are being used. And gene therapy has already been successful in treating some types of hereditary diseases.[12]

Given the coming universality of electronic health records (EHRs), computers will allow all of a patient's physicians to have access to the same data, eliminating duplication of tests and procedures. In the future, even more sophisticated computers and software programs will further improve patient evaluation, both from a preventive standpoint and to treat illnesses. When a patient sees a physician, the latter will have vast amounts of information, including every aspect of the past history and family history. In addition to body scans, physiologic determinations, and genetic profiles, EHRs will store a compendium of previous illnesses, responses to therapy, allergies, and so forth. Computers will assist in analysis of this encyclopedic body of data, helping physicians arrive at differential diagnoses and appropriate therapy. Once a diagnosis is established, the computer can review the medical literature, presenting the physician with all the therapeutic options and their probabilities of success. Finally, computers will then be used to keep tabs on the patient during treatment, to see whether the plan is working and the patient is recovering. If expected progress is not occurring, the physician will be alerted and different treatment can be utilized.

Within several decades, nanotechnology will also play a major role in diagnosing and treating various ailments. Machines, sensors, and robots too small to be seen by the human eye will be placed in people's bodies to travel through their blood streams and lymphatic pathways, and around different organs and body cavities to monitor their status and perform certain tasks. These devices may destroy cancerous cells, clean away atherosclerotic plaques, repair damaged joints, or deliver drugs to targeted cells.

In the years ahead, the ravages of age, degenerative disorders, and diseases affecting each organ system will be able to be attacked and reversed by various means, including increased replacement of body parts, giving credence to the fantasy of the "bionic man." Research and development by technology companies and medical schools are already active in this area.

Cardiovascular System

In the second decade of the twenty-first century, diseases of the cardio-vascular system remain the paramount cause of death in the industrial-ized world. A number of different techniques are being used to stem these disorders including cardiac bypass surgery, angioplasty, stenting, thrombolysis, valve replacement, and permanent pacemakers. Threaded by catheter into arteries in different areas of the body, lasers and microscopic scalpels as well as expandable balloons can open up narrowed vessels. Rhythm disorders of the heart can be treated by ablation of aberrant cardiac electrical systems, as well as by catheter techniques. These procedures have been continually improved since they were first introduced, decreasing associated risks and complications.

Veins from different areas of the body, animal blood vessels, or Teflon grafts can also be used to replace obstructed sections of arteries. In time, new blood vessels grown in cell cultures, as well as in genetical-ly engineered animals, will be employed as substitutes for blocked or damaged human arteries. Or with special techniques, new arteries may be encouraged to grow within the person requiring them, providing blood flow to tissues that were lacking it. All of these advances will benefit midlifers and older people, for whom atherosclerosis causes so many problems. Moreover, in the future, it is also likely that various medications and gene therapy may greatly reduce the ubiquity and severity of atherosclerosis, eliminating blockage of the arteries and rendering many of these procedures unnecessary.

A half century ago, the transplantation of a human heart was viewed as science fiction, until Dr. Christian Barnard performed the first one in South Africa in 1967. Now, given the advances in drugs that suppress rejection, they are seen as extraordinary surgical feats, but achievable with a high rate of success. Heart transplants, employed only when a person's heart has been irreparably damaged and can no longer function effectively, replace the damaged heart with the heart of someone who has died from a non-cardiac cause. However, the utility of this operation has been limited by the small number of hearts available, with many good candidates dying before organs can be found. In the future, genetically engineered animal hearts (or hearts grown from our own cells) may be used to fill the need, though artificial mechanical hearts are also being developed and may ultimately serve as substitutes. Eventually, as the supply of hearts increases, older people who until now have not been considered for heart transplants may become candidates.

The Brain and Central Nervous System

The brain is a network of billions of interconnected neurons, with a multiplicity of pathways linking cells. Transplanting sections of the brain that are damaged or not working properly is not believed feasible. However, there are other ways to approach central nervous system problems. When transplanted into animal brains, stem cells harvested from various sources, both fetal and nonfetal, have been shown to migrate to damaged areas and replace some of the dead tissues. The significance of this is immense for people with neurological diseases or injuries, holding out the possibility their deficits may be able to be reduced in the future.[13] Potentially, these could be used in brains damaged by strokes, Parkinson's disease, Alzheimer's, and head trauma, and could restore severed pathways in spinal cord injuries.

However, finding susceptible individuals and cleaning out their blocked arteries before strokes happens will substantially reduce the incidence of stroke, the major cause of brain injuries. Medication may be given that prevents clots from forming in these vessels, or cholesterol and other blood lipids may be lowered so that atherosclerosis does not even begin. It may also be possible to use specific substances immediately after a stroke to protect brain tissues and minimize damage. Presently, arterial clots that cause strokes can be dissolved and function restored if a patient receives thrombolytic (clot dissolving) drugs quickly enough.[14] But if none of the above avenues have been successful, stem cells may be employed to repair brain areas that have been damaged or destroyed.

Compounds preventing the deposition of abnormal substances (beta amyloid and/or tau) in the brain may eliminate Alzheimer's disease. Studies in 2012 revealed that the changes of Alzheimer's begin at least twenty years before the disease is manifest.[15] This means prophylaxis is necessary early in life. Various biomarkers in blood, brain, and spinal fluid already alert investigators to patients' predilection to Alzheimer's.[16] Brain scans with special compounds can also diagnose Parkinson's disease now at an early stage. This may allow the disease to be halted by substances that preserve damaged cells. Transplants of primitive stem cells in involved regions of the brain may also be used to reconstitute neural pathways that have been lost. But in both Alzheimer's and Parkinson's diseases, gene therapy may ultimately be utilized to prevent the degenerative process from even starting.

Various treatments for multiple sclerosis are now available and generally successful in arresting the disease or slowing its progress. Actual cures for MS and for ALS (Lou Gehrig's Disease) remain evasive, but breakthroughs will likely occur in the next few decades. It can also be expected that genetic diseases such as Huntington's chorea will be solved through gene manipulation. One of the major causes of disability, traumatic brain injuries, may be lessened as new techniques replace damaged cells with transplants of stem cells that will evolve into the neurons needed. Implanted electrical stimulators will be employed to control seizures and tremors.

Mental Illness

Diseases that affect mood, thought processes, and behavior, including garden variety anxiety and depression, will also be better managed in the future with new medications, genetic modification, and possibly new behavioral techniques. Special types of brain imaging may be helpful in diagnosis and determining what medications should be utilized.

Sensory Systems

Techniques that improve hearing and vision will greatly enhance quality of life for many older people in the decades ahead. Some of the disorders that impair these senses are genetic in origin and may be treatable when the underlying abnormalities are elucidated. Others are caused by different types of injuries, either direct or indirect, that result in damage to the sensory organs. These can often be alleviated by replacement of the damaged part (a new lens after removing a cataract), or augmenting function still remaining (use of a hearing aid). These approaches should work even better as design of the substituted elements is further refined. On the horizon, the possibility also exists of replacing useless eyes and ears with small cameras or receivers that connect to the appropriate pathways in the brain to restore lost function. There has already been some experimental work with "artificial eyes" that are able to detect gross movement and black and white forms. In addition, certain compounds or new populations of cells placed in designated locations may be able to correct taste and smell, which decline with age.

Musculoskeletal System

Many of the problems in this area involve degenerative joint disease and arthritis that cause pain and limit activities. Joint replacement with artificial joints of metal and plastic is already a well-established option for people with these conditions. Usage will only increase as better joints are fabricated and operative techniques evolve. New substances may also be developed that retard wear and tear in the joints and strengthen joint cartilage. Implanting new cartilage from cell cultures into deteriorated joints may be effective as well in restoring mobility. Utilizing cells in the damaged joints to manufacture new cartilage is another mechanism that might prove efficacious.

Osteoporosis is presently being treated with various drugs that promote calcium deposition in the bones. Muscle weakness is common as well in older people, leading to the appearance of infirmity. In the future, through exercise programs and newer medications, osteoporosis will be reduced and muscle strength dramatically improved. Frailty and weakness in seniors will be replaced by vigor and robustness that will heighten self-esteem and permit activities previously abandoned. But much of this improvement will depend on the willingness of people to adopt exercise programs at an early age and stick to them.

Organ Replacement

Besides the heart, various organs such as the liver, kidney, lungs, or pancreas, which can be destroyed by infectious agents or chemicals, will be replaced more easily in the years ahead, allowing people with these damaged organs to survive into and through old age. The substitute organs may come from animals (pigs, sheep,) that are raised for this purpose, with genetic engineering to make the donor organs more compatible with the recipient. Growing these organs from the person's own cells in cell culture may also become feasible. Improvements in dialysis and artificial livers may be used as well to increase short- and long-term survival and better quality of life.

Laboratories have been able to culture primitive human stem cells capable of developing into many different types of mature cells. This heightens the possibility that specific tissues and even organs from particular individuals will be able to be produced in the laboratory using a person's own genetic material. These tissues or organs, with no danger of rejection, could then be surgically implanted back into the donors to substitute for malfunctioning organs. Initially, this scenario will occur in people who have seriously damaged vital organs. However, as the technique becomes more commonplace and less costly, it will be used to replace organs or tissues worn-out or less effective because of aging. Thus a person may ask for a new heart because he or she can't exercise as vigorously as in the past. Or an individual may request a skin graft for cosmetic reasons, because the skin is wrinkled and pigmented, even though it is still functional. The day will come when our own genetic material in newly grown cells and organs will be used routinely to rejuvenate each of us by replacing old or dysfunctional body parts.

Cancer

Cancer and the aging process appear to be interrelated problems currently being tackled in various scientific laboratories. Many researchers believe the secret of what makes cells cancerous will also reveal the mechanisms of aging. While surgery and chemotherapeutic agents may be successful now in curing specific cancers, they are crude treatment options. As the genetic abnormalities in different cancers are elucidated, treatments targeted to abnormal genes or proteins will be able to cure or arrest most of them. A number of cancers are already being controlled or cured by therapy that blocks enzyme systems necessary for the cancer cells to replicate. Targeted immunotherapy utilizing antibodies manufactured to attack particular cancer cells have also been successful in some patients and this approach will be enhanced in the future. (A study published in *JAMA* in 2012 suggests that multivitamins modestly reduces the total risk of cancer.[17])

As mentioned earlier, like a biologic clock and programmed with a finite number of divisions from the time the organism itself was conceived, the telomere in a cell's genetic material controls how many times that cell may divide. If this mechanism fails, then the cell becomes able to reproduce wildly and cancerous growth ensues. When scientists determine how telomeres work, they may possibly be able to reprogram normal cells and allow them to divide longer without becoming cancerous, replacing damaged cells with new ones to rejuvenate the recipient.

OTHER ASPECTS OF THE AGING PROCESS

Other aspects of aging need to be addressed as well to improve functioning and quality of life. Included are decrements in memory and cognition that occurs as we grow older, present in everyone to varying degrees. As we search for answers to Alzheimer's and dementia, we may find answers to the less severe impairment of memory and intellectual ability commonplace in normal aging. We may discover that particular nutrients, vitamins, or drugs are helpful in arresting or preventing cognitive decline by augmenting chemical transmission between neurons, by encouraging new connections (synapses) between these cells, or by growing new neurons. Or perhaps there is a genetic solution to this problem. Or perhaps an answer we have not even considered. Increasing amounts of research dollars in both the public and private spheres will be directed to this area in the years ahead. Only when this problem is solved and our minds are able to perform better as we age, will we be able to fully enjoy the extra time we have been granted.

Some preliminary studies suggest that metformin, the diabetes drug, may promote neurogenesis, the growth of neurons in the brain.[18] And another study notes that low-level light therapy may boost memory. Larger, more inclusive studies need to confirm these reports, but they are examples of research occurring in this area. An extremely sophisticated study conceived using carbon-14 dating of people's cells after the nuclear bomb testing that occurred between 1955 and 1963, showed that neurogenesis occurred in the hippocampus of the brain throughout the human lifespan.[19] This means that by finding ways to stimulate neurogenesis, we may be able to improve memory and cognitive abilities later in life.

Another question that needs to be answered is why some ninety-year-old people are able to live on their own and manage quite well, while others of the same age, though not demented or physically ill, need significant assistance. The reasons for these differences, when not the result of disease, have to be explored. Perhaps depression or mental outlook play a role. Or perhaps a brain center for initiative and self-reliance is more developed in some people.

In our quest for eternal youth, continued sexuality is part of the formula, as perceived by most individuals and by society. With different therapeutic measures now in use, sexual function in middle-aged and older people has been enhanced significantly and will only improve further with new medications. At some point perhaps, in our idealized world, we can imagine men and women one hundred years old, but looking young, making love, and rushing off to play tennis or some other activity, fully enjoying life after retirement.

An AARP publication a number of years ago summarized what we might all expect from medical science during the twenty-first century:

- A scan of your genetic structure (with billions of bits of data about the estimated 80,000 genes in your body) will detect symptoms or susceptibility to particular diseases.
- Nanobots (minuscule robots) will deliver medications to affected cells to prevent or treat disease. Or they will clear clogged arteries or repair damaged tissue.
- You will be able to have your checkup anywhere, anytime. You will have your vital signs tested by machines at the drugstore and send the results by the Internet to your doctor for analysis.

- Hospitals will fade away. A surgeon in Boston will do your hip replacement at your home in Cleveland via virtual reality. The doctor will view the surgical site on a screen and remotely manipulate surgical instruments inserted by a technician.
- Implanted biochips will monitor your vital signs, alerting you or your doctor to an impending crisis.
- Replacing diseased or worn-out body parts will be as routine as replacing auto parts today.[20]

The four ways survival and quality of life will be bolstered in the future include replacement of organs, genetic manipulation of cells, new drugs that work in various ways upon our cells, and lifestyle changes. Though the promise is there of greater longevity and a healthier, more rewarding life for all of us, self-destructive behavior by some individuals may negate the possibilities of new therapies and relegate these people to an early demise or significant disabilities. We each have to take care of our own bodies and cannot expect medical science to undo all the abuse to which we subject ourselves. The most obvious self-destructive behavior includes cigarette smoking, immoderate alcohol intake, and the use of drugs. Repeated dietary indiscretions, overeating, a sedentary lifestyle, and lack of physical exercise also exact a toll on our bodies. In addition, driving recklessly or at excessive speeds, taking physical risks or engaging in violence, can potentially result in severe injuries that can foreshorten life or make it less pleasurable—or even cause death. But if we act reasonably and show proper respect for our bodies, old age may be long and satisfying.

SOCIAL CHANGES

In the future, with seniors comprising a larger segment of our population, changes will occur in social mores and beliefs and the workings of society. Two factors guarantee a transformation. The first is the increased political power of older people because of their greater numbers and willingness to participate in the political process. The second is the heightened economic power of seniors, with an even higher proportion of national wealth controlled by them in the years ahead.

Older people will also learn how to better use their power. This means politicians will have to pay more attention to the needs of seniors and pass legislation that meets their expectations. In a time when national debt is soaring, this may be a difficult balancing act. American corporations will also aim more of their products at seniors and new businesses that cater to older people will come into being. Thus, the smart cars, smart homes, robotic companions, and other innovations we mentioned earlier are more likely to be developed and produced in quantity, as consumers will be ready and able to buy them. More mass entertainment will be directed toward seniors as well, with movies and television stressing themes of interest to older audiences. More programs for midlifers and seniors will be developed and streamed over the Internet and smart TVs. Advertising content on television and the radio will be directed at this demographic, with older men and women pitching products instead of young, nubile kids. This has started already with television ads for treatment of erectile dysfunction, osteoporosis, and elevated cholesterol. In Japan, a mall has been built that targets seniors, with products that invoke nostalgia or cater to older people's needs.[21] It has been extremely successful, and other similar ventures can be expected to follow.

Though society's attitudes toward older people may well improve in the future, some generational conflict can still be anticipated. Envy of seniors' wealth and influence will still exist, and some younger men and women will be confrontational and discourteous, as is true today. Another reason for animosity between the generations is that in the next few decades, smaller numbers of young people will be working to support greater numbers of seniors on Social Security and Medicare. Though the heightened productivity of American workers may make this sustainable for a while, some adjustments to entitlement programs will undoubtedly be necessary to insure that those needing Social Security will get it, without putting undue pressure on those still working.

The increase in life expectancy will raise questions about when people should retire and the suitability of mandatory retirement ages in the corporate world, academia, and government. If people live to one hundred twenty and are in good health, should they retire at age sixty-five? That would mean they would work an average of forty years and be retired an average of fifty-five years. (If current survival is to age seventy-nine, the numbers are forty and fourteen.) Not only would longer survival put a greater burden upon society to assist these retirees, but one can assume the retirees would be subject to boredom and malaise. However, if we allowed these individuals to keep working, maintaining their positions and seniority until age eighty or ninety, younger people would be frustrated by their inability to advance and assume leadership roles. And perhaps innovation would be stifled by having the same employees in place for years.

If they are cognitively and physically sound, older people should be able to work longer than the current retirement ages and setting a mandatory retirement age should depend on changes in life expectancy in the years ahead. Working longer, seniors would also have time to accumulate more wealth by putting money away in tax free retirement accounts and allowing it to compound. With people employed into their seventies and eighties, the Social Security system would be aided as well, as these workers would be putting more money into the fund, rather than taking it out. However, it would not be good policy to permit individuals to remain ensconced in specific jobs indefinitely, as that would be unfair to those below them and might lessen worker productivity. One solution to this problem might be to place limits on the length of time a person could continue in one position regardless of age, perhaps rotating people into different roles. This would insure upward and lateral mobility for everyone, and fresh approaches to management and problem solving.

Older people may also be encouraged to embark on second careers, even though they may have been on a particular track most of their lives. This may be in a completely divergent area, rather than an allied field. Many individuals may find satisfaction in new careers that are emotionally and socially productive, rather than financially lucrative, especially if they have been well compensated before; for example, teaching or social work instead of investment banking. Or if they had been in low paying service jobs previously, after returning to school or receiving additional training, they could opt for something that was more economically rewarding. Perhaps some financially secure people may perform volunteer work, or help out nonprofit agencies without remuneration. Or they may work for political parties or special interest groups, or fulfill creative impulses. Though currently, people-oriented jobs rather than technical ones appear to be the strong suit of those we call seniors, in the future, enhanced cognitive function should allow older people to handle the most intellectually demanding positions.

Some researchers in gerontology and cell biology believe human life expectancies of 160 to 180 years are feasible, with good qualities of life for most people. If they are correct, think of what this might portend for the Social Security system, or the allocation of time between work and retirement. Yet, we may find there are fewer available jobs for everyone because of increased productivity fueled by the computer revolution, which permits businesses and government to operate with fewer personnel. Then the priority would have to be employment for younger people to stem any social unrest. Indeed, society may actually have to create make-work jobs to keep people occupied. However, the number of individuals in service jobs can certainly be increased to provide better levels of assistance, even though that increase may neither be absolutely necessary, nor help the corporate bottom line. And older people could play a role here. With more teachers, we could reduce class sizes to help students learn. With more doctors and nurses, each would be able to spend more time with patients. With more salesclerks, each would be able to pay more attention to customers. And more computer support personnel would cut waiting time and provide greater support. Though hiring all these people would be costly, society would benefit greatly from this expense.

Continuing Education

Currently, we attend school during childhood and our early adult years, perhaps taking a course here and there afterward. However, it might make sense as we live longer lives, to return to school periodically, not only to improve skills in our chosen fields, but to learn about living, with courses in the humanities, philosophy, literature, and psychology. We would derive so much more out of these subjects in the light of our life experiences. Studying would also give us opportunities to explore new areas of interest and possibly discover new careers. We might envision a year or two of further university study for those who desired it at ages forty to forty-five, sixty to sixty-five, and eighty to eighty-five, or at any age. While people could take courses over the Internet, it would be preferable for individuals to return to the classroom, where there would be social interaction with new people and stimulating discourse. Corporations might even encourage employees to take these study sabbaticals, then return to work fresh and invigorated. Many people already pursue lifelong learning, which should be supported.

Leisure Time

Regardless of measures taken to increase the number of jobs, in the future, people will have huge amounts of additional leisure time that they must find ways to fill. Particularly for those living into their nineties, hundreds, and beyond, this will be the overwhelming fact of their lives—a challenge that individuals must meet themselves, with the help of society. Playing golf or cards every day for fifty or sixty years will not be enough for most older people, who will want to use their minds and bodies more productively. Perhaps there will be special schools and training centers set up for seniors (who would actually be considered middle-aged), with counselors, therapists, and teachers to assist them in finding activities that are rewarding and make their extra years of life satisfying.

The world of today is due for major changes.

11

DOING IT YOUR WAY—PREPARING FOR LIFE'S END

For what is it to die but to stand naked in the wind and to melt into the sun?
And what is it to cease breathing, but to free the breath from its restless tides,
that it may rise and expand and seek God unencumbered?

—Kahlil Gibran[1]

Most of us hope death will visit us while we are sleeping. We imagine going to bed one night when we are old and simply not awakening the next morning. Unfortunately, for the vast majority, death does not follow this script. For some, there may even be a slow process of weeks to months to years of illness and deterioration before death intervenes. Not that overt pain is a problem, as that can be controlled. Rather there is a cumulative loss of function and an inability to manage our daily tasks. If our minds remain unscathed during this period, depression may be part of the process, because of the realization we are steadily declining.

Living well as we age also requires preparation for the end of life. Two aspects must be considered. The first is when to withdraw therapy and life support if we are being treated for a grave illness and will not recover. This requires advance directives that detail our end-of-life decisions, to be implemented if we are cognitively impaired or otherwise unable to decide ourselves. By doing this, we make it more likely we will not be kept alive in circumstances that would be repugnant to us, such as in a persistent vegetative state (PVS), or with terminal cancer, severe dementia, and so forth. The second is the possibility of arranging to die if our quality of life does not meet a minimum standard we have set for ourselves and we conclude it is no longer worth living. In making this kind of decision and acting upon it, we must have the knowledge and means to do so successfully, for a failed attempt may result in a further erosion of our status.

There are some individuals however, who cannot or will not contemplate dying, no matter what their situations might be. They may even expect continuation of life support when brain death has been certified, or insist on cardiopulmonary resuscitation when the prognosis is hopeless. Religion may be causing some of them to hold on to any thread of life, a fear of dying may motivate others to reject the cessation of medical care. There are also people who fear not only death itself, but also that mistakes might have been made by the medical community, and notwithstanding assurances, they may be permitted to die without having had a fatal illness. More often, however, when a patient is terminally ill, that person and/or the family gradually accept the inevitability of death. This is usually coupled with a reluctant willingness to allow it to occur, or even hasten its arrival.

SOCIAL CONSEQUENCES OF CHOOSING TO DIE

Choosing to end our lives when quality of life is poor and the outlook is bleak, not only affects ourselves and our families, but also impacts society in general. Because society has a limited amount of funds for medical care, if we are sick and consuming medical services, electing to die saves money that can be allocated to others. Thus, the choice by someone with a terminal illness to be taken off a ventilator and removed from the Intensive Care Unit can result in considerable savings, as can stopping renal dialysis if a person has complications of end-stage kidney disease. An individual's decision to die may allow physicians, nurses, and other medical personnel to spend more time with other patients needing care. It may also free up beds in hospital ICUs that others can utilize.

In other nations, older people often do not have an option to receive the medical care we allow. The society rather than the individual chooses whether to provide care to keep a person alive. In other words, there is rationing of medical services. This is true not only in Third

World nations where expenditures on health care are minimal, but also in developed countries with high standards of living, where it is considered too expensive to permit every person to have every medical service, regardless of age, physical, and cognitive status. Of course, using age alone as a parameter can result in arbitrary decisions that may not make sense, and an individual's overall condition should be factored into any choices of whether to provide particular types of therapy.

The Debate over Choosing to Die

Some people and groups believe for religious reasons or reasons of conscience that allowing someone to choose to die cheapens all life. They hold that life is sacred and people should be kept alive by every means possible for as long as possible, notwithstanding the cost (economic, emotional, physical) to that person, his or her family, and society. They insist that physicians should never stop caring for anyone whose heart is still beating, no matter how futile circumstances may seem. This is not a realistic way to approach end-of-life decisions, but these people do not want any decisions to be made as life winds down— merely aggressive treatment and life support until the very end. It should be remembered, however, that choosing to die is not euthanasia. It is the individual making the choice for him or herself, not society imposing its will upon helpless people.

Part of the difficulty in the debate over whether or not to sustain life is how to actually define human life and death. Pro-lifers interpret death as the cessation of a person's heartbeat, and until that point, consider him or her alive. Others, including most of the medical establishment, believe that brain function is a better determinant of whether someone is alive, with "brain death" indicating no possibility of an individual surviving independently, even if the heart continues beating for hours, days, or months. Precise physiologic criteria that have achieved general acceptance in the medical community are utilized to ascertain brain death and usually result in the withdrawal of life support.

However, in other situations that don't fit into the category of brain death, brain function may be severely compromised, the person's quality of life is extremely poor, and the possibility of independent living has been eliminated. Most notably, this includes persistent vegetative states (PVS), in which the thinking part of the brain is irreversibly damaged and the person exists on a primitive level, not interacting meaningfully with his or her environment. Karen Ann Quinlan and a number of other well-known cases are examples of people with PVS. A question can be raised as to whether these unfortunates should be considered alive when they are incapable of thinking. This is more an ethical, philosophical, and religious question than a medical one. But if someone has previously made a decision not to continue living in this state, should any group or individuals be permitted to interfere with that choice?

There are additional circumstances as well in which a person may not be brain dead but is severely impaired and has previously requested he or she not be kept alive in this condition. One of these are major strokes, which may result in someone's being paralyzed on one side of his or her body, unable to speak, or unable to understand. Another is an entity known as the "locked in" syndrome where a brain stem stroke paralyzes someone completely. Though cognitive ability remains intact, the only way the person can communicate is through eye blinking. A third might be a spinal cord stroke or injury that can leave a person quadriplegic (paralyzed in all four extremities), though able to speak. The actor Christopher Reeves had this occur after a fall from a horse. Though he elected to continue his life, an older person, or one with less financial resources might not be willing to take the same path and might ask to be allowed to die. An individual might also prefer dying to living with an advanced dementia, unable to comprehend anything about his or her circumstances or relate meaningfully to friends and family. People might want to die sooner as well with various terminal afflictions, such as metastatic cancer or ALS (Lou Gehrig's Disease), instead of watching themselves slowly deteriorate.

Futile Care

The converse issue is "futile care," where a patient or family wants treatment given or the person maintained in a hopeless situation. As medical science has advanced and people have been kept alive with serious illnesses, doctors have been wrestling with a concept known as "medical futility": a patient has a terminal or preterminal condition that cannot be corrected by therapeutic intervention. According to one definition, "futile treatment might be thought to include those that, even when successful, provide a quality of life well below a threshold considered minimal, or those in which the likelihood of achieving medical goals is exceedingly low. . . . Medical treatment is futile if it has less than 1 chance in 100 of success or if it merely preserves unconsciousness or dependence on intensive medical care."[2] Should physicians render "futile care" if patients or families request it? This would obviously squander money and resources on individuals who cannot be helped. Indeed, most physicians now will not provide care if they consider it futile, but if patients have advance directives spelling out their desires, it can make it easier to stop treatment. If families choose to fight the medical decision to withdraw life support through the courts, they may be able to significantly delay the process if there are no advance directives.

The Physician's Role in Dying

In terms of acquiescing to a person's wishes and hastening his or her death, physicians can play active, or passive roles. By *active* we mean actually doing something affecting the patient's survival, whereas *passive* means doing nothing (which may also affect the patient's survival). Though most physicians find the latter preferable and less conflicting, they may play active roles in certain circumstances. Actively helping a person to die, at times falls into the realm of "physician-assisted suicide." This is illegal in the United States aside from Oregon, which passed the Death with Dignity Act in 1994, and several other states. Dr. Jack Kevorkian, who had been assisting patient suicide in Michigan, was convicted of manslaughter and sent to jail. Legality aside, many physicians hasten patients' death when they have terminal illnesses or conditions causing undue suffering. This occurs through what is known as the "principle of double effect therapy": a medication may work in two opposite ways—beneficially by relieving anxiety and pain, and harmfully by interfering with breathing. In a hospital setting, physicians may order sedative or pain control medications that also depress respiration and brain function in high doses, leading to comatose states and eventually death. For patients outside hospitals with terminal illnesses, physicians may prescribe similar compounds.

Withdrawing medications that sustain someone's life puts the physician in an active role, but cannot be regarded as assisted suicide. A physician also actively intercedes in measures keeping a person alive if he or she stops ventilatory support, renal dialysis, or other interventions necessary for life. (Of course, if patients have incurable illnesses and want to die, physicians are merely following their wishes.) However, it is much easier playing a passive role in helping patients die, from the standpoint of both physician misgivings and of potential legal liability. This may involve not starting particular therapies rather than withdrawing them. It may appear there's little difference between the two courses, but there is a wide gap emotionally for many physicians. Medical ethicists also differentiate between the two approaches.

Because of natural inclination, previous teaching, or religious faith, some physicians have difficulty making decisions that might hasten a patient's demise. In the past, doctors were trained to believe their role was to preserve life without any qualifications and that this determined their success. Only in the last few decades have medical schools begun to understand that good physicians can't reflexly prolong everyone's life without considering its quality and have given courses on medical ethics that dissect end-of-life care. But some doctors still give undue weight to survival alone in assessing therapy and not enough to the condition in which the patient is surviving.

Terminal Dehydration

If a patient is suffering or has a terminal illness, there are various other ways death can be accelerated, both with and without the aid of physicians. One method gaining acceptance is that of terminal dehydration. Cessation of all intake of fluids and food will result in death within a short period and can be done voluntarily by patients who are cognitively intact and wish to gain control over the dying process. Death will usually occur in days to weeks, depending on the patient's reserves and overall condition. Aside from some mild initial discomfort, this method of dying does not cause significant pain or suffering. A deficiency of food and fluids is also the natural way most people die when they have serious illnesses and no access to modern care. Providing nutrients to patients with no appetites, experiencing nausea and vomiting, or who are just too sick to eat can be viewed as being contrary to nature.

In instances when the patient is comatose or incapable of making the decision to stop all fluids and food, and has previously expressed a desire not to live in the state he or she is in, the family or health care agent may choose terminal dehydration as a way to hasten death, if the prognosis is for a prolonged course of weeks to months. In this situation, there should be agreement by the physician and family there is no chance of recovery and the patient would have wanted to take this path. When this occurs in a hospital setting, the choice should be thoroughly documented to preclude legal problems later on.

Hospice Care

When someone has a terminal illness and death is expected within weeks or months, if the patient does not wish to accelerate death, hospice is a reasonable alternative. The patient can receive palliative care and be made comfortable, while being allowed to come to terms with dying. This care includes emotional support from the hospice staff who are accustomed to dealing with dying patients. The time spent in the hospice setting also provides an opportunity for the family to communicate with the loved one who is dying, to express their love, and to learn to accept what is happening. In most areas, hospice care can also be arranged at the patient's home.

PLANNING FOR THE END OF LIFE

If we all remained in command of our faculties until we were ready to die, planning ahead would be unnecessary. Unfortunately, this is often not the case. We may become cognitively impaired months or even years before death is on the horizon, or we may be comatose, stuporous, or confused when the time is at hand to make decisions regarding life and death. For these reasons, it is important to spell out those circumstances in which we wish to be kept alive and those in which we wish to be allowed to die, also noting whether particular methods of dying are acceptable (terminal sedation or dehydration). If this is not done, we effectively lose control over the process of dying and measures may be taken against our religious beliefs, moral or ethical sensibilities, emotional leanings, or intellectual convictions. This can happen whether our family members are making the decisions, or physicians with whom we may have had a passing acquaintance.

Ideally, we should plan for death in terms of living wills and choose health care advocates when we are healthy and able to make rational judgments, unclouded by physical disease, intellectual decline, or emotional illness. But it is not easy to talk about our deaths and how we wish to be cared for, and frequently people are unwilling to focus on dying when in good health. The shock of illness or the death of friends or family members may galvanize us into action and force us to consider how we ourselves want to deal with dying.

The steps we take in terms of preparing living wills and detailing our wishes to a health care agent often depends on our level of sophistication and social environment. Those who have not gone far in school, or are not aware of the problems encountered in the course of dying, frequently do not consider this type of planning. And if other people in our community—our friends and peers—are neither making advance directives, nor specifying the kind of care they expect in various situations, then we are less likely to do so ourselves. Even if we live in a rural area without a modern medical facility, we could wind up on a ventilator at a hospital hundreds of miles away, or a nursing home in another city, being kept alive in a demented and incontinent state. No matter what our neighbors and family are doing, to remain in control of what happens to us, we should plan ourselves for our period of decline and dying.

(Note: It is also worthwhile for each of us to have executed an ordinary will as we grow older. Whether we have significant wealth or material possessions, by composing a will we know our families will not fight over our property after we are gone and that cherished items will go to the people we want to get them. A will also provides a method for us to express our love to those important to us. Absence of a will may also tie up estates for long periods, not allow those who need it to use the money, and permit lawyers to extract hefty fees.)

Advance Directives

Medical progress over the last half century has made advance directives a necessity for everyone. Death no longer occurs suddenly for most people, a catastrophic event due to the cessation of a heartbeat and respiration. Instead, medical intervention often delays inevitable demise. The widespread use of CPR (cardiopulmonary resuscitation) and the development of the medical ICU have resulted in maintenance of innumerable patients on life support after they have suffered devastating anoxic brain damage, and have no hope of long-term survival or useful lives. Patients with incurable metastatic cancer or other debilitating or fatal illnesses, or who have suffered massive strokes, may also be kept alive through artificial means, even though the outlook for them is grim. And newer drugs, machines, and treatment regimens have further enabled physicians to sustain life in questionable circumstances. (Life sustaining treatments are utilized to replace or support a failing essential bodily function necessary to keep you alive. For example, a ventilator [respirator] supports or replaces breathing; dialysis cleans the blood when kidney failure is present.) Because of these developments, many of us may face the possibility of lingering in a state abhorrent to us, causing emotional distress for our families, while draining financial resources. Death with dignity entails choosing which support mechanisms are acceptable to us and defining when they may be utilized.

Life-sustaining treatments are certainly worthwhile on a temporary basis if they will help us survive for a period afterward in a condition we deem reasonable. Thus, a ventilator might assist us in breathing during an acute illness such as pneumonia, until our lungs start working again. However, if there is no hope of restoration of normal function at any point in the future and our survival will be dependent indefinitely on life support, questions arise of whether to initiate or continue these types of treatment. Similarly, if we have an underlying condition that will soon be fatal, or one that has severely reduced our quality of life, treatment to sustain life may not be deemed beneficial.

In the past, operating under a paternalistic medical system, physicians made the life and death decisions for patients, choosing treatments they thought in the patient's best interest. (Of course, life support was not an issue in those days.) Gradually however, this course of action was supplanted by the idea that patients, after the options are explained, have the right to determine what medical care they will or will not receive. With extension of life now commonplace with modern technology, people have to make choices previously unnecessary— about which measures they wish to be taken and in which circumstances, to allow them to survive.

Advance directives are documents that establish how we want to be treated by physicians, other medical caregivers, and family members, before and during the time we are dying, if our condition prevents us from making our wishes known. These documents encompass two types of statements—living wills and health care proxies. If we are conscious and cognitively intact during the period when we are dying, our written instructions will be superseded by our expressed desires, but our directives will come into play if we are intellectually compromised or unable to communicate. The Patient Self-Determination Act passed by Congress in 1990, requires hospitals and nursing homes to discuss advance directives with us whenever we are admitted to one of these institutions and to provide us with help if we want to put them into effect. However, it is not prudent for any of us to delay creating advance directives until hospital admission, as our status at that time might preclude studied deliberation and completion of these documents. Every person over fifty, no matter how healthy, should have these instructions in place, in case unforeseen accidents or illnesses occur. The forms commonly used can be obtained from local hospitals or nursing homes, home care agencies, or social workers, or through organizations such as Partnership For Caring. (There is not a standard document as there are differences in content from state to state.)

Once the forms are acquired, most individuals (if not cognitively impaired) can execute advance medical directives without legal assistance or special help. However, it is important to discuss our intentions with our spouses, children, and anyone who we might designate as our health care advocate, receiving feedback from them as we explain our requests, to be certain those requests are not unreasonable. We should also try to understand our advocates' feelings about the instructions we are giving and whether they will be comfortable carrying them out. In many states, signing of the documents may require witnesses and possibly participation of a notary public to make them binding. But whatever advance directives we record, they do not have to remain in effect in perpetuity. If at any point we change our minds about any of the provisions, we can easily rescind them and rewrite them to reflect our new wishes. In fact, it is probably worthwhile for us to review them periodically, to be certain they are still in accord with our current beliefs.

Advance directives are derived from the concept that each of us has the right to accept or reject any medical care after discussion of the pros and cons of that therapy with our physicians. But because of the possibility our reasoning powers may be compromised at the point when decisions have to be made about various types of treatment, our orders about health care have to be in place before they are needed—thus *advance* directives. Indeed, with most of us living longer now and with the incidence of dementia increasing as a byproduct of longevity, our cognitive abilities have a greater chance of being diminished before we die. Thus, by constructing a living will and health care proxy (advance directives) when we are healthy and clear minded, our desires regarding end-of-life options can be carried out later on.

In the early decades of the twentieth century, most of us died in our homes, surrounded by families and loved ones. Today, few people find themselves in this scenario. "Research has shown that 80 percent of us will die in a medical facility such as a hospital or nursing home,"[3] though the percentage has dropped slightly in the last decade. And given the frequent dispersion of family members around the country, there may be no close relatives available when we become seriously ill. Our children may not be aware of our wishes about life and death anyway, unless they've been specifically discussed. In addition, our caregivers may not be longstanding family physicians who know our way of thinking, but instead strangers designated to treat us. Hospitalists, subspecialists, and other new physicians with whom we have no history, may not have the time to learn our thoughts about dying. Many of these subspecialists are interested in preserving life and at times may ignore the issue of quality of life. In fact, their competence may be measured according to the survival rates of their patients, reinforcing their need to prevent us from dying. Having clear instructions on when and how we wish to live or be allowed to die, will give us, instead of a physician who may have a conflict of interest, the final say about what is to be done.

That a conflict might exist was brought home to me by a surgeon who had done amputations of parts of all of a middle-aged woman's limbs because of gangrene from an overwhelming infection (septicemia) that had also severely injured her brain. Though the patient was in a persistent vegetative state on a respirator for months afterward, the surgeon refused to discontinue the respirator to allow her to die.

Similar problems may arise if we are relegated to a nursing home that is paid as long as we are alive, whatever our condition may be. Their staff did not know us previously when we were vibrant, intact human beings, fully independent and unwilling to live in any other manner. I have seen many instances of patients with severe dementia, or paralysis and aphasia (inability to speak) from strokes, with incontinence and contractures of their extremities, treated for intercurrent illnesses (such as with antibiotics to combat pneumonia), rather than being permitted to die peacefully. Ideally, this should not happen with advance directives in place.

Unfortunately, the circumstances advance directives encompass are extremely complex and no matter how carefully these are crafted, some situations will not be covered. That is why a health care advocate should also be available to make decisions in areas that have not been included in the advance directive. Theoretically, as noted by Dr. Alan Lieberson in his reference book *Advance Directives*, the following five clinical situations that should be addressed:

1. Terminal conditions, (like cancer)
2. Persistent unconsciousness,
3. Progressive dementias, (like Alzheimer's disease)
4. Sudden extensive physical incapacity associated with limitations of mental function, (like strokes)
5. Chronic irreversible disease states.[4]

In addition, there are seven therapeutic modalities that must be considered:

1. Mechanical devices,
2. Medical therapeutics,
3. Surgery,
4. Diagnostic procedures,
5. Cardiopulmonary resuscitation,
6. Management of pain and discomfort,
7. Artificially administered nutrition and hydration.[5]

Obviously, it is not an easy task to have all-inclusive instructions, though it is important to do the best we can, projecting the essence of our beliefs. If a situation is not covered by our living will, our health care advocate can see to it our wishes are observed.

Living Wills

Common law has long held that any person of sound mind has the right to refuse medical treatment. The concept of living wills originated in the 1960s as medical technology became increasingly capable of prolonging life for extended periods in situations where many people would prefer not to be kept alive, but were unable to make their wishes known. In the mid-1970s, the first living will statute was passed by the California state legislature, with most, but not all states subsequently following California's lead. These statutes vary considerably from state to state in terms of what they are called, when they go into effect, and what treatments are covered. Notwithstanding their variability, they all provide immunity to physicians from criminal and civil actions when they observe a patient's instructions, even if this results in that person's premature death.

Stated simply, "a living will is a type of advance directive in which you put in writing your wishes about the medical treatment you desire at the end of your life in the event you are unable to communicate these wishes directly."[6] It becomes operative if we have a fatal condition and death is expected shortly, or if we are in an irreversible coma or persistent vegetative state. In most states two physicians must certify our status. The more explicit we are about our desires, the easier it may be when we are dying for medical professionals to adhere to them. Family and health care agents should be involved in the writing of living wills since they will be playing roles in the decisions when we are dying.

I will give an example of part of a living will used in Connecticut to show how these documents are structured.

LIVING WILL

If the time comes when I am incapacitated to the point when I can no longer actively take part in decisions for my own life, and am unable to direct my physician as to my own medical care, I wish this statement to stand as a testament of my wishes.

I, [name], the author of this document, requests that, if my condition is deemed terminal, or if I am determined to be permanently unconscious, I be allowed to die and not be kept alive through life support systems. By terminal condition, I mean that I have an incurable or irreversible medical condition which, without the administration of life support systems, will, in the opinion of my attending physician, result in death within a relatively short time. By permanently unconscious I mean that I am in a permanent coma or persistent vegetative state which is an irreversible condition in which I am at no time aware of myself or the environment and show no behavioral response to the environment.

Specific Instructions:

Listed below are my instructions regarding particular types of life support systems. This list is not all-inclusive. My general statement that I not be kept alive through life support systems provided to me is limited only where I have indicated that I desire a particular treatment to be provided

	Provide	Withhold
Cardiopulmonary Resuscitation	_____	_____
Artificial Respiration (including a respirator)	_____	_____
Artificial means of providing nutrition and hydration	_____	_____
_____	_____	_____
_____	_____	_____

Other specific requests:

I do want sufficient pain medication to maintain my physical comfort. I do not intend any direct taking of my life, but only that my dying not be unreasonably prolonged.[7]

In addition to what is shown above, the Connecticut living will also has a section for appointment of a health care agent to stand in for the patient if he or she is unconscious or incompetent, to insure the person's wishes are observed. There are also sections for the appointment of an alternative health care agent, documentation of an anatomical gift, designation of a conservator of the person and an alternative conservator, and affirmation by two adult witnesses. The witnesses are required to show that our cognitive abilities are sufficient for us to comprehend the declaration we are signing. In the section for other specific requests, it is worthwhile listing any additional types of therapy we wish to be withheld that might sustain life, such as antibiotics, blood transfusions, chemotherapy, or surgical procedures. An emphasis should also be placed on the desire to achieve adequate pain control to alleviate any major distress or suffering we might experience, even if it accelerates death (double effect). It is also valuable to have a statement in our living wills giving our health care agents the right to interpret our instructions and determine how they might be best carried out.

Attempts have been made at developing a universal structure for living wills throughout the United States in the hope that with simplification, a greater proportion of the citizenry would complete these documents. The National Conference of Commissioners on Uniform State Laws produced the Uniform Rights of the Terminally Ill Act (URTIA) in 1985[8] (revised 1989) as a guideline for state legislatures to move to a common format for living wills and health care proxies. A number of states subsequently enacted URTIA, but many have not. However, because of its simplicity, there is some ambiguity in its definitions and it does not necessarily cover all areas of concern. If these forms are utilized, it is essential to elaborate further.

Having our wishes regarding dying carefully delineated in our living wills should make it easier for our health care agents and family members to deal with the process of our dying. Ideally, it lessens the burden of guilt on loved ones and reduces conflicts among family members as they have to follow our instructions about terminating life support.

Medical Power of Attorney

"A medical power of attorney is a document that lets you appoint someone you trust to make your decisions about medical care if you cannot do so yourself."[9] It is also known as a *health care proxy, durable power of attorney for health care*, or *appointment of a health care agent*. If our condition does not allow us to make our own decisions, the designated person acts as a surrogate for us in matters involving health care. Those chosen as our agents may be spouses, children, other family members, or close friends, but should always be someone knowledgeable about our desires regarding end-of-life care.

As an example of the form that might be utilized for appointing a health care agent, I am reprinting the one used in Connecticut[10] that is part of the living will.

Appointment of Health Care Agent

I appoint [health care agent], [telephone number], to be my health care agent. If my attending physician determines that I am unable to understand and appreciate the nature and consequences of health care decisions and unable to reach and communicate an informed decision regarding treatment,

[Health care agent] is authorized to:

1. Convey to my physician my wishes concerning the withholding or removal of life support systems;
2. Take whatever actions are necessary to insure that any wishes are given effect.

The exact document necessary to designate a health care agent also varies from state to state, including the need for witnesses, notarizing, and the number of physicians who must attest to our inability to comprehend health care decisions, and so forth.

When specifying health care agents, it is important to remember that these people may have to make choices about us regarding life and death. While it may be easiest to appoint a close family member to this position, we do not want someone overly emotional, or who may be overcome by grief, or who may feel guilty about this role, or who may have difficulty following our instructions for other reasons. By presenting our beliefs and the available options regarding the process of dying to this person beforehand, we can get a better understanding of how he or she might react, and whether we want him or her to be given this responsibility. If the discussion includes other family members and/or close friends, the health care agent may have a support apparatus in place when decisions have to be made. In addition, the health care agent should be someone who is not intimidated by physicians or figures of authority and who would be willing to advocate for our beliefs.

When our advance directives (living will and medical power of attorney) are complete, copies should be made and given to our health care agents, family members, physicians, clergy, and other professionals who may be involved in our care. The documents that remain in our possession should be placed in a safe but readily accessible niche, to be available for scrutiny if we are incapacitated. Upon admission to a hospital or nursing home, copies of our directives should be entered into the medical records.

Unfortunately, our instructions may not be followed in emergencies outside the hospital, even if our condition is hopeless. Emergency medical technicians (EMTs) and ambulance personnel must administer cardiopulmonary resuscitation (CPR) to all people they are called to see who have stopped breathing or had a cardiac arrest. Specific signed orders from a physician (non-hospital do-not-resuscitate orders) may prevent this, if someone is present to show these orders to the EMTs, but it is not mandatory that these orders be observed in all states.

In my neurologic practice of over forty years, the value of advance directives in managing end-of-life care has been evident on a number of occasions. As one example, several years ago, a ninety-year-old woman was brought to the hospital with a massive cerebral hemorrhage, causing right-sided paralysis and coma. She had no living will or health care advocate. In the Emergency Room after her CT scan, she had a respiratory arrest, was intubated and placed on a ventilator. I explained to her two daughters the situation was hopeless and suggested we take her off the ventilator and allow her to die. One daughter agreed, but the other insisted that everything possible be done for her mother. Because of this, the patient was moved to the ICU and kept on life support for another six days before she finally expired. With advance directives, she would have been allowed to die in the Emergency Room.

CHOOSING TO DIE

> Death, be not proud, though some have called thee
> Mighty and dreadful, for thou art not so;
> —John Donne[11]

For each of us, the pendulum swings between pleasure and pain, happiness and sadness, health and illness, as part of the normal rhythm of life. Whenever the motion carries us to pain or illness, we take solace knowing our situation is only temporary and that the pendulum will swing back in the other direction at some point. Though for many individuals there may be a tilt toward one pole or the other and not a complete balance between competing elements, we can usually anticipate that movement away from physical or emotional discomfort will be forthcoming. But what if a time comes when the motion ceases and we are trapped in a quagmire of pain and suffering from which we see no escape? Or we have a debilitating illness that will only progress? Or there is nothing ahead in our lives that promises even a modicum of joy?

When the totality of pain and suffering in one's existence outweighs pleasure and happiness, and there is no possibility of change on the horizon, most people would agree that life is no longer worth living. In those circumstances, at least for many of us, death is a logical choice, and by our own hand if there is no other way. "Rational suicide" can allow us to control when we die, when continuing to live might entail greater dependency on people or medications, inability to perform simple tasks for ourselves, loss of mastery over bodily functions, or loss of mental acuity and our own autonomy.

(I am not advocating rational suicide for anyone, or in any particular circumstances. It is being presented as an option for those who desire it if they believe conditions warrant it.)

Death should never be chosen hastily, but only by a slow deliberative process, that allows for mood changes to serve as a restraint. The longer we take to make our decisions before acting, the greater the chances we will choose wisely. The decision to end one's life should also not be made during or immediately after an acute crisis, when one might not be able to accurately assess the quality of one's life and what the future holds. Similarly, it is not a choice that should be made or acted upon during a period of depression, when one sees life through a dark lens, with an outlook not necessarily realistic. When we're depressed, things seem hopeless and we feel worthless, which distorts our view of the world. (However, if in an older person, the cloud of depression does not lift after a long passage of time and quality of life is severely compromised, perhaps suicide is not unreasonable.)

It is important that we discuss what we are contemplating with our families and friends before proceeding, both to give them the opportunity to talk us out of it, and also to spare them from shock and surprise. Family members and friends may be able to project a truer picture for us of our own situation, as well as future expectations, as they may spot flaws in our thinking we cannot see. Thus, they may try to convince us we are making a mistake, or they may be supportive and reinforce our choice. But whatever we think they might tell us, and whether or not they might try to prevent us from acting, we owe it to our loved ones to let them know what is on our minds, before we take that final step.

Before ending our lives, we should also speak about our concerns with professionals, particularly those who deal with dying. If we are experiencing excessive physical pain, our physicians may be able to alleviate it with medication if they are aware of what is happening, eliminating the necessity for suicide. If the anguish is emotional, medication may be of some benefit as well, but discourse with a trained therapist may be even more valuable. (A psychotherapist may not always be required. The primary care physician, oncologist, oncology nurse practitioner, social worker, or visiting nurse can also be effective in this role.) Sometimes, group therapy involving other people with the same or similar problems may help us recognize we are not unique and may reduce our anger and anxiety.

In addition, our attorneys should be informed if we are considering suicide. We want to be sure our will and legal documents are in order, so that our estate will not be tied up after our deaths, causing additional difficulties for our loved ones. We should also inquire whether our insurance policies would be voided if we killed ourselves, penalizing our heirs. (There is usually a waiting period after a policy is issued before they will pay death benefits for suicide.) If we are worried about the financial burden generated by our illness and the process of dying, our lawyers might be able to find ways to help us relieve that concern. For instance, some life insurance policies can be cashed in (for less than full value) before death if someone has a terminal illness and is expected to die within a short period.

Our thoughts about suicide, the hardships of living, and the reasons we want to die should also be discussed with our clergymen and religious guides before acting. Though they might be expected to discourage us from taking our life, if our faith matters to us, it would be important to know their viewpoints on this issue, as we might not want to do anything contrary to religious doctrine. Some religions have admonitions against suicide, proposing that salvation will be withheld from those who kill themselves. Many religions also accept man's suffering as God's will and a normal part of living, and do not see physical or emotional pain, or an incurable illness, as a valid reason for suicide. They can point to Job in the Old Testament as a model for extreme suffering who still did not kill himself, or renounce God.

> Man that is born of woman
> Is of few days, and full of trouble.

He cometh forth like a flower, and withereth.
                              —Book of Job 14:1 [12]

No stone should go unturned before we make our final decision and opt
for suicide. Before acting, we must reaffirm in our own minds that we
are making the right choice.

Why Choose Death?

As we have shown, if the pain in our lives outweighs pleasure and there
is little chance of change, or if we have an incurable illness that is
unbearable, death may be a reasonable way out. It is not a path for
everyone, but an elective planned death can be more fulfilling for both
the person and his or her family than one prolonged and filled with
agony and unhappiness. This decision allows loved ones to say their
goodbyes and remember the dying person while he or she is alert and
able to communicate, rather than confused or in a narcotic stupor. But
being able to take one's life entails being able to evaluate the circumstances and make the choice, then plan the action and follow it through
to completion. Thus an individual who is bedridden cannot take an
overdose of narcotics without someone's assistance. Or a person too
weak to walk cannot go out into the garage and turn on the car to die of
carbon monoxide poisoning.

Even if we are free of major diseases or overwhelming pain, there
might be other instances that would lead us to contemplate ending our
lives. As we age, with each passing year, we lose a small percentage of
what we were previously able to do. (These were discussed in the chapter on losses.) Included are mobility, cognitive function, cardiac activity,
pulmonary function, visual and auditory acuity, sexual ability, urinary
and bowel control, and so forth. At which point do these cumulative
insults add up to make life enough of a burden we no longer wish to
bear?

Growing older may also mean the deaths of spouses, friends, and
peers. If we live long enough and have no children, we may find ourselves totally alone, with no friends and no relatives; with no one who
cares for us and no one about whom we care. For most of us, interaction with friends and loved ones is pleasurable and provides us with
something to which we can look forward. Their absence can make it
difficult for us to continue our daily routines and plodding existence,

draining away energy and resolve. Even having children, grandchildren, and other relatives, we may still feel alone if they are distant and there are no opportunities to see them regularly. And our feelings of loneliness combined with a deteriorated physical state and limited activity may cause us to speculate about dying.

Whatever the contributing factors, when we consider taking our own lives, we are trying to maintain our autonomy and control what happens to our minds and bodies. This allows us to preserve some semblance of dignity even when we have deteriorated physically, or have been overwhelmed emotionally. The final step and ultimate choice still remains in our own hands.

How Do We Decide

There are situations where most people would agree that dying is a reasonable option and others where the choices may not be clear cut and perceptions might vary. Though we should discuss our feelings with friends and family, we must remember that only we are able to actually assess our own conditions and states of mind. Pain and suffering, as well as pleasure and joy, are mainly subjective. Some of us may find one kind of pleasure particularly important to our own happiness, or one type of pain particularly distressing. Yet for others, these elements may be of minor significance. For instance, physical activity may be of prime importance to some of us and of no consequence to others. Or reading may be a major pleasure for some people and of little interest to others. Of course, for most of us, there are usually a number of pleasures that make our lives worth living, rather than just one. Similarly, certain types of pain may be manageable for some people and intolerable for others.

Above all, it is essential that the scale be weighted for us on the side of pleasure and happiness, versus the total amount of pain and sadness we are experiencing—or at least that we can expect the scale to be weighted in a positive fashion for us at some time in the future. Only each of us can say whether or not we are satisfied with the way things are and if our lives remain worthwhile. And for each of us, the threshold for choosing death may be different. In addition, we can never judge the choices other people make, since we are not walking in their shoes. Hopefully, death will not be chosen when depression or only minimal impairment is present, but rather when the quality of life is truly poor, suffering is great, or a terminal illness exists. This type of death can be called a "rational suicide," because it is thought out carefully by the person killing him- or herself and is an action others can understand, whether or not they would have taken the same course.

Conducting an Inventory

When contemplating the possibility of suicide because of what we perceive as an unendurable situation, we should first conduct an inventory of what we find pleasurable and painful in our lives, then add them all up and tabulate the results as objectively as we can to determine whether we really want to die. There are a number of pleasures and pains we should include in this inventory, some of which we rarely think about, although they may be quite important to us.

Pleasures

Our pleasures might include the following:

The pleasures of love. Not only love in a physical sense, but the special rapport and communication possible with a lover. And also the love of a child by a parent, or by a child for a parent. And the love for other relatives and dear friends.

The pleasures of sexuality, intimacy, and physical closeness. Though sexual drive wanes as we grow older, there is still pleasure in touching and intimacy with those we love. Even when sick we can delight in a hug or a caress.

The pleasures of friendship. The comfort of a common history and the understanding of another human being, with the tolerance required to maintain relationships. Conversations with friends, speaking about goals and dreams, and debating beliefs and ideas.

The pleasures of spirituality. Finding peace through prayer and faith in God, or meditation and communing with one's inner self.

The pleasures of helping others. The ability to give of ourselves and provide assistance and sustenance to other human beings.

The pleasures of solitude. Being alone and content, in the forest, in a quiet room, on an early morning stroll, or sitting silently.

The pleasures of nature and the world around us. A sunrise over the water, the grandeur of the night sky, standing in a storm, walking against the wind, the smell of pine trees, skimming over the sea, surveying the world from a mountaintop, watching a doe nuzzling its fawn.

The pleasures of the city. Immersing ourselves in the frenzied activity of urban life.

The pleasures of eating. Enjoyment of the tastes and textures of different foods, both the familiar and the exotic.

The pleasures of reading. Getting involved in a complex plot, or appreciating lovely narrative; the excitement of a good story. Delighting in a verse of poetry. Being enthralled by a book of history, or marveling at a biography.

The pleasures of music. Losing ourselves in an operatic aria or a country and western lament, a soulful blues or a rock ballad, a symphonic theme or a jazz riff.

The pleasures of art. Reveling in the visual beauty of a lush landscape or a stark portrait, while trying to comprehend the artist's vision. Attempting to decipher abstract forms and concoctions of color.

The pleasures of photography. Discovering a reality unknown to our own eyes, with forms and lines often beyond our perception.

The pleasures of the theater. Being caught up in a dramatic performance, stretching our emotive capacity. Watching old plays with disparate interpretations and new plays that explore the boundaries of human relationships.

The pleasures of the movies. Escaping life for a few hours in a temporary reality of motion and color. Frenzied action, improbable romance, unusual characters, incredible stories.

The pleasures of creating. Using our own minds and hands to produce a painting, a sculpture, a photograph, a verse, an article. Singing a song our own way, or playing a theatrical role as we see it. Knitting a sweater, making a quilt, or any other type of creative endeavor.

The pleasures of cooking. Preparing food with our own flair and instincts, while following or not following other's recipes, then sharing it with people we care about.

The pleasures of physical activity. The joy that comes from the body's motion, whether walking, running, bike riding, or swimming. The excitement of competing in sports, individually or as a part of a team.

The pleasures of learning. Experiencing and understanding new concepts and new ideas, and learning to perform new tasks.

The pleasures of contemplation. Thinking about anything and everything, or nothing at all. Daydreaming, or imagining the way things might have been, or might be at some time in the future.

The pleasures of sleep. Lying down and allowing ourselves to drift away after a long, hard day. Feeling the mantle of fatigue lifting as our minds and bodies dissolve into oblivion.

The pleasures of a hot shower. Having the jets of hot water buffeting our bodies, washing away the tightness and tension in our muscles, the heat infiltrating every facet of our beings.

The pleasures of collecting. Discovering objects we covet and being able to acquire them. Surveying our collections and rediscovering all the pieces we love.

The pleasures of a pet. Having another living thing that seems to love us and is dependent upon us, greeting us when we return home and snuggling up to us on a cold night.

The pleasures of traveling. Experiencing new people and new places that force us to change our usual patterns of existence. Looking at life through the lens of a different culture.

The pleasures of gardening. Arranging the land in accordance with our vision. Feeling the earth in our hands as we plant and nurture. Seeing our flowers bloom and eating our vegetables.

The pleasures of being a sports fan. Identifying with a team or player. Watching the games and marveling at the athletic feats.

The above list gives some of the pleasures that come to mind immediately, though all of these are not universal perceptions. There are also many others that some of us might find equally, or more, important. We merely have to think about those things that make our lives worth living and connect us to the world in various ways.

Pains

Though certain physical conditions universally cause pain, how we regard this and the degree of distress present is an individual matter. Other types of pain may be even more subjective, depending on our own experiences and our own life view. And chronic pain is often associated with sadness and anxiety. (Suffering might be thought of as the way the mind perceives pain, whether the basis is physical or emotional.) Different types of pain might include the following:

Pain of physical origin: Pain is an unpleasant sensation caused by stimulation of the sensory nerves anywhere throughout the body, transmitted through central nervous system pathways and interpreted by specific areas of the brain. Many illnesses and degenerative processes cause pain, but only those that are chronic, severe, and unremitting make suicide a consideration. The most feared pain is that associated with metastatic cancer that progressively destroys bones and other normal tissues.

Although a number of conditions can cause debilitating pain and make people think about killing themselves, virtually all physical pain can be controlled with medication or other modalities. Surgical procedures, which can alleviate different kinds of pain, may involve cutting nerve roots or spinal tracts, or ablating areas of the brain. Medication pumps can also be implanted surgically to relieve pain. However, medication often has side effects that lessen quality of life and surgical procedures may also have downsides. Some of us may be able accept and coexist with severe chronic pain if other aspects of our lives are rewarding and help us maintain a positive balance even with our discomfort.

Pain associated with loss of function: While this type of pain is mainly emotional, there are usually physical reasons for the loss. The amount of pain resulting is directly proportional to how important that function is to us and how we perceive its loss. This pain may be due to an inability to walk (from any cause), an inability to use our arms or hands, vision loss, hearing loss, diminished cognitive ability, incontinence, loss of sexual function, loss of a limb, loss of an organ that is surgically removed, difficulty breathing, inability to eat or drink.

Pain due to loss of a loved one: As noted, though this pain may be
emotional, it can produce physical symptoms. The death of a
child may be most devastating because it violates the expected
script of life and protective parental instincts, but the death of a
spouse is usually the most disruptive. Widowed men have more
difficulty than women, since they appear to have greater problems adapting to living alone. The loss of a parent or sibling can
also cause considerable anguish, though as we age, we generally
anticipate parental demise . And the death of a good friend may
even be more distressing than that of a family member, if he or
she had played a significant role in our world. A loved one may
also be lost to us without dying, because of illness or injury, with
the pain reinforced by that person's invalidism and need for care.
Pain may also be caused by a spouse leaving or asking for a
divorce, or a child cutting off contact or marrying someone unacceptable to us. Even a child moving far away may be very painful.

Pain due to loss of financial security: Losing a great deal of money or
one's financial security can be catastrophic for some people, as
evidenced by the suicides after the stock market crash in 1929.
Financial misfortune makes us feel vulnerable and fearful. While
losses in the market are expected by the sophisticated investor,
older people sometimes don't understand the risks inherent in
equities. They may also be placed in improper investments by
unprincipled brokers and are prey for con artists. The pain that
results is not only because of the financial loss, but also from the
embarrassment of having been duped. People may have worked
and saved all their lives to have a nest egg for their later years,
only to see it all gone.

Pain due to general decline: Lacking a specific illness or major problem, age may still take its toll in terms of our inability to do things
once important to us. This difficulty with activities and functioning may eventually reach a point where we decide life is no longer
worth living.

Pain due to approaching death: Even without physical discomfort,
we may feel emotional distress if we have an illness and know we
are dying. We may be unable to find pleasure in the time remaining, being convinced we have nothing to look forward to. In this

situation, some might opt for suicide, while others might simply
give up the fight and passively allow themselves to die earlier.

Pain from anhedonia: Anhedonia means the inability to experience
pleasure. This is usually the result of severe depression or other
psychiatric illnesses. But being unable to feel pleasure can in
itself be painful and can make one uninterested in continuing to
live.

Pain from "existential suffering:" This usually occurs at the end of
life, when we are aware death is near. Much has been written
about this state in the medical literature that deals with the process of dying. By *existential suffering* we mean the feeling that life
is meaningless, that there is nothing afterward, and we have accomplished nothing during our time here on earth. Feelings of
hopelessness and failure, abandonment and dependency, guilt
and worthlessness are part of this. Obviously, religion has a role
to play in alleviating existential suffering if the person is a believer, but reassurance by family members and loved ones, counselors and physicians can also be helpful, and medications can be
beneficial at times.

It is important to try to differentiate the pains we have listed from
depression, though at times it may be difficult to do so, since they are
intertwined. Depression is a general emotional state of unhappiness
that colors all of our perceptions in a negative fashion. Having various
pains can result in a person being depressed and depression can height-
en different kinds of pain. Many of the feelings we noted, particularly in
existential suffering and anhedonia, are commonly seen in depressive
states. When contemplating suicide and trying to make a rational assessment of the quality of our lives, it is better if we are not depressed.
Depression introduces a substantial bias to any decisions we might
make. If we choose to die, it should be after a valid appraisal of how
things are and if they are indeed intolerable, we should be certain there
is no likelihood of improvement in the future.

Double suicide, a couple deciding to die together, is seen occasionally. It may happen when both are sick and no longer want to live, or
when one is very sick and the other partner does not want to live
without his or her mate. Sometimes, neither one has a specific illness,
but both are old and feeble, with a poor quality of life. This makes death
a desirable option. When love is very strong and two people have lived

together for many years, there may be a great interdependency and dying together is preferable to going on alone.

KILLING ONE'S SELF

Once a decision is made to end one's life and reaffirmed after discussions with family, friends, and professionals, the question arises of how to do it. People speak of having a good death, but no death is actually good. Some are just less bad. Ideally, life should be terminated quickly, painlessly, and nonviolently, but it is not always possible to achieve all three goals. It might be easier if it were done with a physician's assistance, but that is a crime and can have serious repercussions for the physician. There are still many doctors, however, who will help patients in the right circumstances. But even without a physician, if one is committed, one can generally kill oneself, unless a severe handicap is present. A short book on this matter helpful for those considering suicide is *Final Exit* by Derek Humphry, who speaks of good planning, attention to detail, and quality assistance to aid in the process of "self-deliverance."[13] He explains various methods in detail including the necessary doses of different compounds.

If it is done properly, choosing to die by one's own hand should allow a dignified end under one's own control at a time he or she decides upon, after closure with family and friends. It is important to have a will in order and a living will with the appointment of a health care agent should also be in place. A note of explanation to one's family, friends, and the legal authorities to minimize recriminations afterward is also essential and should include a pronouncement absolving anyone else of blame. This note should state that we conceived of the plan in its entirety and executed it by our own hand and that we take full responsibility for what has transpired.

For those of us who might decide on rational suicide, it is critical that we act at the right time. Even with an incurable illness, we would not want to die too early or we might lose opportunities for pleasurable moments with our families and friends, shared time we could spend together that they would treasure and we would enjoy. Or we may find other activities meaningful for a short while before we died. On the other hand, we would not want to die too late, when our disease might have progressed too far and we were in a condition that was abhorrent to us. If it were too late, we also might not be able to complete the act because of physical infirmities or cognitive impairment. A list follows of various ways to take one's life, with pros and cons.

Death by Violent Means: In this category, we are speaking of any method that causes physical injury or disfigurement to oneself. It includes death by gunshot, hanging, drowning, blood loss (slitting one's wrists), ingestion of a corrosive substance, or blunt trauma to the head or body (jumping off a building or causing a motor vehicle accident). Though this type of suicide is relatively easy to effect, it is not a dignified way to die and in some instances may be quite painful. It may be very distressing to family and friends as well, and should be avoided. And if the attempt is unsuccessful, we may be kept alive on life support afterward, or maintained in a brain-damaged state, unless we have left specific instructions to the contrary.

Carbon Monoxide Poisoning: This method has been used for suicide for some time and accidental deaths from carbon monoxide are seen frequently. Inhaling carbon monoxide blocks the uptake of oxygen by hemoglobin in the red blood cells, resulting in a lack of oxygen to the brain and the rest of the body. This leads to coma and eventually death. There is great variability in the success of this technique and it probably should not be used for rational suicide. The process can take several hours for completion and may be interrupted. Also the person may possibly be left alive but brain damaged.

Death by Overdose: Once the decision has been finalized, this is the preferable method—painless, relatively quick, and nonviolent. Theoretically, one would merely take medication, go to sleep and never awaken, with death usually caused by respiratory arrest. But it is never quite that simple. Medication has to be obtained from some source in the proper amount and then administered in a way that will produce the expected results. (Many suicides in the past have been accomplished with cyanide, which appears to work fairly quickly and effectively. However, there are questions about whether some people who take cyanide experience pain prior to death.)

There are a number of compounds that have been utilized in rational suicides, but certain barbiturates (Seconal and Nembutal) and morphine appear to be most efficient. (Different tranquilizers, antidepressants, and painkillers have been used with varying degrees of success, depending on the circumstances and dosages. (See Humphry's book *Final Exit* for information.) Medication can often be obtained from a physician who knows us well, is aware of our situation and is sympathetic, seeing us in pain or with a terminal illness. But the drugs will usually be given under another guise. For instance, if we ask for something to kill ourselves, the physician might give us a prescription and say, "These are pills to help you sleep better, or to relieve your anxiety. But don't take more than so many of them, or you might die." This way, the physician is legally not assisting us in suicide, although he or she is furnishing us with the means. If the physician does not respond to our request for medication to help us die, we can ask for sleeping pills or morphine for pain, allowing the physician a greater degree of cover. But if he or she is totally uncooperative, it is usually not difficult to find another doctor who is more compassionate and willing to help. (Though unwilling to actually kill their patients, many physicians believe they are ethically bound to help patients die if their condition is hopeless or they are suffering.) Dr. Timothy Quill in his book *Death and Dignity*, portrays a poignant story of his relationship with a patient dying of leukemia and how he, without actually assisting in the suicide, provided support and medication, allowing her to end her life when she could no longer stand the suffering. [14]

When the time has come and we are ready to act, rather than dying alone and feeling abandoned, it is helpful to have a good friend or family member in attendance to lend support and comfort. This person should not assist us in any way, but just remain a presence. (Otherwise, he or she might be breaking the law and be legally at risk.) We want someone who will remain with us to the end and not call for an ambulance or EMS. Afterward, he or she could report the death to our doctor, or simply leave and allow someone else to find us. If our physician certifies our death as due to cancer or another disease process, it is unlikely there would be an investigation or legal ramifications.

An hour prior to using the medication, it is probably a good idea to take an antiemetic like Compazine or Reglan to prevent vomiting due to stomach irritation from the compounds. A light meal might also be worthwhile in this context. The use of alcohol with these substances enhances their effects and makes it more likely they will work. Taking morphine and barbiturates together has an additive effect as well.

Voluntary Terminal Dehydration: Voluntarily stopping food and fluid intake to end one's life is the ultimate act of autonomy and control, but requires a significant degree of self-discipline. Unlike terminal dehydration, when we are comatose or in a persistent vegetative state and the decision is being made by our health care agent according to our advance directives, we are aware of what we are doing and choosing this course. Before acting, we should discuss our decision with our families, who hopefully will be in agreement. Once we start on this path, death may supervene in days to weeks, depending on our underlying state and how rigidly we abstain from food and liquids. (Taking small amounts will prolong the dying process.) Mild abdominal discomfort can occur early on, but can be managed with analgesics or narcotics, which can be obtained from a physician who is not helping with the suicide, but is just making us comfortable. Ice chips may also be used to moisten the lips. Hallucinations and confusion are possible before we lapse into a coma prior to death. Again, someone should always be in attendance, preferably family members or friends who can provide solace. Because of the length of the process, a number of people may be required and shifts may have to be scheduled. The major drawback to this method is its duration and the uncertainty of when the end will come.

Physician-Assisted Suicide: While a majority of the American population[15] believes physician-assisted suicide is the proper way to assure that people with terminal illnesses or unrelenting suffering are able to end their lives quickly and painlessly, the law in most states does not agree with this premise. And with the political clout of those who support the sanctity of life, it will probably be awhile before this activity is legalized. Though common sense tells us that people who are suffering and want to die should be helped, there is resistance to allowing physicians (or anyone else) to assume that role. If legislation were passed to this end, it would not be difficult to assure that adequate safeguards were in place and that this ability were not abused, but we have not gotten to that point yet.

Physician-assisted suicide is available legally in the Netherlands, where physicians can end life by prescribing pills or by giving lethal injections (voluntary euthanasia), combining barbiturates and muscle relaxants. In the United States, the Oregon Death with Dignity Act of 1994 permits physicians to prescribe lethal drugs to individuals with terminal diseases who want to end their lives. It is also legal in the states of Washington, Vermont, and Montana. In January 2014, the New Mexico Supreme Court ruled that physicians could provide patients with lethal prescriptions and proclaimed a constitutional right for "a competent, terminally ill patient to choose aid in dying."[16] It appears that an increasing proportion of Americans now favors the right of patients with terminal illnesses to seek physicians' assistance in ending their lives.

To live our lives well, we must retain an element of control over the way we die if we are afflicted with chronic or terminal illnesses, or unchecked pain. Preparing advance directives expressing our wishes about dying if we are impaired and unable to do so, and considering "rational suicide" when our lives are no longer worth living, allows us to remain autonomous through our final hours.

12

OBSERVATIONS AND CONCLUSIONS

Ultimately, man should not ask what the meaning of his life is, but rather he must recognize that it is *he* who is asked. In a word, each man is questioned by life; and he can only answer to life by *answering for* his own life; to life he can only respond by being responsible.

—Viktor E. Frankl, *Man's Search for Meaning*[1]

Growing old is a succession of steps on the path of life that eventually ends in death. By a number of actions, we can choose the route we take and improve the quality of our lives as we age—even increasing survival. To those Baby Boomers still in midlife, dying may still seem distant, with peer groups intact and physical limitations minor. But over time, this will change. Notwithstanding the final outcome, we should attempt to protect our minds and bodies as much as possible from the ravages of aging. This does not entail battling to remain young, but merely trying to remain in control of as much of our lives as we can for as long as we can. Our situation is quite different from what it was a millennium ago or even a century ago, when life expectancy was shorter and seniors were isolated survivors among multitudes of the young. Now, older people are a growing minority with their own subculture that crosses race, ethnicity, and gender. Still, their voices are not always heard.

Even though we are living longer and better than in the past, nature and society still conspire to try to rob us of self-respect and vitality as we age. And the older we get, the more successful these adversaries seem to be in their depredations against us. Our cells and tissues are less efficient, and different diseases take their toll. Our organs may be damaged and stop working normally, and expected bodily functions may no longer be as reliable. And in addition to these changes, society puts up barriers that make it even more arduous for us to live well, causing us to feel obsolete and subservient. Because of this discrimination, having to deal with societal slights and insults as well as physical changes, we find it more difficult to fulfill our potential and enhance our happiness in our later years. Yet many of us manage to resist and carry on our lives with satisfaction and zeal.

At any age, we can still fight to secure our dignity against the consequences of growing older and society's attempts to dismiss us. The earlier in life the resistance starts, the better the odds of improving our circumstances. That does not mean we will always be successful, but the struggle itself is essential if we are to preserve our self-esteem. It is also important for us to understand there are aspects of our lives that we can affect and others over which we have no power. The parts within our domain must be managed to our advantage and we must take responsibility there for our actions—for our failures as well as our achievements. And that which is beyond our control, must be accepted—illnesses, disabilities, loss of loved ones, and so forth. True dignity is not complaining over the cards that life has dealt us and being envious of others, but making the most of the cards we have. We cannot go around feeling sorry for ourselves, lamenting our situations or what has occurred in the past, for that accomplishes nothing. At this point in our lives, we are who we are and the past cannot be changed.

We must also recognize that time is precious for all of us and is an irreplaceable commodity. The only time we have is the present, the past being gone and the future being uncertain. When we are young, decades are in the offing, but when we are old, our years are meager. We must use them well. Working within our limitations, we must try to overcome the afflictions imposed upon us by chance or our own missteps. We must utilize our remaining potential to the fullest extent possible, for our self-respect is at least partially determined by what we do with what we have. No matter what our status may be, we must try to maximize both our productivity and pleasure—to make our lives worth living.

EFFECTS OF AGING

As mentioned, normal aging occurs both on a cellular level and throughout each organism. The changes that take place in cells are manifest in various tissues and organs of the body, and are visible as diminished functional abilities. The actual mechanism responsible for aging is not yet clear, but we do know that as cells become old, their capacity to divide decreases and that this is programmed in genetically. Their metabolism also slows, reducing the production of proteins, while also affecting carbohydrates, fats, enzyme systems, and DNA. With cellular performance faltering, the organism as a whole becomes more susceptible to disease, with impairment of the immune system and less reserve in all the body's systems. Strength and stamina diminish and memory and cognitive ability are less acute, though for many, self-sufficiency is maintained.

Diseases with a predilection for older people compound the normal changes that are part of aging, magnifying any decline. Illnesses affecting the brain are the most devastating, with cardiopulmonary compromise also imposing limitations on many older people. Hip fractures may hinder walking and mobility, with degenerative spine disease causing back and leg pain. Multiple complications can develop from diabetes and hypertension, with different types of cancers also more common in older people—some catastrophic, others curable.

Because of the effects upon us of the aging process and diseases, we are more likely to have our protective armor of dignity chipped away as we grow older. Our ability to walk and get around may decrease, with our balance deficient and weakness or pain restricting our movements. We may be short of breath or have chest pain on exertion. Problems may also develop with vision, hearing, or bowel or bladder function. In addition, anxiety or depression may limit our activities and we may stay in our houses more, interacting less with other people. For some, cognitive difficulties signal the end of autonomy and independence, and we find we are no longer in charge of our own lives. Our peers have died off as well and we have fewer friends and family available to provide love and support. And our pride, self-confidence, and self-esteem begin to wane.

Unless a specific illness or injury supervenes, loss of independence is usually a gradual process, during which we cede certain functions to others willingly, or have them seized despite our opposition. We may find that we are being helped with physical tasks we may or may not be able to handle ourselves. The administration of our lives and the daily decisions begin to be made by someone else. Living in our own homes may become impractical and we may have to move in with one of our children or perhaps to an assisted living residence. Though at the onset the help we are given may be minimal, it continues to increase over time. And eventually, family members can no longer furnish the care we may require. Home health care aides may step into the breach and we may be allowed to remain at home with their assistance—strangers giving us medication and helping with the tasks of daily living. However, even this may not be enough for some of us and we may be sent off to spend our final days in the confines of a nursing home, where any shred of dignity we might have left is torn from us.

On top of our physical and cognitive difficulties, society is not kind to us as we grow older. Younger individuals tend to overlook older people's experience, while society as a whole disregards seniors and does not pay enough attention to their needs. If we wish to work and are capable, we may be unable to retain a job or find new employment because of ageist bias. The media either ignores our needs and interests, or depicts us in stereotyped ways. Many of us reside in age-related ghettos because we are uncomfortable out in the world and not enough of an effort is made to help us fit in. Because older people are vulnerable, we are also victims of a disproportionate amount of crime, both scams and violent offenses. And we are the butt of ageist jokes that ridicule us because of our limitations and disabilities.

STRATEGIES FOR MAINTAINING SELF-RESPECT AND VITALITY

Given all the elements arrayed against older people, what can be done to preserve self-respect and vitality as we age? As I have shown in this book, there are a number of strategies, both major and minor, that can be employed in this battle, but it is essential to maintain a positive mind-set. If we feel that whatever we do is of no value and will not help us, it is useless to try, for our efforts certainly will not help. But if we believe we can modify our fate, at least to some degree, our struggle can be rewarding. Some of the strategies are as follows:

- The aging process must be accepted. It is normal to grow old with all the attendant difficulties that are part of aging.
- We must try to remain physically fit, as our physical status impacts on many other aspects of our lives. Aerobic conditioning is vitally important and we should attempt at least an hour of exercise daily, unless there are medical contraindications.
- Proper nutritional rules should be followed and we should eat a well-balanced diet, avoiding excessive calories, fats, cholesterol, and so forth. We should not smoke and we should avoid abuse of alcohol and drugs, including prescription medications.
- Regular medical check-ups can lead to early diagnosis of a number of conditions, allowing certain cancers to be cured, diabetes and hypertension to be treated, and a percentage of heart attacks and strokes to be prevented.
- Sexuality and intimacy among older people are normal and desirable, and we should not make value judgments about what other people do.
- We must remain intellectually and socially relevant so that other segments of society do not marginalize us.
- We must do whatever is necessary to remain independent as long as possible and in every way possible, taking into account illnesses or disabilities. This is not to underestimate the problems this may entail for some people.
- If limitations on our activities are unavoidable, a shared dependency with a group of our peers should be sought if this is feasible, We can help them with some aspects of their lives and they can help us with others.
- We should be candid about our disabilities and shortcomings, rather than trying to hide them from the world at large and looking foolish in our attempts.
- We should avoid constantly complaining about any hardships. It is undignified and people soon become desensitized and less sympathetic.

- It is important that we pay attention to our appearance. Appearances do matter and we lose dignity if we are careless in our dress or hygiene.
- Goals and objectives are vital at every stage of life and are necessary for all of us as we grow older. When careers are over and children are out of the house, we need to have reasons to get up every morning and look forward to each day. We need to have activities that excite us—our own personal goals that give our lives substance and motivate us to keep going.
- We must be able to deal with grief and loneliness, for as we age, more of our relatives and friends will die. If we allow grief to continuously overwhelm us, our lives will no longer be worth living. We must find ways to conquer loneliness and make new friends.
- We should not ignore the spiritual aspect of our existence, for spirituality can bring us peace and contentment, and help us in our search for meaning.
- We should prepare for being old when we are younger, as that will make the transition easier.

Whatever our goals and objectives are in later life, we should try to derive as much pleasure as we can in the time we have. We will not have other opportunities. Aging well means enjoying life. However, we should also try to give something back to others—those who are close to us, our communities, and the world at large. Being totally self-involved will not bring us happiness. There should be a balance between what we do for ourselves and what we do for others. And relationships are important and should not be neglected. Shared time with our spouses, children, friends, and other loved ones should be held dear.

We should also not try to tidy up our lives in preparation for death. There should always be projects that remain unfinished when we die.

I have mentioned a number of factors that play a role in empowering us as we age, while helping us to preserve our self-respect and vitality. Four of these are critical. They can be recalled by the acronym PIRO.

- Physical activity. We must condition ourselves through regular exercise.

- Independence. No matter how difficult it may be, we should try to maximize our independence and self-sufficiency.
- Relevance. We must be aware of what is happening in the world around us.
- Objectives. As we age, we must have goals and objectives, some of which we are passionate about.

As one grows older, time moves faster. This is almost a universal perception as people age, our mind playing tricks with us, though it is unclear why this is. Intuitively, one would expect the opposite to be true, since people are less active and proceed more slowly when older, with fewer tasks to occupy their time. Perhaps it is because the passage of any unit of time is a smaller fraction of our existence and the totality of our experiences as we grow older. For example when a child goes from two to three years of age, the additional year is 50 percent of its life, while a person going from age fifty to fifty-one only adds another 2 percent to his or her experiences. The more reason to use our remaining time well.

We all have an essence, individuality, and innate dignity shaped through the years by experience hammering on the template of our genetic composition, becoming strong, but malleable. It is who we are, our personalities, that provide protection from life's misfortunes, the abuses of society and those of our fellow human beings, and allow us to live according to our own precepts and beliefs, unable to be broken by external forces or internal doubts. We should do everything in our power never to relinquish these.

NOTES

I. INTRODUCTION

1. Marcus Aurelius, *Meditations, Marcus Aurelius and His Times* (Roselyn, NY: William J. Black, Inc., 1945), 43.

2. Satchel Paige—well-known comment.

3. Mick Jagger and Keith Richards, "Mother's Little Helper," on *Flowers* album, 1967.

4. Sabrina Tavernise, "Life Expectancy Rises Around World, Study Finds," *New York Times*, December 14, 2012, New York edition, A4.

5. Ibid.

6. Rosemary Yanick and Lynn G. Ries, "Cancer in the Aged—an Epidemiologic Perspective on Treatment Issues," *Cancer* 68 (1991): 2502.

7. Peter Peterson, *Gray Dawn* (New York: Times Books, 1999), 12.

8. Robert Katzman and Robert D. Terry, *The Neurology of Aging* (Philadelphia, PA: F. A. Davis Company, 1983), 10.

9. Bernice Neugarten, reported by John W. Rowe and Robert L. Kahn, *Successful Aging* (New York: Pantheon Books, 1998), 9.

10. Rowe and Kahn, *Successful Aging*, 10.

11. K. A. Pillemer and D. Finkelbor, "The Prevalence of Elder Abuse: A Random Sample Survey," *Gerontologist* 28, no. 1 (1988): 51–57.

12. Deborah Roberts and Joan Martelli, "Brooke Astor Trial Verdict Latest in Long Family Drama," ABC *20/20*, October 8, 2009, http://abcnews.go.com/20/20/Astor/brooke-astor-son-athony-marshall-guilty-fraud-larceny/.

13. Bradley A. Sharp, "Community Acquired Pneumonia (CAP)," 3, http://sfgh.medicine.ucsf.edu/education/resed/intern_half_day/pdf/dyph_cap.pdf.

Sharpe, assistant clinical professor, Department of Medicine, UCSF, is quoting William Osler, M.D., 1898.

14. Lindsay Abrams, "Study: Attitude about Aging Improves with Age," *The Atlantic*, December 10, 2012, www.theatlantic.com/health/archive/2012/12/study-attitude-about-aging-improves-with-age/266064.

15. Thomas Cole, *The Journey of Life* (Cambridge: Cambridge University Press: 1992), xxv.

16. Rowe and Kahn, *Successful Aging*, 39.

17. Dylan Thomas, "Do Not Go Gentle into That Good Night," in *The New Oxford Book of English Verse*, ed. Helen Gardner (Oxford: Oxford University Press, 1984), 942.

2. THE BABY BOOMERS: AGING RELUCTANTLY

1. Alexander Pope, "The Triumph of Vice," in *The New Oxford Book of English Verse*, ed. Helen Gardner (New York: Oxford University Press, 1972), 421.

2. D'Vera Cohn and Paul Taylor, "Baby Boomers Approach Age 65—Glumly," Pew Research Center, December 20, 2010, http://pewresearch.org/pubs/1834/baby-boomers-old-age-downbeat-pessimism.

3. Ibid.

4. "Baby Boomers Climb on GOP Wagon," *The Daily Caller, Yahoo News*, November 3, 2011, http://news.yahoo.com/baby-boomers-climb-gop-wagon-034608469.html.

5. "Baby Boom Generation, 2001 and Beyond, United States History," accessed May 10, 2012, www.u-s-history.com/pages/h2061.html.

6. Cohn and Taylor, "Baby Boomers Approach Age 65."

7. Jerry Adler and Julie Scelfo, "Finding and Seeking, Born in Affluence, the Baby-Boomers Were Driven to Ask Big Questions about Fulfillment and the Meaning of Life: How Their Legacy Has Changed Us," *Newsweek*, September 18, 2006.

8. Debra Sartelle, "Baby Boomers and Religion," *Examiner.com*, December 12, 2009, www.examiner.com/article/baby-boomers-and-religion.

9. Daniel Lippman, "Young Americans More Loyal to Religion Than Boomers," Reuters, August 6, 2010. Analysis of report from Phillip Schwadel in the *Journal for the Scientific Study of Religion* based on the General Social Survey 1973–2006.

10. George Barna, "Generational Change," State of the Church Series, part 2, 2011, http://garyrohrmayer.typepad.com/yourjourneyblog/2011/08/barnas-state-of-the-church-report-part-2.html.

11. "Aging Baby Boomers in a New Workforce Development System," report from Department of Labor, 2000, www.doleta.gov.

12. Sherle Schwenninger and Samuel Sherriden, "Manufacturing and the U.S. Economy," New America Foundation, July13, 2009, http://newamerica.net/publications/policy/manufacturing_and_u_s_economy.

13. "Aging Baby Boomers in a New Workforce Development System."

14. Linda Levine, "Retiring Baby Boomers = a Labor Shortage?," Congressional Research Service Report for Congress, January 30, 2008, http://stuff.mit.edu/afs/sipb/contrib/wikileaks-crs/wikileaks-crs-reports/RL33661.pdf.

15. Gordon Mermin, Richard Johnson, and Dan Murphy, "How Long Do Boomers Plan to Work?," Brief #12 in the Older Americans' Economic Security series, Urban Institute, January 30, 2009, www.urban.org/url.cfm?ID=311415.

16. "Aging Baby Boomers in a New Workforce Development System."

17. Carol Morello, "If Baby Boomers Stay in Suburbs, Analysts Predict Cultural Shift," *Washington Post*, June 28, 2011.

18. Ibid.

19. Penelope Green, "Under One Roof, Building for Extended Families," *New York Times*, November 20, 2012.

20. Christian Nordqvist, "Obesity Is Baby Boomers' Main Health Problem," *Medical News Today*, July 19, 2011, www.medicalnewstoday.com/articles/231350.php.

21. Ibid.

22. "Baby Boom Generation," United States History, accessed May 10, 2012, www.u-s-history.com/pages/h2061.html.

23. Rachael Swarns, "More Americans Rejecting Marriage in 50s and Beyond," *New York Times*, March 1, 2012.

24. Jeff Kunerth, "Baby Boomers Boost Divorce Rate among Older Adults," December 25, 2011, *Seattle Times*.

25. Ibid.

26. Swarns, "More Americans Rejecting Marriage in 50s and Beyond."

27. Cohn and Taylor, "Baby Boomers Approach Age 65."

28. Ibid.

29. Dean Baker and Kevin Hassett, "The Human Disaster of Unemployment," *New York Times Sunday Review*, May 13, 2012, New York edition, SR9.

30. Derek Thompson, "Why Older Americans Have the Worst Long-Term Unemployment Crisis," *The Atlantic*, May 15, 2012, www.theatlantic.com/

business/archive/2012/05/why-older-americans-have-the-worst-long-term-unemployment-crisis/257228/.

31. Baker and Hassett, "The Human Disaster of Unemployment."

32. "Baby Boomer Handouts Hamper Savings," *Wall Street Journal*, May 1, 2012, http://blogs.wsj.com/totalreturn/2012/05/01/baby-boomer-handouts-hamper-savings/.

33. Alyce Lomax, "How Getting Robbed by Bernie Madoff Led Her to a Happier Life," *DailyFinance*, May 11, 2012, www.dailyfinance.com/2012/05/11/how-getting-robbed-by-bernie-madoff-led-her-to-a-happier-life/. Quoting Geneen Roth from her book *Lost and Found: One Woman's Story of Losing Her Money and Finding Her Life* (New York: Viking Penguin, 2011).

34. Laurence Kotlikoff, "Baby Boomers: The Greediest Generation," *Forbes*, November 11, 2010, www.forbes.com/2010/11/11/greedy-boomers-social-security-medicare-cuts-personal-finance-kotlikoff.html.

35. Bill Keller, "The Entitled Generation," *New York Times*, July 29, 2012.

36. Jessica Rao, "Bust of the Baby Boomer Economy: 'Generation Spend' Tightens Belt," CNBC.com, January 21, 2010, www.cnbc.com/id/34941331/Bust_of_the_Baby_Boomer_Generation_Economy_Generation_Spend_Tightens_Belt.

37. Catherine Rampell, "Big Income Losses Hit Those Near Retirement," *New York Times*, August 27, 2012, B1.

38. Vincent Fernando, "70% of the Elderly Aren't Retiring Because They Can't Afford to Anymore," Business Insider, March 3, 2010, www.businessinsider.com/70-of-the-elderly-arent-retiring-because-they-cant-afford-to-2010-3.

39. Jeff Love, "Approaching 65: A Survey of Boomers Turning 65 Years Old," AARP Research and Strategic Analysis, December 2010, www.aarp.org/personal-growth/transitions/info-12-2010/approaching-65.html.

40. Carol Keegan et al., *Boomers at Midlife 2004: The AARP Life Stage Study, Wave 3*, 2004, 18,http://assets.aarp.org/rgcenter/general/boomers_midlife_2004.pdf.

41. Ibid.

42. Ibid., 35.

3. THE GREATEST GENERATION AND THE SILENT GENERATION: LIFE BEFORE THE BOOMERS

1. Marcus Aurelius, *Meditations, Marcus Aurelius and His Times* (Roselyn, NY: William J. Black, Inc., 1945), 40.

2. Robert Margo, "Employment and Unemployment in the 1930s," *Journal of Economic Perspectives* 7, no. 2 (Spring 1993): 43.

3. Mitchell Landsberg, "Study on Religion Finds Young Adults Less Affiliated but Not Less Believing," *Los Angeles Times*, February 10, 2010, http://articles.latimes.com/2010/feb/10/loca/la-me-beliefs22-2010feb22.

4. William Strauss and Neil Howe, *Generations: The History of America's Future, 1584 to 2069* (New York: William Morrow, 1991), 264.

5. Anne Tergesen, "Counting On an Inheritance? Count Again," *Wall Street Journal*, June 11, 2012, http://online.wsj.com/news/articles/SB10001424052702303990604577370001234970954.

6. Strauss and Howe, *Generations*, 261.

7. Yolanda Williams, "The Silent Generation: Definition, Characteristics & Facts," Education Portal, http://education-portal.com/academy/lesson/the-silent-generation-definition-characteristics-facts.html#lesson.

8. Strauss and Howe, *Generations*.

9. James Brett, "The Silent Generation," http://jamesrbrett.com/TheSilentGeneration/.

10. Strauss and Howe, *Generations*, 279.

11. Landsberg, "Study on Religion."

12. Strauss and Howe, *Generations*, 284.

13. "Divorce in the Silent Generation," *rocketswag.com*, http://www.rocketswag.com/elderly/generation/silent-generation/Divorce-In-The-Silent-Generation.html.

14. Strauss and Howe, *Generations*, 284.

4. THE IMPACT OF TIME AND THE AGING PROCESS

1. Ernest Hemingway, *The Old Man and the Sea* (New York: Scribner Paperback Fiction, 1995), 10.

2. Ralph Waldo Emerson, *Essays: First Series* (1841), http://izquotes.com/quote/227188.

3. Michael Fossel, *Reversing Human Aging* (New York: William Morrow and Company, 1996), 10.

4. Leonard Hayflick, *How and Why We Age* (New York: Ballantine Books, 1996), 122.

5. Ibid.

6. Michael Fossel, "Telomerase and the Aging Cell—Implications for Human Health," *JAMA* 279, no. 21 (1998): 1732–35; Nicholas Wade, "Cell Rejuvenation May Yield Rush of Medical Advances," *New York Times*, January 20,

1998, www.nytimes.com/1998/01/20/science/cell-rejuvenation-may-yield-rush-of-medical-advances.html; Nicholas Wade, "Cells' Life Stretched in Lab," *New York Times*, January 14, 1998, www.nytimes.com/1998/01/14/us/cells-life-stretched-in-lab.html.

7. Nicholas Wade, "How a Gamble on an Obscure Theory of Aging Paid Off," *New York Times*, February 17, 1998.

8. Leonid Gavrilov and Natalia Gavrilova, "Evolutionary Theories of Aging and Longevity," *Scientific World Journal* 2, (2002): 339–56.

9. Ibid.

10. Roger Rosenberg, "Editorial: Time and Memory," *Archives of Neurology* 59, (2002): 1699–1700.

11. See, for example, Nicholas Wade, "Scientists Say Aging May Result from Brain's Hormonal Signals," *New York Times*, Science Section, October 10, 2000, www.nytimes.com/2000/10/10/health/scientists-say-aging-may-result-from-brain-s-hormonal-signals.html.

12. Nicholas Wade, "A Pill to Extend Life: Don't Dismiss the Notion Too Quickly," *New York Times*, September 22, 2000, www.nytimes.com/2000/09/22/us/a-pill-to-extend-life-don-t-dismiss-the-notion-too-quickly.html.

13. Amy Maxmen, "Calorie Restriction Fails to Lengthen Life Span in Primates," August 29, 2012, *Nature Magazine*, www.scientificamerican.com/article.cfm?id=calorie-restriction-fails-lenghten-lifespan-primates.

14. Nicholas Wade, "Study Spurs Hope of Finding Ways to Increase Human Life," *New York Times*, August 25, 2003, A10.

15. Anne Trafton, "3 Questions: MIT Biologist on New Resveratrol Study," *MIT News*, March 7, 2013, http://web.mit.edu/newsoffice/2013/3q-leonard-guarente-resveratrol-study-0307.html.

16. Brian Vastag, "Cause of Progeria's Premature Aging Found," Medical News and Perspectives, *JAMA* 289, no. 19 (2003): 2481–82.

17. Philip Horner, "Editorial: Regeneration in the Adult and Aging Brain," *Archives of Neurology* 59 (2002): 1717–20.

18. Ana Pereira et al., "An *In Vivo* Correlate Of Exercise-Induced Neurogenesis in the Adult Dentate Gyrus," *Proceedings of the National Academy of Sciences* 104, no. 13 (2007): 5638–43.

19. Robert Katzman and Robert D. Terry, *The Neurology of Aging* (Philadelphia, PA: F. A. Davis Company, 1983), 15–16

20. Hayflick, *How and Why We Age*, 165.

21. Ecclesiastes, 8:15, *The Holy Scriptures* (Philadephia, PA: The Jewish Publication Society of America, 1955).

22. Hayflick, *How and Why We Age*, 160.

23. See Gina Kolata, "Chasing Youth, Many Gamble on Hormones," *New York Times*, December 22, 2002, www.nytimes.com/2002/12/22/us/chasing-youth-many-gamble-on-hormones.html.

24. Mary Lee Vance, "Can Growth Hormone Prevent Aging?," *New England Journal of Medicine* 348 (2003): 779.

25. Steven, Lamberts, "Editorial: The Endocrinology of Aging and the Brain," *Archives of Neurology* 59 (2002): 1709–11; Marc R. Blackman et al., "Growth Hormone and Sex Steroid Administration in Healthy Aged Women and Men," *JAMA* 288, no. 18 (2002): 2282–92.

26. Susan Schiffman, "Taste and Smell Losses in Normal Aging and Disease," *JAMA* 278, no. 16 (1997): 1357–62; Claire Murphy et al., "Prevalence of Olfactory Impairment in Older Adults," *JAMA* 288, no. 18 (2002): 2307–12.

5. KNOWING YOUR ENEMIES: DISEASES AND DISORDERS COMMON WITH AGING

1. Attributed to actress Bette Davis, wiki.answers.com, http://wiki.answers.com/Q/Who_said_%27getting_old_ain%27t_for_sissies%27.

2. B. Schoenberg, "Epidemiology of Dementia," *Neurologic Clinics* 4, no. 2 (May 1986): 447.

3. Y. Liao et al., "Quality of the Last Year of Life of Older Adults: 1986 vs 1993," *JAMA* 283, no. 4 (2000): 512–18.

4. M. Aronson et al., "Dementia—Age Dependent Incidence, Prevalence and Morbidity in the Old-Old," *Archives of Internal Medicine* 151, no. 5 (1991): 989.

5. Chengxuan Qui et al., "The Influence of Education on Clinically Diagnosed Dementia Incidence and Mortality Data from the Kungsholmen Project," *Archives of Neurology* 58, no. 12 (2001): 2034–39.

6. Robert Wilson et al., "Life-Span Cognitive Activity, Neuropathologic Burden, and Cognitive Aging," *Neurology* 81, no. 4 (2013): 314–21.

7. Walter A. Kukull et al., "Dementia and Alzheimer's Disease Incidence," *Archives of Neurology* 59, no. 11 (2002): 1737–46.

8. Kulkull et al., "Dementia and Alzheimer's Disease Incidence."

9. Harald Neumann and Mark Daly, "Variant TREM2 as Risk Factor for Alzheimer's Disease," *New England Journal of Medicine* 368, no. 2 (2013): 182–83.

10. Brenda L. Plassman et al., "Incidence of Dementia and Cognitive Impairment, Not Dementia in the United States," *Annals of Neurology* 70, no. 3 (2011): 418–26.

11. Oscar Lopez et al., "Incidence of Mild Cognitive Impairment in the Pittsburg Cardiovascular Health Study-Cognition Study," *Neurology* 79, no. 15 (2012): 1599–1606.

12. Kurt Samson, "Why Are Some People Resistant to Dementia?," *Neurology Today* 13, no. 20 (October 17, 2013): 12.

13. P. Murali Doraiswamy et al., "Amyloid-B Assessed by Florbetapir F 18 PET and 18- Month Cognitive Decline," *Neurology* 79, no. 16 (2012): 1636–44.

14. B. Winblad et al., "A 1-Year, Randomized, Placebo-Controlled Study on Donepezil in Patients with Mild to Moderate AD," *Neurology* 57, no. 3 (2001): 489–95; N. Trinh et al., "Efficacy of Cholinesterase Inhibitors in the Treatment of Neuropsychiatric Symptoms and Functional Impairment of Alzheimer's Disease," *JAMA* 289, no. 2 (2003): 210–16.

15. Pauline Anderson, "Can Caffeine Prevent Progression to Dementia," Medscape, June 22, 2012, www.medcape.org/viewarticle/766208.

16. "Bapineuzumab, Drugs in Clinical Trial," Alzheimer's Research Forum, December 2012, www.alzforum.org/drg/drc/detail.asp?id=101.

17. Pauline Anderson, Pauline, "BACE Inhibitor Dramatically Reduces Amyloid-Beta," Medscape, November 12, 2012, www.medscape.com/viewarticle/774280.

18. Vladimir Coric et al., "Safety and Tolerability of the Gamma-Secretase Inhibitor Avagacestat in a Phase 2 Study of Mild to Moderate Alzheimer's Disease," *Archives of Neurology* 69, no. 11 (2012): 1430–40.

19. Laura Baker et al., "Effects of Growth Hormone-Releasing Hormone on Cognitive Function in Adults with Mild Cognitive Impairment and Healthy Older Adults," *Archives of Neurology* 69, no. 11 (2012): 1420–29.

20. Everett Lehman et al., "Neurodegenerative Causes of Death among Retired National Football League Players," *Neurology* 79, no. 19 (2012): 1970–74.

21. Brett Kissela et al., "Age at Stroke," *Neurology* 79, no. 17 (2012): 1781–87.

22. Lauren Sanders et al., "Performance of the ABCD2 Score or Stroke Risk Post TIA," *Neurology* 79, no. 10 (2012): 971–80.

23. Jouni Karppi et al., "Serum Lycopene Decreases the Risk of Stroke in Men," *Neurology* 79, no. 15 (2012): 1540–47.

24. "Deep Brain Stimulation Changes Rhythms to Treat Parkinson's Disease and Tremor," *Science Daily*, August 28, 2012, www.sciencedaily.com/releases/2012/08/120828093040.htm.

25. Ibid.

26. Maurice Mittlemark et al., "Prevalence of Cardiovascular Diseases among Older Adults," *American Journal of Epidemiology* 137, no. 3 (1993): 311.

27. Graeme Dewhurst et al., "A Population Survey of Cardiovascular Disease in Elderly People: Design, Methods and Prevalence Results," *Age and Aging* 20, no. 5 (1991): 353.

28. Economics and Statistics Administration, "Table Number 131: Deaths by Age and Leading Cause, 1993," *Vital Statistics* (Washington, DC: Economics and Statistics Administration, 1996).

29. Gina Kolata, "Vast Advance Is Reported in Preventing Heart Illnesses," *New York Times*, August 6, 1999, www.nytimes.com/1999/08/06/us/vast-advance-is-reported-in-preventing-heart-illnesses.html.

30. "Heart Disease Facts and Statistics," *National Vital Statistics Reports* 60, no. 3 (2011), www.cdc.gov/heartdisease/statistics.htm.

31. Russell Ross, "Mechanisms of Disease: Atherosclerosis—an Inflammatory Disease," *New England Journal of Medicine* 340 (1999): 115–26.

32. "High Blood Pressure Frequently Asked Questions," Centers for Disease Control and Prevention, accessed December 2012, www.cdc.gov/bloodpressure/faqs.htm.

33. Aram V. Chobian et al., "The Seventh Report of the Joint National Committee on Prevention, Detection, Evaluation and the Treatment of High Blood Pressure," *JAMA* 289, no. 19 (2003): 2560; and Thomas Kottke et al., "JNC 7: It's More Than High Blood Pressure," *JAMA* 289, no. 19 (2003): 2573.

34. Chobian et al., "The Seventh Report of the Joint National Committee," 2560.

35. Mark Williams, *Complete Guide to Aging and Health* (New York: Random House, 1995), 389.

36. Edward O. Laumann et al., "Sexual Dysfunction in the United States," *JAMA* 281, no. 6 (1999): 537–44.

37. Williams, *Complete Guide to Aging and Health*, 32.

38. Sara Rimer, "For Aged, Dating Game Is Numbers Game," *New York Times*, December 23, 1998, A1.

39. Henry Fountain, "Human Muscle Regrown on Animal Scaffolding," *New York Times*, September 17, 2012, www.nytimes.com/2012/09/17/health/research/human-muscle-regenerated-with-animal-help.html.

40. Diane Fesanich, Walter Willett, and Graham Colditz, "Walking and Leisure-Time Activity and Risk of Hip Fracture in Postmenopausal Women," *JAMA* 288, no. 18 (2002): 2300–2306.

41. "Conditions and Treatments: Hip Fracture," Massachusetts General Hospital, accessed February 3, 2014, www.massgeneral.org/conditions/condition.aspx?id=223.

42. "Cancer Facts and Figures 2013," American Cancer Society, accessed February 3, 2014, www.cancer.org/acs/groups/content/@epidemiologysurveilance/documents/document/acspc-036845.pdf.

43. Catherine Boring, Teresa S. Squires, and Tony Tong, "Cancer Statistics, 1993," CA—a Cancer Journal for Clinicians 43, no. 1 (January/February 1993): 7.

44. Rosemary Yanick and Lynn Ries, "Cancer in the Aged—an Epidemiologic Perspective on Treatment Issues," Cancer 68, (1991): 2502.

45. Ibid.

46. "Cancer Facts and Figures."

47. Zamosky, Lisa, "When to Get a Screening Mammogram," WebMD, 2, accessed February 3, 2014, www.webmd.com/breast-cancer/features/starting-mammography-screening.

48. Gina Kolata, "Drugs Aim to Make Several Types of Cancer Self-Destruct," New York Times, December 22, 2012, www.nytimes.com/2012/12/23/health/new-drugs-aim-to-make-cells-destroy-cancer.html?pagewanted=all.

49. "What Percentage of People with Cancer Are Cured?," Cancer Research UK, accessed April 22, 2013, www.cancerresearchuk.org/cancer-help/about-cancer/cancer-questions.

50. "Fact Sheet on Older Adults Depression and Suicide," National Institute of Mental Health, 2012.

51. Ibid.

52. Brenda Penninx et al., "Depressive Symptoms and Physical Decline in Community Dwelling Older Persons," JAMA 279, no. 21 (1998): 1720–26.

53. Jane Brody, "Hidden Plague of Alcohol Abuse by the Elderly," New York Times, April 2, 2002, F7.

54. Chrisopher Wren, "Many Women 60 and Older Abuse Alcohol and Prescribed Drugs, Study Says," New York Times, June 15, 1998, A12.

55. James Lubitz et al., "Health, Life Expectancy, and Health Care Spending among the Elderly," New England Journal of Medicine 349 (2003): 1048–55.

56. James Lubitz, James Beebe, and Colin Baker, "Longevity and Medicare Expenditures, New England Journal of Medicine 332, no. 15 (1995): 999–1003.

57. James Fries, "Reducing Disability in Older Age," JAMA 288, no. 24 (2002): 3164–66.

58. Cynthia Ogden et al., "Prevalence of Obesity in U.S. 2009–2010," NCHS Data Brief Number 82, January 2012, www.cdc.gov/nchs/data/databriefs/db82.pdf.

59. Anthony Vita et al., "Aging, Health Risks, and Cumulative Disability," New England Journal of Medicine 338, no. 15 (1998): 1035–41.

60. Francis Beaumont, "On the Tombs in Westminster Abby," http://
izquotes.com/author/francis-beaumont/2.

6. LOSS: AGING'S COMPANION

1. Yamanoue Okura, "The Impermanence of Human Life," trans. Bownas
and Thraite, *Be Not Defeated by the Rain*, http://benotdefeatedbytherain.
blogspot.com/2009/11/yamanoue-okura.html.

2. Sara Rimer, "Families Bear a Bigger Share of Long-Term Care for the
Frail Elderly," *New York Times*, national edition, June 8, 1998, www.nytimes.
com/1998/06/08/us/families-bear-a-bigger-share-of-long-term-care-for-the-
frail-elderly.html.

3. Peter Kilborn, "Disabled Spouses Are Increasingly Forced to Go It
Alone," *New York Times*, May 31, 1999, www.nytimes.com/1999/05/03/us/
disabled-spouses-are-increasingly-forced-to-go-it-alone.html.

4. Richard Schulz and Scott Beach, "Caregiving as a Risk Factor for Mortality," *JAMA* 282, no. 23 (1999): 2215–19; and Janice Kiecolt-Glaser and Richard Glaser, "Chronic Stress and Morbidity among Older Adults," *JAMA* 282,
no. 23 (1999): 2259–19.

5. Schulz and Beach, "Caregiving as a Risk Factor for Mortality," 2215.

6. Tamar Lewin, "Report Looks at a Generation and Caring for Young and
Old," *New York Times*, July 11, 2001, www.nytimes.com/2001/07/11/us/report-
looks-at-a-generation-and-caring-for-young-and-old.html.

7. Sara Rimer, "Study Details Sacrifices in Caring for Elderly Kin," *New
York Times*, November 27, 1999, www.nytimes.com/1999/11/27/us/study-
details-sacrifices-in-caring-for-elderly-kin.html.

8. Lewin, "Report Looks at a Generation and Caring for Young and Old."

9. Sara Rimer, "Blacks Carry Burden of Care for Their Elderly," *New York
Times*, March 15, 1998, www.nytimes.com/1998/03/15/us/blacks-carry-load-of-
care-for-their-elderly.html.

10. Nicholas Kristoff, "Once Prized, Japan's Elderly Feel Abandoned and
Fearful," *New York Times*, August 4, 1997, www.nytimes.com/1997/08/04/
world/once-prized-japan-s-elderly-feel-abandoned-and-fearful.html.

11. Sana Siwolop, "The Many Life Styles of Senior Housing," *New York
Times*, May 16, 1999, www.nytimes.com/1999/05/16/realestate/the-many-life-
styles-of-senior-housing.html; and Sara Rimer, "A Niche for the Elderly, and
for the Market," *New York Times*, May 9, 1999, www.nytimes.com/1999/05/09/
us/a-helping-home-a-special-report-a-niche-for-the-elderly-and-for-the-
market.html.

12. Assisted Living and Senior Care Facilities, accessed February 4, 2014, www.assistedlivingfacilities.com.

13. "They Didn't Live So Long for This," *New York Times* editorial, April 26, 1999, www.nytimes.com/1999/04/26/opinion/they-didn-t-live-so-long-for-this.html.

14. Hila Richardson, "In Long Term Care," in *Health Care Delivery in the United States*, ed. Anthony Kovner (New York: Springer Publishing, 1990), 175–208.

15. A. Scitovsky and A. Capron, "Medical Care at the End of Life: The Interaction of Economics and Ethics," *Annual Review of Public Health* (impact factor 3.27) 7 (February 1986): 59–75, www.researchgate.net/publication/20069661-medical-care-at-the-end-of-life-the-interaction-of-economics-and-ethics.

16. Richardson, "In Long Term Care."

17. National Center for Health Statistics, "Americans Less Likely to Use Nursing Home Care Today," *HHS News*, January 23, 1997, http://archive.hhs.gov/news/press/1997pres/970123b.html.

18. "Nursing Home Care," FastStats, Centers for Disease Control, updated May 2013, accessed February 4, 2014, www.cdc.gov/nchs/fastats/nursingh.htm.

19. Sheryl Stolberg, "Study Finds Pain of Oldest Is Ignored in Nursing Homes," *New York Times*, June 17, 1998, www.newyorktimes/1998/06/17/us/study-finds-pain-of-oldest-is-ignored-in-nursing-homes.html.

20. "They Didn't Live So Long for This."

21. Sara Rimer, "An Aging Nation Ill-Equipped for Hanging Up the Car Keys," *New York Times*, December 15, 1997, www.nytimes.com/1997/12/15/us/an-aging-nation-ill-equipped-for-hanging-up-the-car-keys.html.

22. U.S. Department of Transportation, "Licensed Drivers by Age and Sex," Federal Highway Administration, last updated April 4, 2011, www.fhwa.dot.gov/ohim/onh00/onh2p4.htm.

23. Wayne A. Ray, "Safety and Mobility of the Older Driver," editorial, *JAMA* 278, no. 1 (1997): 66–67.

24. Thomas Cole, *The Journey of Life* (Cambridge: Cambridge University Press: 1992), xix.

7. AGEISM—MARGINALIZING OLDER PEOPLE

1. William Shakespeare, Act 1, Scene 2, *King Lear* (New York: The Signet Classic Shakespeare, 1986), 17.

2. Betty Friedan, *The Fountain of Age* (New York, Simon and Schuster, 1993), 40–41.

3. Thomas Cole, *The Journey of Life* (Cambridge: Cambridge University Press, 1992), 64–65.

4. Ibid., 163–65.

5. David Rosenblum, "Social Security: The Basics, with a Tally Sheet," *New York Times*, January 29, 1999, www.nytimes.com/1999/01/28/us/social-security-the-basics-with-a-tally-sheet.html.

6. John Tagliabue, "In France, Nothing Gets in the Way of Vacation," *New York Times*, August 24, 2003, www.nytimes.com/2003/08/24/weekinreview/ideas-trends-in-france-nothing-gets-in-the-way-of-vacation.html, and Fred Brock, "Victims of the Heat: Victims of Isolation," *New York Times*, Business section, September 14, 2003, www.nytimes.com/2003/09/14/business/seniority-victims-of-the-heat-victims-of-isolation.html.

7. Alladi Venkatesh, Debora E. Dunkle, and Amanda Wortman, "Evolving Patterns of Household Computer Use 1999–2010," Center for Research on Information Technology and Organization, The Paul Merage School of Business, University of California, Irvine, accessed Februry 5, 2014, http://crito.uci.edu/papers/2011/HouseholdComputerUse.pdf.

8. Julie Flaherty, "A Company Where Retirement Is a Dirty Word," *New York Times*, Section 3, December 28, 1997, www.nytimes.com/1997/12/28/business/earning-it-a-company-where-retirement-is-a-dirty-word.html.

9. Fred Brock, "Slow to Learn the Lessons of Ageism," *New York Times*, Sunday business section, December 2, 2001, www.nytimes.com/2001/12/02/business/yourmoney/02SENI.html.

10. Francis X. Clines, "Glenn Is Ready to Say Goodbye to All That," *New York Times*, June 13, 1998, national edition, www.nytimes.com?1998/06/13/us/glenn-is-ready-to-say-goodbye-to-all-that.html.

11. Robert N. Butler and Alice V. Luddington, "Aging Research: John Glenn's New Mission," *Geriatrics* 53, no. 9 (1998): 42–48.

12. Steven Greenhouse, "Working Late, by Choice or Not," *New York Times*, special section on retirement, May 10, 2012, www.nytimes.com/2012/05/10/business/retirementspecial/for-many-reasons-older-americans-remain-at-work.html?pagewanted=all&_r=0.

13. Don Terry, "In This Brand-New City, No Shortage of Elders," *New York Times*, March 4, 1999, www.nytimes.com/1999/03/04/us/in-this-brand-new-city-no-shortage-of-elders.html.

14. Sara Rimer, "New Needs for Retirement Complexes' Oldest," *New York Times*, March 23, 1998, www.nytimes.com/1998/03/23/us/new-needs-for-retirement-complexes-eldest.html.

15. Ibid.

16. Alan Feuer, "Haven for Workers in Bronx Evolves for Their Retirement," *New York Times*, August 5, 2002, www.nytimes.com/2002/08/05/

nyregion/haven-for-workers-in-bronx-evolves-for-their-retirement.html?ref=
alanfeuer.

17. Ivor Peterson, "As Taxes Rise, Suburbs Work to Keep Elderly," *New York Times*, February 27, 2001, www.nytimes.com/learning/aol/pop/articles/27SUBU.html.

18. Robert Butler, "Commentary: Living Longer, Contributing Longer," *JAMA* 278, no. 16 (1997): 1372–73.

19. Bill Carter, "Faces on TV Get Younger and Comedy Is Not King," *New York Times*, May 24, 1999, www.nytimes.com/1999/05/24/arts/faces-on-tv-get-younger-and-comedy-is-not-king.html.

20. Anne Jarrell, "Models, Defiantly Gray, Give Aging a Sexy New Look," *New York Times*, November 28, 1999, www.nytimes.com/1999/11/28/style/noticed-models-defiantly-gray-give-aging-a-sexy-new-look.html.

21. Cam Marston, "Boomers Saving the Box Office," Generational Insights, August 30, 2012, www.generationalinsights.com/boomers-saving-the-box-office/.

22. Douglas Frantz, "Sweepstakes Pit Gullibility and Fine Print," *New York Times*, July 28, 1998, www.nytimes.com/1998/07/28/us/sweepstakes-pit-gullibility-and-fine-print.html; and Douglas Frantz, "Phone Swindles Steal a Page from Publishers' Playbook," *New York Times*, July 29, 1998, www.nytimes.com/1998/07/29/us/phone-swindles-steal-a-page-from-publishers-playbook.html?pagewanted=all&src=pm.

8. THE QUEST: STRATEGIES FOR CONTROL

1. Lao-Tzu, Number 9, *Tao-Te-Ching*, trans. Stephen Mitchell (New York: Harper and Row, 1988).

2. Ruth La Ferla, "Over 60: Fashion's Lost Generation," *New York Times*, Sunday styles section, December 3, 2000, www.nytimes.com/2000/12/03/style/over-60-fashion-s-lost-generation.html?pagewanted=3.

3. Kenneth Mukamal et al., "Roles of Drinking Pattern and Type of Alcohol Consumed in Coronary Heart Disease in Men," *New England Journal of Medicine* 348, no. 2 (2003): 109–18.

4. Ana Pereira et al., "An *In Vivo* Correlate of Exercise-Induced Neurogenesis in the Adult Dentate Gyrus," *Proceedings of the National Academy of Science* 104, no. 13 (2007): 5638–43; Nicola T. Lautenschlager, "Effects of Physical Activity on Cognitive Function of Older Adults at Risk for Alzheimer's Disease," *JAMA* 300, no. 9 (2008): 1027–37; Gunnar Eriksson et al., "Changes in Physical Fitness and Changes in Mortality," *Lancet* 352, no. 9130 (1998): 759–62; S. Blair et al., "Influences of Cardiorespiratory Fitness and Other

Precursors and All-Cause Mortality in Men and Women," *JAMA* 276, no. 3 (1996): 205–10; E. Simonsick et al., "Risk Due to Inactivity in Physically Capable Older Adults," *American Journal of Public Health* 83, no. 10 (1993): 1443–50; Pekka Kannus, "Preventing Osteoporosis, Falls and Fractures among Elderly People," *BMJ* 318, no. 7178 (1999): 205–6; Steven Blair et al., "Changes in Physical Fitness and All-Cause Mortality," *JAMA* 273, no. 14 (1995): 1093–98; Amy Hakim et al., "Effects of Walking on Mortality among Nonsmoking Retired Men," *New England Journal of Medicine* 338, no. 2 (1998): 94–98; Linda Fried et al., "Risk Factors for 5-Year Mortality in Older Adults," *JAMA* 279, no. 8 (1998): 585–92; L. Sandvik et al., "Physical Fitness as a Predictor of Mortality among Healthy Middle-Aged Norwegian Men," *New England Journal of Medicine* 328, no. 8 (1993): 533–37; Ralph Paffenbarger et al., "The Association of Changes in Physical Activity Level and Other Lifestyle Characteristics with Mortality among Men," *New England Journal of Medicine* 328, no. 8 (1993): 538–45; and William Kraus et al., "Effects of the Amount and Intensity of Exercise on Plasma Lipoproteins," *New England Journal of Medicine* 347, no. 19 (2002): 1483–92.

5. Lawrence Kushi et al., "Physical Activity and Mortality in Postmenopausal Women," *JAMA* 277, no. 16 (1997): 1287–92; I-Min Lee, Chung-cheng Hsieh, and Ralph S. Paffenbarger Jr., "Exercise Intensity and Longevity in Men," *JAMA* 273, no. 15 (1995): 1179–84; and Michael Pratt, "Benefits of Lifestyle Activity vs Structured Exercise," *JAMA* 281, no. 4 (1999): 375–76.

6. Jane Brody, "Panel Urges Hour of Exercise a Day: Sets Diet Guidelines," *New York Times*, September 6, 2002, www.nytimes.com/2002/09/06/health/06DIET.html.

7. R. Butler et al., "Physical Fitness: Exercise Prescription for Older Adults," *Geriatrics* 53, no. 11 (1998): 45–56; Holcomb Noble, "A Secret of Health in Old Age: Muscles," *New York Times*, October 20, 1998, www.nytimes.com/1998/10/20/science/a-secret-of-health-in-old-age-muscles.html; Sara Rimer, "Older, Wiser, Stronger: Grandmas Head for the Weight Room," *New York Times*, June 21, 1998, www.nytimes.com/1998/06/21/health/older-wiser-stronger-grandmas-head-for-the-weight-room.html; Maria Fiatarone et al., "High-Intensity Strength Training in Nonagenerians," *JAMA* 263, no. 22 (1990): 3029–34.

8. Gretchen Reynolds, "WELL; Phys Ed: A Bit Here, a Bit There, Exercise Pays Off," *New York Times*, July 31, 2012, http://query.nytimes.com/gst/fullpage.html?res=9F0DE1DA1731F932A05754C0A9649D8B63.

9. Gretchen Reynolds, "The Rise of the Minimalist Workout," *New York Times*, June 24, 2013, http://well.blogs.nytimes.com/2013/6/24/the-rise-of-the-minimalist-workout?php=true&-type=blog_r=0.

10. Pauline Anderson, "Regularly Breaking a Sweat May Protect against Stroke," Medscape, July 19, 2013, www.medscape.com.

11. B. M. van Gelder et al., "Physical Activity in Relation to Cognitive Decline in Elderly Men," *Neurology* 63, no. 12 (2004): 2316–21; Jennifer Wueve et al., "Physical Activity, Including Walking, and Cognitive Function in Older Women," *JAMA* 292, no. 12 (2004): 1454–61; Robert Abbott et al., "Walking and Dementia in Physically Capable Elderly Men," *JAMA* 292, no. 12 (2004): 1447–53.

12. Olga Rukovets, "Midlife Fitness Associated with Decreased Dementia Later in Life," *Neurology Today* 13, no. 7 (April 4, 2013): 1.

13. Pereira et al., "An *In Vivo* Correlate of Exercise-Induced Neurogenesis."

14. Megan Brooks, "Resistance Training May Delay Dementia Onset," Medscape, May 2, 2012, www.medscape.com/viewarticle/763105.

15. Butler et al., "Physical Fitness: Exercise Prescription for Older Adults."

16. Ibid.

17. L. Partridge, "Diet and Healthy Aging," *New England Journal of Medicine* 367, no. 26 (December 27, 2012): 2550–51.

18. I-Min Lee et al., "Body Weight and Mortality," *JAMA* 270, no. 23 (1993): 2823–28; June Stevens et al., "The Effect of Age on the Association Between Body-Mass Index and Mortality," *New England Journal of Medicine* 338, no. 1 (1998): 1–7; and Anthony Vita et al., "Aging, Health Risks, and Cumulative Disability," *New England Journal of Medicine* 338, no. 15 (1998): 1035–41.

19. Kevin Fontaine et al., "Years of Life Lost Due to Obesity," *JAMA* 289, no. 2 (2003): 187–93; and JoAnn Manson and Shari Bassuk, "Obesity in the United States—a Fresh Look at Its High Toll," *JAMA* 289, no. 2 (2003): 229–30.

20. Gina Kolata, "Mediterranean Diet Shown to Ward Off Heart Attack and Stroke," *New York Times*, February 25, 2013, www.nytimes.com/2013/02/26/health/mediterranean-diet-can-cut-heart-disease-study-finds.html?pagewanted=all.

21. Georgios Tsivgoulis et al., "Adherence to a Mediterranean Diet and Risk of Incident Cognitive Impairment," *Neurology* 80, no. 18 (2013): 1684–92.

22. Ying Bao et al., "Association of Nut Consumption with Total and Cause-Specific Mortality," *New England Journal of Medicine* 369, no. 21 (2013): 2001–11.

23. William Thompson et al., "Mortality Associated with Influenza and Respiratory Syncytial Virus in the United States," *JAMA* 289, no. 2 (2003): 179–86.

24. Susan Jacoby, "Great Sex—What's Age Got to Do with It? The AARP/ *Modern Maturity* Survey on Sexual Attitudes and Behavior," *Modern Maturity* (September/October 1999): 41.

25. Edward Laumann et al., "Sexual Dysfunction in the United States," *JAMA* 281, no. 6 (1999): 537–44.

26. Robert Butler, "Editorial—the Viagra Revolution," *Geriatrics* 53, no. 10 (1998): 8–9.

27. Jane Gross, "Wielding Mouse and Modem, Elderly Remain in the Loop," *New York Times*, June 15, 1998, www.nytimes.com/1998/06/15/ nyregion/wielding-mouse-and-modem-elderly-remain-in-the-loop.html? pagewanted=all&src=pm.

28. Benedict Carey, "Sleep Therapy Seen as an Aid for Depression," *New York Times*, November 19, 2013, www.nytimes.com/2013/11/24/health/sleep-therapy-is-expected-to-gain-a-wider-role-in-depression-treatment.html?ref= benedictcarey.

29. Karlene Ball et al., "Effects of Cognitive Training Interventions with Older Adults," *JAMA* 288, no. 18 (2003): 2271–81.

30. Howard Fillit et al., "Achieving and Maintaining Cognitive Vitality with Aging," *Mayo Clinic Proceedings* 77, no. 7 (2002): 681–96.

31. Robert Wilson et al., "Life-Span Cognitive Activity, Neuropathologic Burden, and Cognitive Aging," *Neurology* 81, no. 4 (2013): 314–21.

32. Christine Cassel, "Editorial—Use It or Lose It," *JAMA* 288, no. 18 (2002): 2333–35.

9. IT'S IN YOUR HANDS: ADDITIONAL STRATEGIES

1. "Even Such Is Time Which Takes in Trust," Dictionary.com, Columbia World of Quotations, Columbia University Press, 1996. http://quotes. dictionary.com/Even_such_is_Time_which_takes_in_trust.

2. Elizabeth Pope, "A Longer Life Is Lived with Company," *New York Times*, September 11, 2012. www.nytimes.com/2012/09/12/business/ retirementspecial/for-older-adults-close-connections-are-key-to-healthy-aging. html.

3. Thomas Moore, "Spring and Autumn," BrainyQuote.com, 2014, www. brainyquote.com/quotes/quotes/t/thomasmoor384582.html.

4. Jane Brody, "Ways to Make Retirement Work for You," *New York Times*, July 24, 2001, www.nytimes.com/2001/07/24/health/personal-health-ways-to-make-retirement-work-for-you.html.

5. Frank Bruni, "89 and 2000 Miles to Go for 'Democracy'," *New York Times*, April 27, 1999, www.nytimes.com/1999/04/27/us/89-and-2000-miles-to-go-for-democracy.html.

6. Harold Koenig et al., "Does Religious Attendance Prolong Survival? A Six-Year Follow-Up Study of 3,968 Older Adults," *Journal of Gerontology* 54A, no. 7 (1999): M370–M376.

7. Ibid.

8. Brett Pulley, "Glitzy Pastime, Gambling, Entices Elderly," *New York Times*, July 2, 1998, www.nytimes.com/1998/07/02/us/glitzy-pastime-gambling-entices-elderly.html?pagewanted=all&src=pm.

9. Ibid.

10. Suzi Levens et al., "Gambling among Older, Primary-Care Patients: An Important Public Health Concern," *American Journal of Geriatric Psychiatry* 13, no. 1 (2005): 69–76.

11. Sara Rimer, "An Alaska Trek Makes Elders of the Aging," *New York Times*, September 2, 1998, www.nytimes.com/1998/09/02/us/an-alaska-trek-makes-elders-of-the-aging.html.

12. "Elderhostel," *Wikipedia*, last modified August 30, 2013, http://en.wikipedia.org/wiki/elderhostel.

13. Edwin McDowell, "Travel Industry Finds Adventure Is Now Ageless," *New York Times*, February 20, 1999, www.nytimes.com/1999/02/20/business/travel-industry-finds-adventure-now-ageless-many-older-vacationers-shun-tour-bus.html.

14. Ibid.

15. Jodi Wilgoren, "Golden Years Now Bring New Emphasis on Learning," *New York Times*, December 26, 1999, www.nytimes.com/1999/12/26/golden-years-now-bring-new-emphasis-on-learning.html.

16. David Wetzel, "Why Older Adults Are Going Back to School," Suite 101, July 27, 2010, https://suite101.com/article/why-older-adults-are-going-back-to-school-a266406.

17. Jay Tokasz, "White Hairs Settle In among the Ivy," *New York Times*, March 21, 2001, www.nytimes.com/2001/03/21/business/21RETI-TOKA.html.

18. Thomas Glass et al., "Population Based Study of Social and Productive Activities as Predictors of Survival among Elderly Americans," *BMJ* 319, no. 7208 (1999): 478–83.

19. Joe Verghese et al., "Leisure Activities and the Risk of Dementia in the Elderly," *New England Journal of Medicine* 348, no. 25 (2003): 2508–16.

20. J. Coyle, "Use It or Lose It—Do Effortful Mental Activities Protect against Dementia?," *New England Journal of Medicine* 348, no. 25 (2003): 2489–90.

21. Douglas Martin, "Work First, Invest Later? Not These Days; To Be Old, Gifted and Employed Is No Longer Rare," *New York Times*, January 14, 2001, www.nytimes.com/2001/01/14/business/work-first-invest-later-not-these-days-be-old-gifted-employed-no-longer-rare.html.

22. Vincent Fernando, "70% of the Elderly Aren't Retiring Because They Can't Afford to Anymore," Infowars.com, March 3, 2010, www.infowars.com/70-of-the-elderly-arent-retiring-because-they-cant-afford-to-anymore/

23. E. S. Browning, "Too Much Debt to Retire," September 7, 2011, Smart-Money.com, www.smartmoney.com/rwetirement/planning/too-much-debt-to-retire-1315407838873/.

24. Patricia Marx, "Golden Years," *New Yorker*, October 8, 2012, www.newyorker.com/reporting/2012/10/08/121008fa_fact_marx.

25. Ted Barrett, "GOP Senators Propose Raising Age for Social Security Benefits," April 13, 2011, CNN: *Political Ticker*, http://politicalticker.blogs.cnn.com/2011/04/13/.

26. "Medicare and Beyond," Columbia Forum, *Columbia College Today* (Fall 1998): 40.

27. Sara Rimer, "Older People Want to Work in Retirement, Survey Finds," *New York Times*, September 2, 1999, www.nytimes.com/1999/09/02/us/older-people-want-to-work-in-retirement-survey-finds.html.

28. Ibid.

29. Marci Alboher, "A Switch at Midlife, to Make a Difference," *New York Times*, December 8, 2012, www.nytimes.com/2012/12/09/jobs/switching-careers-at-midlife-to-make-a-difference.html?_r=0.

30. Jessica Silver-Greenberg, "A Risky Lifeline for the Elderly Is Costing Some Their Homes," *New York Times*, October 14, 2012, www.nytimes.com/2012/10/15/business/reverse-mortgages-costing-some-seniors-their-homes.html.

31. Patricia Marx, "Golden Years."

32. John Cutter, "Coming to Terms with Grief after a Longtime Partner Dies," *New York Times*, June 13, 1999, www.nytimes.com/specials/women/061399hth-women-widow.html.

33. Ibid.

34. Ernest Hemingway, *For Whom the Bell Tolls* (New York: Charles Scribner, 1968): 463.

35. Associated Press, "E-Mail and the Internet Brighten Nursing Homes," *New York Times*, November 23, 1999, www.nytimes.com/1999/11/23/science/e-mail-and-the-internet-brighten-nursing-homes.html.

36. Fred Brock, "Catering to the Elderly Can Pay Off," *New York Times*, Business Section, February 3, 2002, www.nytimes.com/2002/02/03/business/seniority-catering-to-the-elderly-can-pay-off.html.

37. Mary Duenwald, "Power of Positive Thinking Extends, It Seems, to Aging," *New York Times*, November 19, 2002, www.nytimes.com/2002/11/19/ science/power-of-positive-thinking-extends-it-seems-to-aging.html.

10. WHAT THE FUTURE HOLDS—AGING IN THE NEW MILLENNIUM

1. Lao-Tzu, Number 74, *Tao Te Ching*, trans. Stephen Mitchell (New York: Harper and Row, 1988).

2. Dana Canedy, "Gadgets Go Gentle into Age," *New York Times*, October 17, 1998, www.nytimes.com/1998/10/17/business/gadgets-to-go-gentle-into-age-a-market-grows-and-modernizes-as-demand-increases.html; and Thomas Claburn, "Google Autonomous Cars Get Green Light in California," *Information Week*, September 27, 2012, www.informationweek.com/government/ policy/google-autonomous-cars-get-green-light-i240008033.

3. Anne Eisenberg, "A 'Smart Home' to Avoid the Nursing Home," *New York Times*, April 5, 2001, www.nytimes.com/2001/04/05/technology/a-smart-home-to-avoid-the-nursing-home.html.

4. University of Hertfordshire, "Robotic Companions for Older People," Product Design and Development, December 2, 2011, www.pddnet.com/ news/2011/12/robotic-companions-older-people.

5. Claburn, "Google Autonomous Cars."

6. Katie Hafner, "Honey, I Programmed the Blanket," *New York Times*, May 27, 1999, www.nytimes.com/1999/05/27/technology/honey-i-programmed-the-blanket.html.

7. John Markhoff, "Intel and Alzheimer's Group Join Forces," *New York Times*, July 25, 2003, www.nytimes.com/2003/07/25/technology/25OLD.html.

8. Claburn, "Google Autonomous Cars."

9. "Could Robots and Smart Devices Help Older People Look After Themselves?," *Science Daily*, March 26, 2010, www.sciencedaily.com/releases/ 2010/03/100324184558.htm; "Companion Robots to Improve Elderly People's Quality of Life in Smart Homes," *Science Daily*, April 6, 2009, www. sciencedaily.com/releases/2009/04/090416083350.htm.

10. Scott Kirsner, "Making Robots, with Dreams of Henry Ford," *New York Times*, December 26, 2002, www.nytimes.com/2002/12/26/technology/making-robots-with-dreams-of-henry-ford.html.

11. Kevin O'Brien, "Robots Are Nearing Reach of Consumers," *New York Times*, December 10, 2012, www.nytimes.com/2012/12/10/technology/robotic-gadgets-are-becoming-within-reach-of-average-consumer.html?_r=0.

12. Ricki Lewis, "Genes as Medicine: Molecular Therapy Comes of Age," Medscape, November 13, 2012, www.medscape.com/viewarticle/774365.

13. Sandra Blakelee, "In Early Experiments, Cells Repair Damaged Brains," *New York Times*, Science section, November 7, 2000, www.nytimes.com/2000/11/07/science/in-early-experiments-cells-repair-damaged-brains.html.

14. Jeffrey Saver, "Thrombolytic Therapy in Strokes—Ischemic Stroke and Neurologic Deficits," Medscape References, updated September 18, 2012, http://emedicine.medscape.com/article/1160840-overview.

15. Lauren LeBano, "Brain Changes May Begin Decades before Onset of Alzheimer's Disease," *Neurology Reviews* 20, no. 8 (August 2012), www.neurologyreviews.com/index.php?id=25318&tx_ttnews[tt_news]=208046.

16. Sid O'Bryant, "Using Blood Markers for Alzheimer's Disease in Clinical Practice?," *Neurology* 79, no. 9 (2012): 846–47.

17. J. Michael Gaziano et al., "Multivitamins in the Prevention of Cancer in Men," *JAMA* 308, no. 18 (2012): 1871–80.

18. Pauline Anderson, "Metformin May Help Renew Neurons," Medscape, July 10, 2012, www.medscape.com/viewarticle/767139.

19. Kirsty L. Spalding et al., "Dynamics of Hippocampal Neurogenesis in Adult Humans," *Cell* 153, no. 6 (2013): 1219–77.

20. Susan Crowley, "Hello to Our Future," *AARP Bulletin* 41, no. 1 (January 2000).

21. Howard French, "Hot New Marketing Concept: Mall as Memory Lane," *New York Times*, January 7, 2003, www.nytimes.com/2003/01/07/world/tokyo-journal-hot-new-marketing-concept-mall-as-memory-lane.html.

11. DOING IT YOUR WAY—PREPARING FOR LIFE'S END

1. Kahlil Gibran, *The Prophet* (New York: Alfred A. Knopf, 1961), 81.

2. N. Jecker and L. Schneiderman, "Futility and Rationing," *American Journal of Medicine* 92, no. 2 (1992): 189–96.

3. Ibid., 6.

4. Alan Lieberson, *Advance Medical Directives* (New York: Clark, Boardman, Callaghan, 1992), 9.

5. Ibid.

6. *Advance Directives and End-of-Life-Decisions*, 5.

7. Ibid., 7.

8. Lieberson, *Advance Medical Directives*, 53.

9. *Choice in Dying*, 5.

10. Ibid., 8.

11. John Donne, "Holy Sonnets III," *The New Oxford Book of English Verse*, ed. Helen Gardner (Oxford: Oxford University Press, 1984), 197.

12. Book of Job, 14:1, *The Holy Scriptures* (Philadelphia, PA: The Jewish Publication Society of America, 1955), 1044.

13. Derek Humphry, introduction to *Final Exit* (New York: Dell Publications, 1996), xiii–xxi.

14. Timothy Quill, *Death and Dignity* (New York: W. W. Norton, 1993), 9.

15. Humphry, *Final Exit*, 123–28.

16. Erik Eckhold, "'Aid in Dying' Movement Takes Hold in Some States," *New York Times*, February 8, 2014, A1, www.nytimes.com/2014/02/08/us/easing-terminal-patients-path-to-death-legally.html?partner=rss&emc=rss.

12. OBSERVATIONS AND CONCLUSIONS

1. Viktor E. Frankl, *Man's Search for Meaning* (New York: A Touchstone Book, 1984), 113–14.

FOR FURTHER REFERENCE

NUTRITION

Fuhrman, Joel. *Eat to Live Cookbook*. New York: Harper Collins, 2013. Two hundred recipes that promote good health.

Herbert, Victor, and Geneel J. Subak-Sharp, eds. *Total Nutrition: The Only Guide You'll Ever Need, from the Mount Sinai School of Medicine*. New York: St. Martin's Griffin, 1995. Voluminous book, old but with a huge amount of information.

Smolin, Lori A., and Mary B. Grosvenor. *Basic Nutrition (Healthy Eating: A Guide to Nutrition)*. New York: Facts on File, 2010. An introduction to basic nutritional concepts. Discusses our need for carbohydrates, proteins, fiber, lipids, vitamins, minerals, and how they function in our bodies.

EXERCISE

Exercise and Physical Activity: Your Everyday Guide from the National Institute on Aging. Guide to various exercises and physical activity for older people. Can be downloaded or ordered online from the National Institute on Aging from their website.

Fenton, Mark. *The Complete Guide to Walking for Health, Weight Loss, and Fitness*. Guilford, CT: The Globe Pequot Press, 2001. All aspects of walking, stretching, exercise, nutrition, and so forth.

Metzl, Jordon D., with Andrew Heffernan. *The Exercise Cure*. New York: Rodale Press, 2013. Shows how exercise can improve overall health and extend life.

Reynolds, Gretchen. *The First 20 Minutes: The Surprising Science of How We Can Exercise Better, Train Smarter, Live Longer*. New York: Hudson Street Press, 2012. The importance of keeping your body in motion, what you can do, and new discoveries in exercise science.

SEXUALITY

Black, Joel D. *Sex Over 50*. New York: Penguin Group, 2008. Describes how older people can have an exciting and fulfilling sex life. Addresses common problems and offers solutions. Also discusses dating scene for single boomers.

Lynn, Doree, with Cindy Spitzer. *Sex for Grown-Ups*. Deerfield Beach, FL: Health Communications, Inc., 2010. How to improve sexual attitudes and performance as we age, with advice on the older dating scene.

Price, Joan. *Naked at Our Age: Talking Out Loud about Senior Sex*. Berkeley, CA: Seal Press, 2011. Challenges and joys of love and sex late in life. Problems and successes, questions and advice.

MEMORY AND COGNITIVE FUNCTION

Amen, Daniel G. *Use Your Brain to Change Your Age*. New York: Crown Archtype, 2012. Techniques for improving cognitive function. Also addresses psychiatric problems, sexuality, and nutrition.

Foer, Joshua. *Moonwalking with Einstein: The Art and Science of Remembering Everything*. New York: Penguin Press, 2011. Strategies and techniques to help boost memory, applicable at every age.

Fotuhi, Majid. *The Memory Cure: How to Protect Your Brain against Memory Loss and Alzheimer's Disease*. New York: McGraw-Hill, 2003. What is memory and how does it work? How does aging affect the brain? How to protect the brain against Alzheimer's and memory loss. (Does not include recent data.)

Hurley, Dan. *Smarter: The New Science of Building Brain Power*. New York: Penguin Group, 2013. Science journalist Hurley expands his *New York Times Magazine* article describing new techniques of learning and solving problems.

Levine, Robert A. *Defying Dementia*. Lanham, MD: Rowman and Littlefield Publishers, 2010. Different types of dementia including Alzheimer's disease described in depth. A comprehensive program to prevent dementia is presented.

COSMETIC SURGERY

Copland, Michelle, with Alexandra Postman. *Change Your Looks, Change Your Life*. New York: Harper Resources, 2003. Describes various cosmetic procedures and what they entail.

Narins, Rhoda, and Paul Jarod Frank. *Turn Back the Clock without Losing Time*. New York: Three Rivers Press, 2002. Guide to various cosmetic procedures, both surgical and nonsurgical.

GENERAL HEALTH AND AGING

Hill, Robert. *Seven Strategies for Positive Aging*. New York: W. W. Norton and Company, 2008. How to find satisfaction in life while aging using various strategies.

Lorig, Kate, and Halsted Holman. *Living a Healthy Life with Chronic Conditions*. Boulder, CO: Bull Publishing Company, 2012. Self-management of major conditions affecting older people. Includes symptoms of diseases, exercise, nutrition, sex, medication, and so forth.

Gurian, Michael. *The Wonder of Aging: A New Approach to Embracing Life after Fifty*. New York: Altria Books, 2013. Addresses spiritual, emotional, and cognitive aspects of aging and how to derive positive benefits from the process.

Lustbader, Wendy. *Life Gets Better: The Unexpected Pleasures of Growing Old*. New York: Jeremy P. Tarcher/Penguin, 2011. What happens when we get older—what's good about it, and how we can make it better.

Weil, Andrew. *Healthy Aging*. New York: Alfred A. Knopf, 2007. Understanding the aging process and some "alternative" approaches to the problems of aging.

INDEX

AARP, 209
AARP 1999 Survey on Sexuality, 187
AARP Report 2001, 132
ABCD$_2$ score, 91
abdominal arterial disease, 95
abortion, 26
abuse of elderly, 12
accelerated aging, 121–122
acceptance of aging, 171–174
acetylcholine, 75, 88
administrative assistance, 126
adrenal, 80
advance directives, 266–270
Afghanistan War, 22
age discrimination, 156–159
ageism, 11–12, 151–169
ageist bias, counteracting, 233–234
ageist jokes, 168–169
age spots, 82
aging process, 67–84; antagonistic
    pleiotropic theory, 71; biologic clock,
    71; cellular aging, 68–70; errors in
    cellular repair, 72; free radical theory,
    71; immune system changes, 72, 112;
    mutations and genetic errors, 71;
    theories of aging, 70–74
aging process—the future, 244–246
aging successfully, 13
AIDS, 33
Al-Anon, 177
alcohol and drugs, 24, 32, 119, 176–177

Alcoholics Anonymous, 177
Ali, Muhammad, 59
alpha blockers, 101
alveoli, 78
Alzheimer's and diabetes, 88
Alzheimer's disease, 51, 87–90, 93–94
American Academy of Anti-Aging
    Medicine, 80
American Graffiti, 25
American Journal of Geriatric Psychiatry,
    212
amyloid, 75, 88, 90
annual physical, 32
antibodies, 72
antioxidants, 71, 80
anxiety, 118, 197
aortic aneurysms, 98
Apocalypse Now, 25
APOE E4, 87
appearance, 201
Apple, 23
Aricept, 90
Armstrong, Neal, 59
arthritis. See osteoarthritis; rheumatoid
    arthritis
artificial support mechanisms, 140
aspirin, 92, 98, 107–108
assets. See finances
assisted living residences, 135–136
Astor, Brooke, 12
atherosclerosis, 67, 91–93, 95–99

atomic bomb, 45
attitudes, 11, 41
Aurelius, Marcus, 1, 43
authors, 25
The Autobiography of Malcolm X, 25
autoimmune diseases, 72

B_6, 96
B_{12}, 96
Baby Boomers, 2, 6, 19–41
balance, 76
bapineuzumab, 90
Barron's, 223
Basie, Count, 46
The Beach Boys, 24
Beard, George Miller, 152
The Beatles, 24, 59
Beat Movement, 59
Beaumont, Francis, 123
Bellow, Saul, 25
benign prostate hyperplasia (BPH), 101
bereavement counselors, 230
Berle, Milton, 58
Berry, Chuck, 58
Beyond Freedom and Dignity, 25
biking, 180
biologic clock, 71
biologics, 108
bipolar disorder, 116
bobby-soxers, 58
bone densitometry, 106
Bonnie and Clyde, 25
books, 25
Brain (journal), 88
brain and central nervous system—the
    future, 247–248
brain atrophy, 75
brain ventricles, 75
Brando, Marlon, 59
breadwinner, 52
breakdown sores, 102
Brokaw, Tom, 43
brotherhood of the aged, 203
Brown, Dee, 25
Brown, James, 59
Brown v. Board of Education, 59
Buck, Pearl, 46
Buckley, William, 59
Buffet, Warren, 11

Burroughs, William, 59
Bury My Heart at Wounded Knee, 25
Bush, George W., 22
Butler, Robert, 11, 222
Byrd, Robert, 159

CABG, 51, 97
calorie restriction, 73, 74
cancer, 112–115; early detection, 113;
    etiologies, 112; prevention, 113; types,
    113
cancer—the future, 250–251
Capitalism and Freedom, 25
carcinogenic, 113
cardiac neurosis, 98
cardiovascular system—the future,
    246–247
caregivers, paid, 134–135
carotid surgery (endarterectomy), 92
Carson, Rachael, 25
cataracts, 111
Catholic Church, 46
causes (organizations or issues), 208
chemotherapy, 115
Cheney, Dick, 59, 97
chicken pox, 109
Chinatown, 25
cholinesterase inhibitors, 90
choosing to die, 261–262, 278–285
chronic obstructive pulmonary disease
    (COPD), 100; alveoli, 100; aspiration,
    100; bronchitis, chronic, 100; dyspnea,
    100; emphysema, 100; oxygen, 100;
    phlegm, 100; pulmonary cripples, 100;
    pulmonary toilet, 100
chronic traumatic encephalopathy, 90
Cialis, 103, 189
Citizen Kane, 46
Civilian Conservation Corps, 44
civil rights, 59
civil rights movement, 23, 58, 59
classification of ages, 10
claudication, 98
Clinton, Bill, 22
A Clockwork Orange, 25
Clooney, Rosemary, 58
clot busters, 91, 97
cognitive vitality, 202
Cold War, 22, 45

Cole, Nat King, 46
Cole, Thomas R., 15, 148
collagen, 82
collecting, 213–214
colonoscopies, 32, 114
Comfort, Alex, 25
The Common Sense Book of Baby and Child Care, 25
Como, Perry, 45
The Complete Book of Running, 25
compliment, 72
compression fractures, 106
compression of morbidity, 120
computers, 23
conservatism, 147
constipation, 101
construction, 48
continuing education—the future, 256
coronary artery bypass graft, 51, 97
coronary artery disease, 95, 96–98
corticosteroids, 108
cosmetic surgery, 174
crash of 1929, 44
C-reactive protein (CRP), 96, 109
creative pursuits, 215
crime and seniors, 166–167
Crosby, Bing, 46
cross-linking, 73
cross-training, 180
CTE. *See* chronic traumatic encephalopathy
Cuban Missile Crisis, 22, 25, 45, 57
cultural causes, 210
cultural influences, 21–27, 44–47, 57–60
cultural relevance, 192–193
CVAs. *See* strokes
cytotoxic drugs, 108

damaged goods, 62
dancing, 175, 218
Darrin, Bobby, 58
DAT scans, 93
Daughters of the American Revolution, 210
Davis, Bette, 85
Day, Doris, 58
Dean, James, 59
Death and Dying, 288
Death with Dignity Act, 263

debulking, 115
deconditioning, 77, 105
decubitus ulcers, 110
deep brain stimulation, 93
deficiency diseases, 115
dementia, 51, 87–90
dementia pugilistica, 90
demographics, 20, 43, 57
dental problems, 84
dependence upon a spouse, 127–129
dependence upon children, 130
dependence upon other family member, 131
dependency, 14
depression, 51, 116–118, 197; endogenous depression, 116; reactive depression, 116
Depression, Great. *See* Great Depression
Detroit bankruptcy, 7
diabetes, 104–105; diabetic coma, 105; diabetic neuropathy, 104; diabetic retinopathy, 104; diabetic ulcers, 104; glucose, 104; hypoglycemia, 105; insulin, 104, 105; islet cells, 104; Type Two diabetes, 104
diastolic. *See* hypertension
diet. *See* nutrition
dietary supplements, 184
differential aging, 8–9
dignity, 4, 16
disability, 120
diseases and disorders common with aging, 85–122; cancer, 112–115; cardiovascular diseases, 95–99; diseases of the brain and nervous system, 87–95; endocrine disorders, 104–105; gastrointestinal diseases, 101; genitourinary system, 101–104; musculoskeletal diseases, 105; respiratory diseases, 100; skin disorders, 109–110; vision, 111. *See also* Alzheimer's disease; essential tremor; Parkinson's disease; peripheral neuropathies; strokes
disinhibition, 89
diverticula, 78
diverticulitis, 101
divorce, 33–34, 36, 63, 104
Domino, Fats, 58

donepezil, 90
Donne, John, 275
dopa agonists, 94
dopamine, 75, 93, 94
The Dorsey Brothers, 46
Douglas, Kirk, 92
downsizing, 156
Downton Abbey, 165
The Drifters, 58
driver's license, loss of, 141–143
driving, 89
drooling, 93
Dr. Strangelove, 25
drug use. *See* alcohol and drugs
Dust Bowl, 44
dying, the physician's role, 263–264
Dylan, Bob, 24, 59
dyspareunia, 80

The Eagles, 24
Easy Rider, 25
Ecclesiastes, 78
edentulous, 84
education, 27, 28, 47–48, 61
Eisenhower, Dwight, 59, 97
elastin, 82
elder hostels, 217
election participation, 21
electronic health records (EHRs), 245
electronic monitoring, 133
elevated cholesterol, 51, 63, 98
Emerson, Ralph Waldo, 67
emotional support, 126
employment, 28–29, 38–39, 47, 48–49,
    61, 221–222
empty nest, 146
encore career, 222
ending life, social consequences, 260–265
end of life, preparation for, 259–290
endorphins, 180, 181
Entitled Generation, 19
entitlement programs, 37
entropy, 68
erectile dysfunction, 103
Erhard, Werner, 26
essential tremor, 94
EST, 26
estrogen, 80
evangelicalism, 26

Everyday Technologies for Alzheimer's
    Care (ETAC), 240
*Everything You Always Wanted to Know
    about Sex*, 25
executive function, 89
Exelon, 90
exercise, 31, 62, 98, 105, 177–183
existential angst, 148
existential suffering, 285
The Exorcist, 25
extended family, 12, 131–132
extrapyramidal system, 93

Facebook, 12, 23
factories, 48
farming, 49, 61
Faubus, Orval, 59
Federal Deposit Insurance Corporation,
    44
feeding tubes, 140
The Feminine Mystique, 25
feminism, 23
Ferber, Edna, 46
Final Exit, 286, 288
finances, 35–38, 40, 54, 61, 65, 223–225
financial aid, 126
financial pressures, 10
fingernails, 82
Fisher, Eddie, 58
fitness. *See* exercise
5-alpha reductase inhibitors, 101
Fixx, Jim, 25
Forbes, 37
Fortune, 223
For Whom the Bell Tolls, 229
The Fountain of Age, 151
4-H, 47
Fox, Michael J., 94
fractures, 106–107
Frankl, Viktor, 291
frankness about shortcomings, 199–201
Friedan, Betty, 25, 151
Friedman, Milton, 25
fronto-temporal dementia, 87
futile care, 262
the future and aging, 237–257

gambling, 212
games, 212

gastroesophogeal reflux disease, 101
Gates, Bill, 23
gay Boomers, 35
gay power, 23
Generation Change, 19
generations, 6
Generations: The History of America's Future, 1584–2069, 57
Generation Spend, 19, 38
genetic profiles, 245
genetic screening tests for cancer, 114
gentrification, 49
GERD. *See* gastroesophogeal reflux disease
gerontology, 68
ghettoization, 160–164
G.I. Bill, 47
Gibran, Kahlil, 259
G.I. Generation, 43
Gilded Age, 44
Gingrich, Newt, 59
Ginsberg, Allen, 59
glaucoma, 111
Glenn, John, 159
global warming, 22
goals, 206
The Godfather, 25
"golden years," 15
Gone With the Wind, 46
Goodall, Jane, 25
Goodman, Benny, 46
Google, 23
Government's National Health Interview Survey of 1994, 127
The Graduate, 25
"granny bashing," 12
The Grateful Dead, 24
Gray Dawn, 7
Gray Panthers, 209
Great Depression, 43, 44
Greatest Generation, 43–56
The Great Gatsby, 44
Great Recession, 22, 38
Greediest Generation, 19, 37
grief, dealing with, 143, 227–232
growth hormones, 80
gyri, 75

Haley, Alex, 25

Hare Krishna, 26
Hayflick, Leonard, 76
Hayflick Limit, 69
Hayworth, Rita, 87
health, 31–32, 50–51
health care agent, 273–274
health care proxy, 273
hearing, 83, 86
heart, 96–97; ablation, 97; angina, 96; angioplasty, 97; antifibrinolytic agents, 97; arrhythmias, 97; cardiac cripple, 96; chest pain, 96, 97; congestive heart failure, 96; coronary angiography, 97; coronary catheterization, 97; edema, 96; heart transplant, 97; implantable defibrillator, 97; myocardial infarction (MI), 96; myocardial ischemia, 96; occlusion (vascular), 96; pacemaker, 97; pulmonary edema, 96; stenosis (vascular), 96
heartburn, 101
Heflick, Leonard, 76
Hemingway, Ernest, 43, 46, 67, 229
Hendrix, Jimi, 24, 59
Hepburn, Katharine, 94
herpes zoster, 109
Heston, Charlton, 87
high blood pressure. *See* hypertension
hip fractures, 107
hippies, 24
hippocampus, 75
hip replacement, 107
Holocaust, 45
home care, 132–133
home health aides, 135
homemaker, 52
homeostasis, 68
homocysteine, 96
hormonal cancer therapy, 115
hospice care, 265, 275–290
House Un-American Activities Committee, 58
housing, 30, 38, 49, 61; suburban, 30, 49, 61
Howe, Neil, 57, 61
hypertension (high blood pressure), 51, 63, 95, 98, 99
hypothalamus, 80
hypothyroidism, 104

ibuprofen, 107
impotence, 103, 104
impulse disorders, 89
inappropriate behavior, 175–176
income, 29, 61
incontinence, 89
independence, 194–198
infectious diseases, 8
inflammation of arteries, 96
infrastructure, 48
Institute of Medicine, 178
integration, 23, 59
integrative exercise, 181
intermittent claudication, 98
Internet, 12, 23, 155, 237–238
interstate highway system, 49
In the Shadow of Man, 25
inventory of pleasure and pain, 280–285
Iraq War, 22

Jagger, Mick, 3
Jaws, 25
Job, Book of, 277–278
job discrimination, 156–159
Jobs, Steve, 23
jogging, 179
John Paul II (pope), 94
Johnson, Lyndon, 97
Jones, Tommy Lee, 165
Joplin, Janis, 24
Journal of Gerontology, 211
The Journey of Life, 15, 148
The Joy of Sex, 25

Kabbalists, 26
Kahn, Robert, 16
Keaton, Diane, 165
keeping up with the Joneses, 52
Kennedy, Robert, 59
Kennedy, Ted, 59
Kennedy assassination, 21, 22
Kerouac, Jack, 59
Kevorkian, Jack, 263
kidneys, 79
killing one's self, 286–290
King, Martin Luther, Jr., 59
King Lear, 151
Kissinger, Henry, 11
knee replacement, 107

Korean War, 57
Kotlikoff, Lawrence, 37
kvetch, 74
kyphosis, 106

lactase, 78
Laguna Woods, 160
lamin A, 74
language ability, 89
Lao-Tzu, 171, 237
L-dopa, 94
leading causes of death, 2000, 86
League of Women Voters, 209
Leary, Timothy, 24
leisure time—the future, 257
Leisure World, 160
Levitra, 189
Levittowns, 49
Lewis, Jerry Lee, 58
Lewy body disease, 87
libido, 102–103, 117
Lieberson, Alan, 270
life expectancy, 6, 8, 9
life support: loss of control, 140–141
LinkedIn, 23
lipofuscin, 73
living environment changes, 238–243
living wills, 270–273
LMNA gene, 74
"locked in" syndrome, 262
loneliness, dealing with, 232–233
losses, 125–149
loss of identity, 145–146
loss of independence, 126–140
loss of initiative, 147
loss of loved ones, 143–144
loss of meaning, 147–148
loss of self-image, 145–146
Lost Generation, 43
lycopenes, 93
lymphoma, 1; non-Hodgkins lymphoma, 1

macular degeneration (AMD), 111
Madmen, 165
Madoff, Bernie, 37
Mailer, Norman, 25
Malcolm X, 25
male pattern baldness, 82
malnutrition, 115

mammograms, 32, 113
manic-depressive illness, 116
Man's Search for Meaning, 291
manufacturing, 48
marginalization of older people, 154–155
marijuana, 177
Marshall, Anthony, 12
Martin Luther King Jr. assassination, 22
master gland, 80
master's competitions, 183
McCain, John, 59
McCarthy, Joseph, 58
McDonald's, 49
Meals on Wheels, 183
media and older people, 164–166
Medicaid, 51
medical power of attorney, 273–275
Medicare, 7, 37, 51, 152–153, 224
medicine: medical care, 32, 63, 185–186;
    training, 27
Mediterranean diet, 184
melanin, 82
melatonin, 80
memantine, 90
memory, 76, 89
memory and cognitive decline—the
    future, 251–252
menopause, 80
mental illness, 51
mental illness—the future, 248
metastasis, 115
Microsoft, 23
Midnight Cowboy, 25
mild cognitive impairment (MCI), 87–88
Miller, Glenn, 46
Miltown, 51
Mini Mental State Exam (MMSE), 88
Mitchell, Margaret, 46
Money, 223
Monroe, Marilyn, 59
moon landing, 23
More, Thomas, 208
Motown, 24
mourning, 143, 227, 229, 230–231, 232
movies, 25
musculoskeletal system—the future, 249

Nader, Ralph, 25
Namenda, 90

nanotechnology, 245
naproxen, 107
National Alliance for Caregivers, 127
National Football League, 90
National Institute of Aging Study, 132
naturally occurring retirement community
    (NORC), 163
natural selection, 67
neuroformina, 108
Neurology (journal), 87, 93
neurons, 75
neurotransmitters, 75, 93
New Age, 26
New England Journal of Medicine, 87,
    184
New York Times, 137, 184, 209
Nicholson, Jack, 165
Nixon resignation, 21, 46
NMDA receptor antagonist, 90
nocturia, 79
non-Hodgkins lymphoma, 1
non-steroidal anti-inflammatory drugs
    (NSAIDs), 107–108
nurse's aides, 135
nursing homes, 136–140
nutrition, 32, 98, 183–184

Oates, Joyce Carol, 25
Obama, Barack, 22
obesity, 31, 121, 183
objectives. *See* goals
observations and conclusions, 291–297
obsessive-compulsive disorders, 197
obsessive conduct, 89
Of Mice and Men, 46
Okura, Yamanoue, 125
The Old Man and the Sea, 67
online dating, 34
On the Road, 59
oral contraceptives, 26
organ replacement—the future, 250
organs, normal aging of, 74–84; brain and
    nervous system, 75–77; cardiovascular
    system, 77; endocrine system, 80;
    gastrointestinal system, 78; general
    changes, 75; genitourinary system,
    79–80; heart, 77; malnutrition, 115;
    musculoskeletal system, 81; psychiatric
    disorders, 116–119; respiratory system,

78; sensory systems, 82–83; skin, 82
Osler, William, 152
osteoarthritis, 81, 86, 105, 107–108
osteomyelitis, 110
osteophytes, 107
osteoporosis, 81, 105, 106
ostomies, 140–141
outdoor activities, 218
ovaries, 80

Page, Patti, 58
Paige, Satchel, 2
palliative therapy, 115
pancreas, 78, 80
panic attacks, 118
pap smears, 32, 114
paranoia, 89, 90
Parkinson's disease, 51, 93–94
Patient Self-Determination Act, 267
Paul, Ron, 59
Pearl Harbor, 45
performance anxiety, 103
periodontal disease, 84
peripheral nerves, 76
peripheral neuropathies, 95
peripheral vascular disease, 95, 98
persistent vegetative state (PVS), 261
Peterson, Pete, 7
pets, 220
Pew Research survey, 20
philosophy of life, 1
phobias, 197
physical activity. See exercise
physical fitness. See exercise
physical help, 126
physician assisted suicide, 263, 290
physiological age, 9
Pick's disease, 87
PIRO, 236, 296–297
pituitary, 80
planning for the end of life, 265–275
The Platters, 58
pneumonia, 8, 13, 100
politics, 64, 159, 208–209
polymyalgia rheumatica, 109
Ponzi schemes, 37
positive thinking, 236
post-herpetic neuralgia, 109
Post-War Generation, 56

potential, fulfilling, 16
premarital sex, 52
preparation for the future, 225–226
presbycusis, 83
presbyopia, 83
Presley, Elvis, 24, 58
pressure sores, 110
preventative maintenance, 244
prevention, 32
progeria, 74
progesterone, 80
Prohibition, 44
proportion of women, 11
prostate biopsy, 114
prostate specific antigen (PSA), 114
Protestant churches, 46
public pensions, 7
purpose of life, 147
purse snatchings, 166
push-ins, 166

quality of life, 2, 13
Quill, Timothy, 288
Quinlan, Karen Ann, 261

radiation, 115
radicular pain, 108
Raleigh, Walter, 203
random thoughts on aging, 234–236
Ray, Johnnie, 58
Reagan, Ronald, 87
Recession, Great. See Great Recession
recreational vehicles (RV's), 217
Reeves, Christopher, 262
reinvention, 145
Reinvention Generation, 19
relationships, 33–34, 52–53, 63–64,
    206–208; children, 11; spouse, 11, 34,
    52–53, 55, 63
relevance, 191–194
religion, 25, 26, 46, 60, 148, 211, 230
renal dialysis, 140–141
Reno, Janet, 94
resistance training, 182
resting tremor, 93
resveratrol, 74
retirement, 40, 55, 63–64, 222
retirement communities, 63
retirement villages, 160–163

Reuben, David, 25
reverse mortgages, 225
rheumatoid arthritis, 108
rivastigmine, 90
Roaring Twenties, 43, 44
Roberts, John, 22
robotic companions, 241–243
rock and roll, 24, 58
Roe v. Wade, 26
The Rolling Stones, 3, 24
Romney, Mitt, 22
Roosevelt, Franklin, 44
Roots, 25
Rosie the Riveter, 45
Roth, Geneen, 37
Roth, Phillip, 25
Rowe, John, 16
running, 179

"sandwich generation," 36
sanitation, 8
scams, 167
Scientology, 26
scouting, 47
Securities and Exchange Commission, 44
sedentary lifestyle, 122
sedimentation rate (ESR), 109
segregation, 49, 59
self-employment, 156
senescence, 69
senile keratoses, 82
seniority, 156, 159
sensory systems—the future, 249
septicemia, 110
sexuality, 79–80, 102–104, 186–191
sexual revolution, 26
Shakespeare, William, 151
shaking palsy, 93
shared dependency, 198
shingles, 109
Silent Generation, 56–65
silent information regulator, 73
silent killer. *See* hypertension
Silent Spring, 25
Sinatra, Frank, 46, 58
sirtuins, 74
SIR2, 73
Skinner, B. F., 25
Skype, 240

sleep, 77
small vessel ischemic changes, 92
smart cars, 241
smart homes, 238–240
smell and taste, 83
smoking, 32, 63, 98, 100, 111
social causes, 209–210
social changes—the future, 253–256
social media, 155
social networks, 12
social relevance, 193
Social Security, 7, 29, 37, 44, 152–153, 224
society's role in care, 133
spinal cord constriction, 108
spinal stenosis, 105, 108
Spock, Benjamin, 25
Spring and Autumn, 208
Springsteen, Bruce, 24
stages of life, 9–10
Stanford, Alan, 37
Star Wars, 25
stasis dermatitis, 110
stay-at-home moms, 48
Steinbeck, John, 46
Steinem, Gloria, 59
stenting, 50, 97
steroids, 108, 109
strategies for control, 171–202, 203–236
Strauss, William, 57, 61
Streep, Meryl, 165
striation, 93
stroke prophylaxis, 92, 93
strokes, 91–93, 95
studying, 219
substantia nigra, 93
successful aging, 16
suicides, 116, 117
sulci, 75
Sullivan, Ed, 58
summer of 2003, France, 154
sunlight, 82, 113
suttee, 143
synopsis, 17–18
systolic. *See* hypertension

Tao-Te-Ching, 171, 237
tau, 90
Taylor, Elizabeth, 59

television, 46
telomerase, 69, 112
telomere, 69–70, 70, 112
temporal arteritis, 109
Tennessee Valley Authority, 44
terminal dehydration, 264
testes, 80
testosterone, 79, 80, 82, 103, 189
Thomas, Dylan, 16–17
Thorazine, 51
Thurmond, Strom, 159
thymus gland, 72
thyroid, 80, 104
TIAs, 91
Time, 57
tissue plasminogen activator. *See* TPA
touch, 83
TPA, 91
Traditionalists, 56
Transcendental Meditation, 26
transient ischemic attack. *See* TIAs
travel, 216–217
TREM2, 87
trophy wife, 104
tumor necrosis factor (TNF), 108
TURP, 101
Twitter, 12, 23
2001: A Space Odyssey, 25

ultraviolet light, 82
unemployment, 35–36, 44
unfunded liabilities, 7
Unification Church, 26
Uniform Rights of the Terminally Ill Act
    (URTIA), 273
unions, 47

Unsafe at Any Speed, 25
Updike, John, 25
urinary frequency, 79
urinary incontinence, 79, 102, 104
urinary retention, 79

vaginal dryness, 103
vaginal lubricants, 189
Valium, 51
Viagra, 53, 103, 189
Vidal, Gore, 59
Vietnam War, 22, 45–46, 57, 59
vision, 83, 86
vitamin C, 71, 74
vitamin E, 71, 74
voluntary terminal dehydration, 289
volunteering, 39
volunteerism, 208

walking, 179
Wall Street, 44
Walmart, 49
Warhol, Andy, 59
Watergate, 21, 22, 47
wealth transfer. *See* finances
weight training, 182
Woodstock, 26
Woodstock Generation, 24
Works Progress Administration, 44
World War I, 43
World War II, 43, 45
Worth, 223
wrist fractures, 107

Your Money, 223

ABOUT THE AUTHOR

Robert Levine was a Ford Scholar at Columbia University, graduating at nineteen with a BA in history. Finishing medical school at Downstate SUNY at age twenty-three, he was an intern and medical resident at Montefiore Hospital in the Bronx, New York. After service in the army, including a tour of duty at the 3rd Field Hospital in Vietnam in 1965–1966, he took his neurology training at Albert Einstein in the Bronx.

Subsequently, Dr. Levine was in the private practice of neurology in Norwalk, Connecticut, for over forty years with a special interest in dementia. He is the former chief of neurology at Norwalk Hospital and an associate clinical professor of medicine (ret) at Yale University. He is a fellow of the American Academy of Neurology and was a consultant to *Cardiology Review* from 1998 to 2007. He is a member of the Ethics Committee at Norwalk Hospital and currently runs the Neurology Clinics at the hospital and Americares in Norwalk.

Aging with Attitude, Dr. Levine's first book, was published in 2004 and won a Choice Award of the American Library Association as one of the outstanding titles of the year. His second book, *Defying Dementia*, was released in 2006. This describes the different forms of dementia and how they can be prevented.

His third book, *Shock Therapy for the American Health Care System* (2009), details the problems of the nation's health care system and presents a comprehensive reform plan that will not cost the federal government additional money and will not raise taxes. His fourth book, *Resurrecting Democracy* (2011), is about the need for a centrist third political party in the United States, as he believes the current system is dysfunctional.

Dr. Levine also has an interest in American folk art. He and his wife, Anne, have a major collection of wood carvings, with a focus on American historical figures. A show at the Westport Historical Society in 2009 featured their collection. Dr. Levine was also a half owner of an Italian restaurant, Anacapri, in the mid-1980s, which received two stars in the *New York Times*. An avid believer in the need for physical activity, Dr. Levine ran nine marathons and currently walks an average of five miles or more every day.